EMPIRE OF SHIVA

The Global Civilization

David Hatcher Childress

Adventures Unlimited Press

Other Books by David Hatcher Childress:

PROJECT RAINBOW & THE PHILADELPHIA EXPERIMENT
VRIL: SECRETS OF THE BLACK SUN
ANDROMEDA: THE SECRET FILES
HAUNEBU: THE SECRET FILES
ANTARCTICA & THE SECRET SPACE PROGRAM
THE LOST WORLD OF CHAM
OBELISKS: TOWERS OF POWER
ANCIENT TECHNOLOGY IN PERU & BOLIVIA
THE MYSTERY OF THE OLMECS
PIRATES AND THE LOST TEMPLAR FLEET
TECHNOLOGY OF THE GODS
A HITCHHIKER'S GUIDE TO ARMAGEDDON
LOST CONTINENTS & THE HOLLOW EARTH
ATLANTIS & THE POWER SYSTEM OF THE GODS
THE FANTASTIC INVENTIONS OF NIKOLA TESLA
LOST CITIES OF NORTH & CENTRAL AMERICA
LOST CITIES OF CHINA, CENTRAL ASIA & INDIA
LOST CITIES & ANCIENT MYSTERIES OF AFRICA & ARABIA
LOST CITIES & ANCIENT MYSTERIES OF SOUTH AMERICA
LOST CITIES OF ANCIENT LEMURIA & THE PACIFIC
LOST CITIES OF ATLANTIS, ANCIENT EUROPE & THE MEDITERRANEAN
LOST CITIES & ANCIENT MYSTERIES OF THE SOUTHWEST
YETIS, SASQUATCH AND HAIRY GIANTS
THE BIGFOOT FILES
BIGFOOT NATION
VIMANA
ARK OF GOD

With Brien Foerster
THE ENIGMA OF CRANIAL DEFORMATION

With Steven Mehler
THE CRYSTAL SKULLS

EMPIRE OF SHIVA

The Global Civilization

Empire of Shiva

ISBN 978-1-948803-76-2

Published by:
Adventures Unlimited Press
One Adventure Place
Kempton, Illinois 60946 USA
auphq@frontiernet.net

Cover by Terry Lamb

AdventuresUnlimitedPress.com

10 9 8 7 6 5 4 3 2 1

A clay seal from the Indus Valley depicting a meditating Shiva.

A typical modern depiction of Shiva at his abode in the Himalayas.

EMPIRE OF SHIVA

David Hatcher Childress

A bronze statue of a four-armed Dancing Shiva (Nataraja).

TABLE OF CONTENTS

A modern Shivite sadhu preist with long hair and three stripes to symbolize Shiva.

Chapter 1

A 20,000-Year-Old Statue of Shiva

There is a coherent plan in the universe,
though I don't know what it's a plan for.
—*Fred Hoyle* (1915 - 2001)

While walking through an airport in Thailand a few years ago, I saw an unusual poster of a strange rock formation I figured was located somewhere in Thailand. It was clearly constructed of megaliths somewhere along a rocky coast. The formation was huge and looked as if it were the remains of some ancient megalithic wall. Where was it?

The poster was mainly in Thai but there were a couple of words in English. They said "Hin Son." I took a photo of the poster, planning to research this odd spot when I had a chance.

Later, back at my office in the USA, I looked at my photo of the curiosity and began to research it. It took me some time to figure out that there was a typo on the Thai poster and that it was not "Hin Son" but rather "Hin Sorn" or more correctly, Koh Hin Sorn. Koh (or ko) in the Thai language means "small island" or islet. I was quite confused for awhile, but eventually I was able to pinpoint the small island and where it lay in relation to other islands in Thailand.

Koh Hin Sorn, I discovered, is one of the southernmost Thai islands, far down along the border with Malaysia in what is generally known as the Adang Archipelago. The Adang Archipelago contains the major islands of Koh Adang, Koh Lipe, Koh Rawi and the far-flung, Koh Tong (or Koh Dong, as it is often spelled—this was also rather confusing). There are many other small islets with beaches, rock outcrops, coral reefs and jungles in the Adang Archipelago. These islands were made into Thailand's first national park in 1974. Named the Tarutau National Marine Park, it consists of more than 60 islands and islets, one of them

A travel poster for the island of Ko Hin Son in southern Thailand.

being Koh Hin Sorn. This park is part of the larger Mu Koh Adang-Rawi National Park.

Most of the hotels and tour operators are located on the smaller island of Ko Lipe. Most tourists visiting the area stay at bungalow hotels on Koh Lipe, which contains the main village of the native sea gypsies called the Chao Leh who roam throughout the islands and the nearby mainland. The area has good coral reef activity and has become famous for snorkeling and diving. It has been call the "Maldives of Thailand" because of its many small islands.

Koh Hin Sorn is certainly the strangest of the all the islands in the Adang Archipelago, and the Mu Koh Adang-Rawi National Park. Yes, the word "Mu," like the famous lost continent of James Churchward fame, is part of the official name for the national park. The rock wall on Koh Hin Sorn has the look of the last remains of an ancient sea wall or other fortification. It seems the Thai people were fascinated by this rock wall, or otherwise it would not be on a giant tourism poster flaunted at an airport. Most of the Thai people are devout Buddhists who believe in the epic tales of the Ramayana and the Mahabharata as quite literal accounts of ancient history that included magnificent kingdoms, ancient technology (like flying machines called vimanas), and great heroes and villains who fought for dominance in the remote past.

According to the great Hindu poet Valmiki, who is credited

A photo of the island of Ko Hin Son in southern Thailand.

with writing the Ramayana circa 800 BC, but speaking of a much older era:

Rama ruled the earth for eleven thousand years.
He gave a year-long festival
In this very Naimisha Forest.
All this land was his kingdom then;
One age of the world ago;
Long, long, ago;
Long before now, and far in the past.
Rama was King from the center of the world
To the four Oceans' shores.

Thinking about these lines from the Ramayana, of a time said to be during the last Treta Yuga, I wondered if some of the Thai people believed that the curious rocks of Koh Hin Sorn were part of some ancient city that was from that time of Rama so long ago. A time when the oceans and land masses looked different from today. Was Koh Hin Sorn the last remaining wall of a now sunken city from the time of the Ramayana? It was a fascinating thought.

One book that promotes the idea of a lost "Lemuria" is Stephen Oppenheimer's 1998 work *Eden in the East*.[7] Oppenheimer maintains that civilization started on a now drowned continental shelf around Thailand, Malaysia and Indonesia that existed over 9,000 ago. Oppenheimer claimed that this civilization was the first to domesticate rice, but that this area drowned with the rising of sea levels at the end of the last ice age. He suggests that people from this drowning land dispersed to become the Neolithic cultures of China, India, Mesopotamia, the Eastern Mediterranean and even Egypt. He also speculates that the Polynesians who settled such remote islands as Hawaii, Tahiti and Easter Island were from this sunken land.

Could the strange rock wall at Koh Hin Sorn be a relic from this submerged land? Koh Hin Sorn is the last bit of Thailand on the southwest coast, and Malaysian territorial waters begin here. Was this curious-looking stone symbolic of the ancient Buddhist-Hindu faith that runs so strong in Thailand, and a subliminal symbol of the ancient past?

Near Koh Hin Sorn is the island of Koh Hin-ngam which

Oppenheimer's map of the drowned world of Southeast Asia.

has "magical" black rock beaches. The small island in Mu Koh Adang-Rawi does not have sand on its beaches but only black rocks, usually in the shape of small discs. Local traditions says that it is bad luck for someone to take any of the rock from this island back to their home, and eventually the person must bring it back to the island because of a spirit known as Tarutao. Another local tradition says that if you want your wish to come true, you must stack 13 of the black rocks in a rock tower that is 13 levels high.

The waters around Koh Hin Sorn and the Adang Archipelago are crystal clear and the snorkeling and scuba diving are excellent in the warm waters surrounding the islands. As more Thais take the time to vacation in their own country, they are curiously drawn to this far rock wall island on their southern border—the last remnants of Rama's ancient kingdom? Or perhaps it is just a curious natural rock formation, one that attracts the imagination of tourists walking through airports.

The Shiva Statue From 26,450 BC

Recently I came across this curious article on the Internet about a brass statue of Shiva that was thought to be over 26,000 years old. The intriguing story includes a mysterious chest from

The bronze statue of Kalpa Vigraha-Shiva.

Tibet, the CIA and a series of tests. The article was from Booksfact.com [https://www.booksfact.com/archeology/kalpa-vigraha-oldest-hindu-idol-of-lord-siva-26450-bc.html] and the date given is June 17, 2015.

Entitled "Kalpa Vigraha Oldest Hindu Idol of Lord Siva (26,450 BC)" the article, no author given, went on to say:

> Around 1959-60, a heavy chest containing the idol was reportedly given to CIA officials for safekeeping at Lo Monthang (called "Mustang" in CIA files) by a Tibetan monk accompanied by Khampa bodyguards. The monk apparently related to the CIA officials the importance of the chest and its contents. A curious CIA official meticulously wrote down the details of what the Buddhist monk told them about the chest and its contents. Why he thought it important to record the Buddhist monk's story is anybody's guess. But it also appears that the Americans were initially not quite impressed with the quaint values attached to objects of Oriental worship at that time when their priority was conducting a guerrilla war against the Chinese forces advancing into Tibet.
>
> In the same week that the CIA officials received the chest a skirmish erupted with Chinese forces in which the Tibetan monk and his guards were killed. The CIA officials not knowing what to make of the curious chest loaded it onto an aircraft and had it sent to a secret airbase in India, afterward transporting it to Camp Hale, a now-abandoned Army base near Vail, Colorado. A few weeks later the chest wound up at a CIA store-room in Washington DC labeled "ST Circus Mustang-0183."
>
> Many months would elapse before someone in the CIA decided to take an interest in the chest and its contents. A strange manuscript found inside and the unusually age-worn chest coupled with its noticeably unique design prompted them to conduct a radiocarbon test of the timber with which the chest was made. The results given to them by the University of California Radiation Laboratory, Berkeley astounded the CIA officials. The antiquity of the worn-out wooden chest and the idol was mind-boggling to say the least. It did not belong to this "yuga" or epoch on the Hindu time scale just as the monk had claimed.

That is to say, it belonged to a period called the Dwapara yuga, making it the oldest human artifact in existence. Radiocarbon (C14) dating conducted by the University of California Radiation Laboratory on the heavy 9-inch thick timber sides and lid of the chest in which it was discovered arrived at readings that indicated a period around 26,450 BCE. That would make it over 28,450 years old today, and about 23,300 years older than the legendary Hindu Kurukshetra war described in Mahabharata. The idol was also tested by experts who concluded that it was the oldest Hindu idol in existence. None of the known ancient excavated civilizations of history—Egyptian,

Painting of Shiva giving the Sudarsana Chakra to Vishnu.

Mesopotamian or Indus Valley—existed before 6000 years ago.

The Kalpa Vigraha idol was reportedly found placed inside this heavy metal-lined wooden chest with a socket-and-pivot hinged lid and an ancient loop-and-rod lock assembly. The chest itself presented a curiosity, as the space within the box was barely 8x8x8 inches while the timber pieces used to construct all its five sides were about 8 inches thick each! The timber of which the lid of the chest was made also measured about 6 inches in thickness. The teakwood timber was further protected by a 1-inch thick bronze-like alloy plate on all sides which despite severe external corrosion had preserved the teakwood of the box to a fair extent. The metal plate appears to have been riveted into the teakwood with nails of some similar metal alloy. Though many rivets were missing, the metal casing held well. The appearance of the chest suggested that it might have lain buried for a considerable period of time, though scrape-marks from attempts made to clean the corrosion on the outside were visible.

Corrosive salts or dampness had not crept into the chest despite its age, though some degree of natural oxidation and decay was noticed in the contents of the chest which included a manuscript written on wooden slats and the small brass-like crude metal idol. The old pre-Rigvedic Sanskrit-type manuscript was translated by the CIA with difficulty. In fact it reportedly took two long years to decipher, employing experts including some Indians and Nepalese. They concluded that the language belonged to the proto-historic period of Hinduism when it was thought no language existed and that the Vedas were being passed down orally. The manuscript appeared to be something akin to Sanskrit, but not quite anything any archaeologist or historian had ever encountered before. The manuscript mentioned the name of the idol—“kalpa maha-ayusham rasayana vigraha” abbreviated in CIA files to “Kalpa Vigraha.”

The Kalpa Vigraha is a small crude brass idol weighing about 47.10 grams depicting a deity resembling the Hindu god Shiva kneeling or seated on one knee, a serpent’s hood forming a canopy above the head of the idol. In the right hand of the figure was a discus or circular weapon, perhaps the "sudharshan-chakra" of Hindu mythology. Around its neck was a string of beads. The metal formed three "loops" on one side caused by the snake, an arm holding a conch-shell and the discus. It measured about 5.3 cm tall and about 4.7 cms wide, with an oval base 2.5 cms long and 1.7 cms wide. There was no doubt the small statue was of some extreme importance to have been preserved with such care in a chest of such strength and durability.

But following the translation of the manuscript, events surrounding the Kalpa Vigraha suddenly took a mysterious turn. The UCRL's records were impounded by the CIA and a shroud of silence was cast over all matters regarding the chest and the Hindu idol. "ST Circus Mustang-0183" was removed from the inventory at the CIA storehouse records, and the whole episode was swept under the carpet for some inexplicable reason.

However, a retired CIA agent, revealed that based on the text of the manuscript found along with the idol, a series of top-secret experiments were conducted by the CIA on unsuspecting human subjects in the United States and elsewhere in the world. According to this unnamed source in Langley, Virginia, an "inner-circle" of the CIA dedicated most of their time in the early 1960s conducting experiments based on the ancient manuscript, and the Kalpa Vigraha idol itself played the most important role in this bizarre research.

The source, who was partially involved in the research, explained that one of the experiments was particularly intriguing. It required a human subject to consume a tumbler of water each day for 3 days. This water was earlier "charged" by CIA agents by simply placing the idol in a large copper vessel containing drinking water for nine days before the human subject was required to drink it. What results the "inner circle" officials expected to see by this innocuous experiment was not known to anybody at that time, but top CIA officials evidenced great interest in it. The "charged" water was also sent to various laboratories under heavy security and all reports and documents received from the labs were sent directly to the CIA director, John McCone.

...The Kalpa Vigraha, the CIA store-room inventory item labeled "ST Circus Mustang-0183", was not seen or heard of for many decades. An audit conducted in 1996 revealed that the heavy metal-lined chest was very much in the store, but that the idol and the manuscript had been "misplaced." In a search conducted over many weeks, spanning many states, and enquiries made to many retired personnel, the agency was able to trace the manuscript from the house of a microbiologist the CIA had many years ago hired for analysis of the "charged" kalpa vigraha water. The manuscript was found but the whereabouts of the Kalpa Vigraha is still a mystery. Following the discovery of the manuscript, a spate of mysterious deaths of microbiologists followed. The media and the internet were rife with conspiracy theories on the death of the rather alarming number of them, but few laid suspicion on the CIA until our above-mentioned source No 2, a serving agent of the CIA spilled the beans. However hard it will be to pin all these inexplicable deaths on the CIA, the coincidences are equally hard to rule out if source No 2 is honest regarding the facts. We would not like to go into the details revealed to us and would rather allow police and the investigation agencies to arrive at their own conclusions with regard to the deaths.

According to CIA source No 2 the Kalpa Vigraha has since been smuggled out of the United States to India. The latest information received at the CIA headquarters is that it lies in the possession of some software employees or IT professionals at Hyderabad, India or moved to some interior place in the state of Andhra Pradesh. For the first time since 1960, photographs of the Kalpa Vigraha, depicting the idol from four different directions, were circulated around the world by the CIA with an enormous cash reward for its recovery.

The "Suaharshan Chakra" referred to in the story is also known as the Sudarsana Chakra. It was given to Lord Vishnu by Lord Shiva who was pleased with Vishnu's devotion. Vishnu who was having a torrid time as preserver god, in controlling the evil asuras, went to Mount Kailasa and began to pray to Shiva. Vishnu chanted many mantras, but there was no sign of Siva. Lord Shiva has a thousand names and Vishnu next started to chant these names. Each day he chanted the thousand names and offered a thousand lotus flowers to Shiva, who decided to litmus test Vishnu. One day, he stole a single lotus flower from the thousand that were to be offered. When Vishnu realized that there was one lotus flower less, he gouged out his own eye and offered it in place of the missing lotus flower. Siva was now pleased and appeared before Vishnu and presented him with the Sudarshana Chakra. The idol shows Shiva with a snake as a crown on top of his head, he is giving Sudarsana Chakra with his right hand to Vishnu.

The use of the Sudarshana Chakra is occasionally mentioned in the Hindu texts of Rigveda, Yajurveda and Puranas, as an ultimate weapon to eliminate the enemy of law, order and preservation.

So, what are we to make of this fascinating article? Was the wood in the chest really dated to 26,450 BC? This is astonishing in itself and it seems that the box still exists in some CIA storage area (you might wonder what else is sitting in CIA storage areas) and it could be dated again to be scientifically accurate. The assumption is that the brass Shiva idol holding the Sudarsana Chakra is the same age as the small chest that it came in. This does seem to be a good assumption, but unfortunately brass itself cannot be dated, only the box that it came in. One might think that such an old metal statue would be made of some gold alloy, rather than brass. The Shiva statue being of brass seems to indicate that it is of recent manufacture, probably within the last 4,000 years. But who knows? Maybe the Kalpa Vigraha Shiva statue was made at a time when Shiva ruled the world—26,450 years ago!

We have the beginnings here of a Hindu realm of Shiva and Rama that spans tens of thousands of years. This Empire of Shiva has many faces and places. It spans continents and oceans. It is epic in its monumental constructions and it has left many traces of its existence. It is a fascinating adventure that spans space and time in a heroic way.

Shiva statue with erection from Mathura, India, circa 300 AD.

Chapter 2

When Shiva Ruled the World

It comes from confusion, all the things I left undone
It comes from moment to moment, day to day
The time seems to slip away
But I've got twenty million things to do, twenty million things
—*20 Million Things,* Lowell George (Little Feat)

Yes, there was a time when Shiva ruled the world. It was a time long ago, and not so long ago, that Shiva and Shaivites, both Hindu and Buddhist, roamed the far reaches of planet Earth, and brought a large part under their domination. I maintain that this realm of Shiva was the largest "nation" that the world has ever seen. It spanned from India to Turkey, Syria, Hungary and Madagascar in the west and from Southeast Asia and its many islands across the Pacific to the west coasts of North and South America. In my research I have found that this vast empire was probably dominated by the Cham, a group of Hindu (and later Buddhists who continued to worship Shiva) people of different races that spanned both coasts of India, coastal areas around the Indian Ocean, and eastward into Southeast Asia, the islands of Indonesia and out into the Pacific. These people were often dark skinned with long black hair. They could be oriental in appearance, or Caucasian or black, with distinct Negroid appearances.

While the Western world centers its maps on the Atlantic Ocean with Europe and Africa on one side and North and South America on the other side, making the Far East the edge of the world, when discussing the time when Shiva ruled the world we need to change this map. We need to look at a map that has the Pacific Ocean in the center.

Now we have a true map of the ancient world, one that was centered on the Pacific Ocean and the many voyages made by large ships into the Indian Ocean, the seas of Southeast Asia and the

Pacific Ocean. This Hindu empire, later to be partially Buddhist, spanned east and west from India and Southeast Asia, the core area of the Shiva nations. To the north was Tibet, where Shiva was said to actually reside, and to the south was southern India, Sri Lanka, the Maldives and other islands.

To the west we have the Shaivite areas of the Indian Ocean, Oman—the land of Sinbad—and areas of East Africa and Madagascar. Also, Hindu-Shiva lands were known to extend in ancient times through what is today Pakistan, Afghanistan, Iran, Turkey and into countries around the Black Sea, including Bulgaria and Hungary. Queen Nefertiti, wife of Akhenaton, was from the royal family of Mittani, a Hindu kingdom in central Turkey, allied with the Hittites.

Similarly, some historians posit that the Israelites, the children of Abraham, were actually a tribe of Hindus. The area around Turkey and Syria was known to be a Hindu area and the name "Abraham" is really a title. Abraham means "A Brahmin" which means a Hindu priest. Ancient India under Hinduism is known for its caste system of Brahmin priests, a military caste, a business class and a peasant class.

Going to the east the Hindu-Shaivites used the gigantic fleet of ships that existed throughout the areas of southeast Asia—an area with many islands, some in close proximity and some far-flung. These many islands were part of an extensive trading network that not only spanned all the coastal areas of Southeast Asia and all of its islands, but also eastward to remote islands in the western Pacific such as Pohnpei (with its fantastic settlement of Nan Madol), Samoa, Tonga and others.

The coastal areas may have been colonized by these Shiva worshippers, friends to seamen and farmers alike, but the mountainous interior of many of these islands remained "wild" much like the land of the headhunters of Borneo and the dangerous island of New Guinea, still a hazardous area of little exploration today.

From the islands of the central Pacific the fleets of huge Cham ships went east across the Pacific to the western coasts of Mexico, Central America and South America. Here they searched for jade, obsidian, medicinal plants, hallucinogenic plants, gold and other metals. They were probably involved with the hybridization of some of the important vegetables such as corn (maize), squash, tomatoes, beans, potatoes and sweet potatoes, among many others.

The oldest known Shvia statue is this carved lingam from 200 BC at Gudimallam, India. It shows Shiva standing on the demon Apasmara.

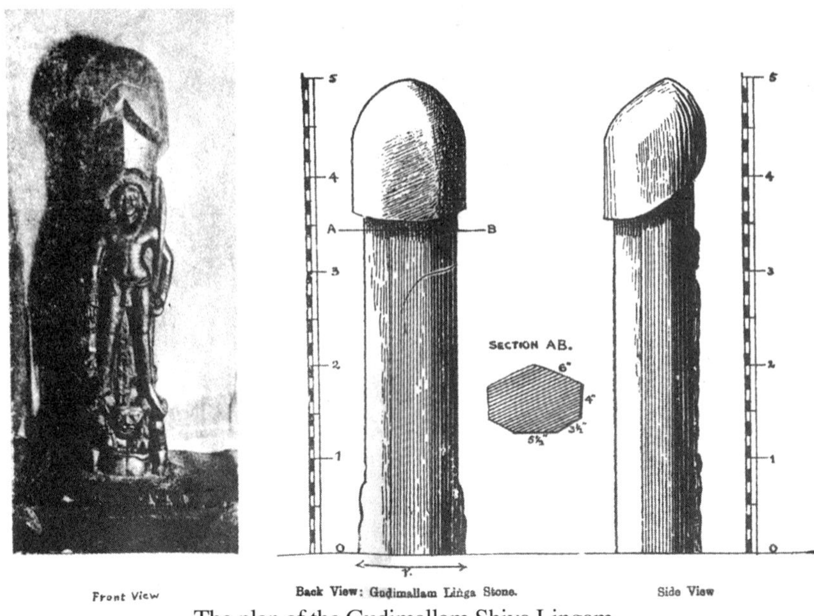

The plan of the Gudimallam Shiva Lingam.

They brought with them the coconut palms and the banana as well as chickens, which have been proven to have originated in Southeast Asia and were brought across the Pacific to coastal areas of South America. The Cham then brought the sweet potato from South America to Pacific Islands such as Easter Island, Tahiti, Tonga and Hawaii. The coconut is actually a cultivated plant that is native to Southeast Asia but exists on nearly every tropical Pacific Island. Brought to Central America by the Cham, the Mayans—and the Olmecs before them—cultivated huge plantations of coconut palms. Even today the remote, uninhabited areas of the Peten jungle of northern Guatemala have hundreds of thousands of coconut palms scattered among the deserted Mayan ruins that cover the area. The area is also crisscrossed with hundreds of disused canals that have been spotted in satellite photos.

What is the Cult of Shiva?

Shiva is one of the three main gods of Hinduism, the other two being Vishnu and Brahma. The iconographical attributes of Shiva are the serpent around his neck, the adorning crescent moon, his matted braided hair coiled as a topknot on his head, the third eye on his forehead, a trident (or trishula) as his weapon, and the damaru drum. He is married to the goddess Parvati and they

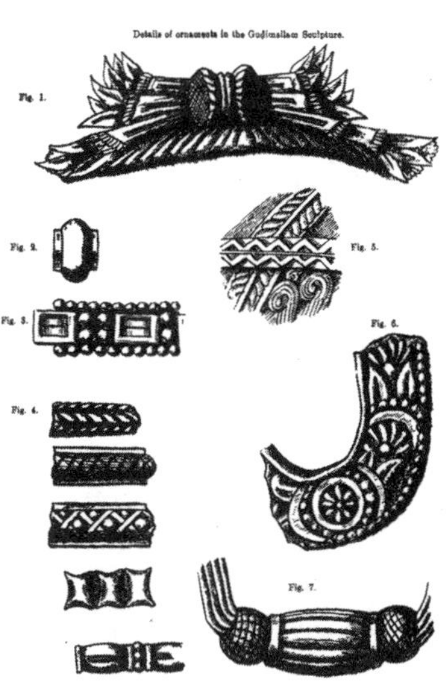

Details of the Gudimallam Shiva Lingam. Note the thick lips.

have a son, the elephant-headed god of good fortune, Ganesh. In benevolent aspects, Shiva is depicted as an omniscient yogi who lives an ascetic life on Mount Kailash in Tibet.

The online Ancient History Encyclopedia gives us this definition of Shiva:

> A complex character, he may represent goodness, benevolence and serve as the Protector but he also has a darker side as the leader of evil spirits, ghosts and vampires and as the master of thieves, villains and beggars. He is also associated with Time, and particularly as the destroyer of all things. Nevertheless, Shiva is also associated with creation. In Hinduism, the universe is thought to regenerate in cycles (every 2,160,000,000 years). Shiva destroys the universe at the end of each cycle which then allows for a new Creation. Shiva is also the great ascetic, abstaining from all forms of indulgence and pleasure, concentrating rather on meditation as a means to find perfect happiness. He is the most important Hindu god for the Shaivism sect, the patron of Yogis and Brahmins, and also the protector of the Vedas, the sacred texts.
>
> ...With Parvati, Shiva had a son, the god Ganesha. The boy was in fact created out of earth and clay to keep her company and protect her while Shiva went on his

> meditative wanderings. However, Shiva returned one day and, finding the boy guarding the room where Parvati was bathing, he enquired who he was. Not believing the boy was his son, and thinking him an impudent beggar, Shiva called up the bhutaganas demons who fought the boy and eventually managed to distract him with the appearance of the beautiful Maya and, whilst he admired the beauty, they lopped off his head. At the commotion, Parvati rushed from her bath and screamed that her son had been killed. Realising his error, Shiva then sent for a new head with which to make the boy whole again but the nearest at hand was of an elephant. And so Ganesha, the elephant-headed god, was born. Other sons of Shiva are Skanda or Karttikeya, the god of war and Kuvera, the god of treasures.
>
> ...Shiva is closely associated with the Linga (or Lingham)—a phallus or symbol of fertility or divine energy found in temples to the god. Following the death of Sarti, and before her reincarnation, Shiva was in mourning and went to the Daru forest to live with rishis or sages. However, the wives of the rishis soon began to take an interest in Shiva. In jealousy, the rishis first sent a large antelope and then a gigantic tiger against the god but Shiva swiftly dealt with them and wore the tiger skin thereafter. The sages then cursed Shiva's manhood which, in consequence, fell off. When the phallus struck the ground, earthquakes began and the rishis became afraid and asked for forgiveness. This was given but Shiva told them to forever after worship the phallus as the symbolic Linga.

Shiva is worshipped today in India, Nepal, Sri Lanka and certain areas of Southeast Asia (such as Bali). All of the Muslim areas of Southeast Asia, including the southern Philippines, were formerly populated by Hindu-Buddhists who worshipped Shiva. In ancient times Shiva was worshipped as far west as Turkey and coins featuring Shiva were minted in the Kushan Buddhist kingdom in northern Pakistan and Afghanistan circa 200 BC. A clay seal from the Indus Valley city of Mohenjo Daro features a seated Shiva in meditation and is dated to circa 2000 BC.

Wikipedia says that Shaivism is one of the four major sects of Hinduism, the others being Vaishnavism, Shaktism and the Smarta Tradition. Followers of Shaivism, called "Shaivas," revere Shiva

A sadhu Shaivite with his long hair in a topknot and three stripes that signify Shiva.

as the Supreme Being. “Shaivas believe that Shiva is All and in all, the creator, preserver, destroyer, revealer and concealer of all that is. He is not only the creator in Shaivism, but he is also the creation that results from him, he is everything and everywhere. Shiva is the primal soul, the pure consciousness and Absolute Reality in the Shaiva traditions.” (Wikipedia)

Normally, in the past, a Hindu male would shave his head and leave a small lock of hair in the back of the head known as a sikha. Hindu brahmins and various devotees, such as Hari Krishnas, are known to shave their heads and leave this bit of hair at the back. In ancient times, every male Hindu was to wear a sikha, and it was one of the few symbols of Hindusism that transcended caste, language and regional barriers. As we will discuss in the next chapter, statues from Gobekli Tepe and Nevali Cori in eastern Turkey show men with the distinctive Hindu ponytail.

Nevalı Cori was an early Neolithic settlement on the middle Euphrates, in the province of Sanliurfa (Urfa), eastern Turkey. The site is famous for having revealed some of the world’s most ancient known temples and monumental sculpture. Together with the site of Göbekli Tepe, it has revolutionized scientific understanding of the Eurasian Neolithic. The site was excavated in 1993 and

Gold alloy statue of Shiva with a mustache from the Goa Anthropology Museum.

dating suggested that the site existed by 9000 BCE, an astonishing 11,000 years ago! Nevali Cori is now under water because of a dam, but artifacts from the site are at the Archeological Museum in Sanliurfa and the most famous piece is the bust of a man whose head is shaved except for the Hindu sikha.

This would suggest to archeologists that the area of central Turkey 11,000 years ago was a Hindu nation. Furthermore, some archeologists maintain that this is the oldest statue of a human in the world, and it is of a Vedic, or Hindu, priest in Turkey.

The Hindu sikha was not worn by all Hindu men, as some chose to not shave their heads and grew their hair very long. This hairstyle is worn today by Hindu ascetics, known as sadhus (and as Shaivas—worshippers of Shiva), wandering holy men who grow their hair out and often carry a trident and a rice bowl or pot.

They typically wear their hair unshaven and very long—never getting a haircut in most cases. This long hair is sometimes worn hanging down over the shoulders and back, or it is tied up in a large bun, or topknot, on the top of the head. This is the way that the Hindu god Shiva wears his hair and it was a popular hairstyle among the Cham, as witnessed by the many statues at the Museum of Cham Culture in Da Nang. This topknot of hair—along with long earlobes—is also seen on the Easter Island statues, to be discussed later. Sometimes this topknot was worn beneath a turban, popular in Fiji and Indonesia.

Says Wikipedia:

> Shaivism is one of the major traditions within Hinduism that reveres Shiva as the Supreme Being. The followers of Shaivism are called "Shaivites" or "Saivites". It is one of the largest sects that believe Shiva, worshipped as a creator and destroyer of worlds, is the supreme god over all. The Shaiva have many sub-traditions ranging from devotional dualistic theism such as Shaiva Siddhanta to yoga-oriented monistic non-theism such as Kashmiri Shaivism. It considers both the Vedas and the Agama texts as important sources of theology. The origin of Shaivism may be traced to the conception of Rudra in the Rig Veda.
>
> Shaivism has ancient roots, traceable in the Vedic literature of 2nd millennium BCE, but this is in the form of the Vedic deity Rudra. The ancient text Shvetashvatara Upanishad dated to late 1st millennium BCE mentions terms such as Rudra, Shiva and Maheshwaram, but its interpretation as a theistic or monistic text of Shaivism is disputed. In the early centuries of the common era is the first clear evidence of *Pāśupata* Shaivism. Both devotional and monistic Shaivism became popular in the 1st millennium CE, rapidly becoming the dominant religious tradition of many Hindu kingdoms. It arrived in Southeast Asia shortly thereafter, leading to the construction of thousands of Shaiva temples on the islands of Indonesia as well as Cambodia and Vietnam, co-evolving with Buddhism in these regions. In the contemporary era, Shaivism is one of

the major aspects of Hinduism.

Shaivist theology ranges from Shiva being the creator, preserver, and destroyer to being the same as the Atman (self, soul) within oneself and every living being. It is closely related to Shaktism, and some Shaiva worship in Shiva and Shakti temples. It is the Hindu tradition that most accepts ascetic life and emphasizes yoga, and like other Hindu traditions encourages an individual to discover and be one with Shiva within. Shaivism is one of the largest traditions within Hinduism.

The origins of Shaivism are unclear and a matter of debate among scholars. Some trace the origins to the Indus Valley civilization, which reached its peak around 2500–2000 BCE. Archeological discoveries show seals that suggest a deity that somewhat appears like Shiva. Of these is the Pashupati seal, which early scholars interpreted as someone seated in a meditating yoga pose surrounded by animals, and with horns. This "Pashupati" (Lord of Animals, Sanskrit paśupati) seal has been interpreted by these scholars as a prototype of Shiva.

...According to Gavin Flood, "the formation of *Śaiva* traditions as we understand them begins to occur during the period from 200 BC to 100 AD."

The curious Indus Valley Seal with Shiva meditating.

Suvarnabhumi: the Land of Gold

Suvarnabhumi is the Sanskrit name for Southeast Asia and the islands of Indonesia. Some historians think that the island of Sumatra was Suvarnabhumi but it is likely that Suvarnabhumi was a very large area and included the coastal areas of many islands. The very modern international airport in Bangkok is named Suvarnabhumi Airport after this legendary land. Scholars argue as to where and how large Suvarnabhumi was. Apparently Suvarnabhumi is the same as Champa—a vast Hindu-Buddhist land of ports and islands beginning with the island of Sumatra and spreading eastward. Says Wikipedia:

> Suvarnabhumi means "Golden Land" or "Land of Gold" and might be a region named Aurea Regio in "India beyond the Ganges" of Ptolemy, also referred to as the Golden Chersonese. The *Periplus of the Erythraean Sea* refers to the Land of Gold, Chryse, and describes it as "an island in the ocean, the furthest extremity towards the east of the inhabited world, lying under the rising sun itself, called Chryse… Beyond this country… there lies a very great inland city called Thina." Dionysius Periegetes mentioned: "The island of Chryse (Gold), situated at the very rising of the Sun." Avienus referred to the Insula Aurea (Golden Isle) located where "the Scythian seas give rise to the Dawn." Josephus speaks of the "Aurea Chersonesus," which he equates with the Biblical Ophir, whence the ships of Tyre and Israel brought back gold for the Temple of Jerusalem. The city of Thina was described by Ptolemy's Geography as the capital city of the country on the eastern shores of the Magnus Sinus (Gulf of Thailand). Some have speculated that this country refers to the Kingdom of Funan. The main port of Funan was Cattigara Sinarum statio (Kattigara the port of the Sinae).

I show in my book *The Lost World of Cham*[8] that the land of Funan and Champa, including Cambodia, were one and the same. If the land of the Champa stretched from Sumatra to Java, to Malaysia, Vietnam, Borneo, Sulawesi, Bali and other islands, then it would naturally be a "Land of Gold" that was not just one island, but a series of them. In my book *Ark of God* I discuss the Biblical land of Ophir—a land of gold—and suggest that it was

Indonesia or beyond. It was a three-year journey going east from the Red Sea to Ophir and back according to the Bible.

Wikipedia mentions that the 3rd century BC Indian emperor Asoka sent Buddhist missionaries to Suvarnabhumi as mentioned in Asoka's edicts and the Sanskrit text known as the "Mahavamsa." The site also says:

> The term Suvarnabhumi ("Land of Gold"), is commonly thought to refer to the Southeast Asian Peninsula, including lower Burma and the Malay Peninsula. However there is another gold-referring term Suvarnadvipa ("Islands of Gold"), which may correspond to the Indonesian Archipelago, especially Sumatra. Both terms might refer to a powerful coastal or island kingdom in present-day Indonesia and Malaysia, possibly centered on Sumatra or Java. This corresponds to the gold production areas traditionally known in Minangkabau highlands in Barisan Mountains, Sumatra, and interior Borneo. An eighth century Indian text known as the "Samaraiccakaha" describes a sea voyage to Suvarnadvipa and the making of bricks from the gold rich sands which they inscribed with the name dharana and then baked. These pointing out to the direction of the western part of insular Southeast Asia, especially Sumatra, Malay Peninsula, Borneo and Java.

It would seem that, at the very least, Suvarnabhumi began at Sumatra and may have included the many islands to the east. It was these islands, especially the small Spice Islands such as Ambon, that were sought for even more valuable commodities than gold—the spices of nutmeg, cinnamon, cloves and allspice. So, it seems that the Hindus

A five headed Cambodia statue of Shiva. 10th century.

in India may have called Sumatra "Suvarnabhumi," while people in the area of the Malay Penninsula, Thailand, Cambodia and Vietnam called themselves Cham or Champa. The Chinese called the area Funan. The Thai peoples are invaders from the north who replaced the darker-skinned Cham and Khmer peoples but kept their Buddhist-Hindu religion. As I have pointed out, the large international airport in Bangkok is called Suvarnabhumi Airport, a nod to the region's ancient history as the land of gold in the old Sanskrit texts.

But a still larger island world spanned farther east into the Pacific—a vast chain of islands through Indonesia, New Guinea, the Philippines, Micronesia, Melanesia, Tonga, Tahiti and beyond. Was there a great fleet of Hindu sailors journeying to these far-flung areas of the western Pacific and leaving megalithic remains behind? The evidence, in my view, points to the Cham and even to earlier Shiva worshipping Indo-Sumerians from the Indus Valley, circa 3000 to 2000 BC. The Nevali Cori statue in eastern Turkey with the Hindu sikha is dated to a staggering 9000 BCE.

Archeologists are now confirming that some sort of Hindu thalassocratic empire existed in Southeast Asia by at least 1000 BC if not before. Stone jars and monuments at Bada Valley on the island of Sulawesi are dated to 2000 BC or older.

Starting by 1500 BC (or earlier) Hindu seafarers began to move through Southeast Asia and Indonesia and into the Pacific. By 500 BC the trade networks of mini port states of the Champa were well formed. Voyages across the Pacific were made. Around 250 BC Asoka began to spread Buddhism east and west. By 200 AD megalithic structures such as My Son, Preah Vihear, Angkor Wat and Borobadur were being built. By 700 AD the Cham Empire had shrunk to central Vietnam. This was a thalassocratic empire that existed for over a thousand years across the entire Pacific Ocean.

But first, what is a thalassocratic empire?

The Thalassocratic Empire of Cham-Kam-Khem 1000 BC

A thalassocratic empire is essentially a maritime empire that maintains naval supremacy through the use of a huge fleet (or fleets) of ships. A country that is a thalassocracy is a maritime trading empire with many port cities on far-flung islands and coastlines. The Phoenicians (who later became the Carthaginians) are a well-known thalassocratic empire that spanned the Mediterranean, North Africa and beyond.

The Merriam-Webster dictionary gives the rather terse definition of thalassocracy as simply "Maritime supremacy." But Wikipedia gives us a much fuller definition:

> A thalassocracy (from Greek language (thalassa), meaning "sea," and (kratein), meaning "to rule," giving (thalassokratia), "rule of the sea") is a state with primarily maritime realms—an empire at sea (such as the Phoenician network of merchant cities) or a sea-borne empire. Traditional thalassocracies seldom dominate interiors, even in their home territories (for example: Phoenician Tyre, Sidon and Carthage or Srivijaya and Majapahit in Southeast Asia). One can distinguish this traditional sense of thalassocracy from an "empire," where the state's territories, though possibly linked principally or solely by the sea lanes, generally extend into mainland interiors (for example: the Bruneian Empire (1368–1888) in Asia). Compare to tellurocracy—land-based hegemony.
>
> The term thalassocracy can also simply refer to naval supremacy, in either military or commercial senses of the word supremacy. The Greeks first used the word thalassocracy to describe the government of the Minoan civilization, whose power depended on its navy. Herodotus also spoke of the need to counter the Phoenician thalassocracy by developing a Greek "empire of the sea."

So, economic powers and their corresponding city-states are divided into two groups: those based on inland cities and control of the roads and rivers (a tellurocracy) and those trading empires based on a vast fleet of ships going from port to port and visiting different continents and far-flung island archipelagos. Some nations may be a combination of the two.

The Shaivite Cham thalassocracy may have been the largest ever known in the ancient world. In modern times it could be argued that the British thalassocratic empire, on which "the sun never set," was the largest in all of history. It is an amazing accomplishment that a small island archipelago in the North Sea would have a maritime empire spanning all the oceans of the earth, to remote areas such as New Zealand, the Falkland Islands and much of North America, Africa and the Middle East. It was the large British navy and other cargo ships that linked this vast network that continues to this day as the British Commonwealth.

It was the Shaivite Cham who built a gigantic naval base out of millions of tons of basalt on the volcanic Micronesian island of Pohnpei, today the capital of the Federated States of Micronesia. From here they moved out into the central Pacific, to Fiji, Tonga, Tahiti and the Marquesas Islands. Easter Island was also colonized by them.

They arrived at the west coast of Mexico where they created ports and began the Olmec civilization that flourished in Mexico, Guatemala and other areas of Central America. Later some of these areas became dominated by the Maya. Others became dominated by the Zapotec or Toltec. The Aztecs came at a much later period.

The Cham continued to the Pacific Coast of Colombia, Ecuador and Peru and interacted with cultures there. In all these places they were after metals of all kinds, including iron, gold, copper, tin and silver. They had iron tools and advanced technology. They set up mining camps in areas that the locals had helped them discover and washed and smelted ores. They worked hard stone such as basalt and granite with relative ease and assembled stone walls that still amaze visitors today at places like Cuzco, Tiwanaku, Ollantaytambo, Machu Picchu and Chavin.

They left stone crucibles that baffle archeologists today as well as stone towers that were used for smelting the ore into the liquid metals. Archeologists today believe these to be burial towers. Despite the fact that archeologists know that bronze metals were poured into granite or sandstone molds at Tiwanaku and Puma Punku, they do not explain where the metallurgical complex is located. As I explain in my book *Ancient Technology in Peru and Bolivia,* the purpose of the megalithic site of Tiwanaku and Puma Punku was the washing and smelting of ores. Ultimately the liquid metals of gold, silver, copper and even iron were created and mixed into their alloys. The Cham were fond of using electrum—a mix of gold and silver—for many of their metal statues and the area around Tiwanaku was a major source of both metals.

Shiva and the Enigma of Bada Valley

Some years ago I became acquainted with the Bada Valley in central Sulawesi Island in Indonesia. I had seen some photos from the Tropen Museum in Holland and realized that a megalithic mystery was to be found in this remote valley of the island in Southeast Asia. I visited Bada in 2012 with my wife Jennifer and a friend, John Feiertag. The ancient statues in this remote valley, which has gold in its rivers, include statues of Shiva.

An old photo of the Shiva statue.

Bada Valley, sometimes called Napu Valley, is located in the Lore Lindu National Park and contains hundreds of finely carved megaliths. They go back to at least 1400 AD and are probably much older. No one knows who the builders were. The locals are apparently as mystified about the megaliths as archeologists are. They are magnificent and enigmatic and testify to a genius and high civilization that we know nothing about.

One of the things that most impressed me was the similarity of some of the Bada Valley statues with Olmec statues in Mexico and Guatemala. This is an area of research that I intend to pursue. I was able to conclude that many of the statues, including the main large statue, are statues of Shiva. Shiva is often shown with an erect penis which is what is detailed in some of the Bada Valley statues.

Here is the article on Bada Valley as it appears by an anonymous author on indahnesia.com:

> An impressive phallic symbol, carved out to express a human shape, rises from the ground. The face—several bend lines, the round eyes and a slightly opened mouth—watches to the west with a timeless expression, unmoved and understandable like the sphinx. This megalithic art, massive and simple, kept its tremendous silent power even after someone tried to brush away the natural erosion.

Together with three other megaliths and many big stone drums, Palindo—as the stone statue is named—lives in the Bada valley, which stretches up to 15 kilometers through Lore Lindu

The Shiva statue in Bada Valley with an erect penis.

An aerial photo of remote Bada Valley on the island of Sulawesi.

National Park. The Sungai Lariang river runs through the entire valley and is crossed by three hanging bridges. This river, together with its smaller feeder rivers, is used to irrigate the terraced rice fields. Gintu, the capital of the sub-district Bada, has only a few thousand inhabitants. This village controls the area with its several government buildings, shops and a handful of televisions. There are about 10.000 people in fourteen villages in the area.

The megaliths in Bada draw a handful of tourists and archeologists. The fierce terrain forms an impressive background for the stone pieces of art. Eroded rows of hills and low mountains at a distance of two kilometers complete the raw gracefulness of the statues. For some, the natural background wasn't enough. In 1984, the government asked the people in the Bada Valley to build a giant wooden house beside Palindo, as well as a vaguely traditional building behind that. They don't serve a clear purpose. The final blow to the statue is a system of paths around it, complete with flat, square stones. There is also a shed with a damaged platform under a raised storage. The purpose of the shed is not known, but you can sit down in its shadow and watch the statue from behind.

The Besoa Valley, at a long days walk north of the Bada Valley, (watch out for leeches), also houses a number of human-like statues, as well as the big stone drums or *kalambu*. In Besoa they are covered in inscriptions, which are missing from the drums in Bada. One of these stone drums has a lid with five carved-out animals on the sides, looking similar to the bronze Dongson drums, which found their way from Vietnam to Indonesia in prehistoric times.

A tiki statue in Bada Valley. Shiva?

In 1902, the first Europeans, Paul and Fritz Sasarin, entered the valley without seeing the megaliths. The Dutch missionary, Dr. Albert C. Kruyt, reports that sacrifices for a wealthy harvest were brought to one of the statues; when there was too little rain, sacrifices of pinang nuts were brought to the statue that is known as Tarai Roi. Other sources also report these kinds of sacrifices. Note that the sacrifices are not of animals but of nuts from a tree. This is the kind of sacrifice that a vegetarian Hindu would make.

Nothing is known for sure about the origin of the stones. When Kruyt reached Bada in 1908, the megalith culture was already gone. The inhabitants could not tell much more than that the statues were already there ever since their ancestors entered the valley. A final survey hasn't been done yet, but estimations of age vary from

A tiki statue in Bada Valley. A statue of Shiva?

3000 BC to 1300 AD. Probably, the sculptures of Bada, as well as those in the Besoa Valley, are remains from a megalith tradition that was once spread over the entirety of Indonesia (and is still continued in Sumba). Central Sulawesi has, together with the stone statues and big drums, a diversity of stone objects that probably originate from the same culture.

A Tiki statue in Bada Valley. Shiva?

Although the statues in the Bada Valley are completely different in size—anywhere between one and four meters—they are almost similar in style: somewhat oval with large round faces. The eyes, somewhat oval as well, are surrounded with a long bend line which marks eyebrows, nose and chin. The face is in high relief, but the arms, hands and genitals (an erected penis or open vagina) are in low relief.

It is suggested that the Palindo is assoctiated with death. For the Toraja, a people who live about four to five days' walk to the south, west is the direction of death. Linguistic and other cultural similarities between the Toraja and the populations of the Bada give this theory at least some credibility. The Bada insist on burying their dead with the head towards the west, even after their conversion to Christianity, and the Toraja used to erect megaliths as a part of their burial ceremonies until not too long ago. The Bada as well as the Toraja sacrifice a water buffalo for the spirits of their deceased.

The inhabitants of the Bada valley have had a very comfortable life since they can remember. The rice fields regularly bring in a surplus of rice, and coffee (an import from Ethiopia) is grown to be sold. The area is now also growing clove and cacao-trees that were introduced by the government. An irrigation project, paid for by the government, enlarged the capacity of rice fields by about 1,000 hectares in the 1990s.

People who are looking for gold, who work in the different rivers and creeks, concentrate on the area called Sungai Malei. It is said that gold brings in about half of the income of the valley. It

One of the stone jars at Bada Valley.

is still dangerous however. In a flash flood in 1986, 25 people that were sleeping on a bank in the middle of the river were washed away and killed.

It is clear that Bada Valley was an ancient Hindu-Shaivite gold mining center. The gold trade stopped for many generations but has now returned. Gold in the rivers seems to be the main reason for the megalithic statues being in this remote location. Also, it is suspected that Bada Valley may be the original site of ancient rice planting, a rather complicated procedure that is thought to have originated in Indonesia and Southeast Asia.

The water buffalo is also traditionally used as dowry. The nobility has mostly lost its privileged status by now, but an aristocrat daughter is still worth several water buffalos. The Bada also accept money nowadays.

Water buffalos, oxen, horses, pigs and chickens are common in the valley. In trading, oxen have the same value as water buffalos (traditionally the highest valued possession in many parts

One of the stone jars with a lid of carved frogs. The many stone jars in Bada Valley were probably crucibles for melting gold ore in a kiln.

of Indonesia); they are in demand for their meat as well as for their working power. Both kinds of animals are used in the rice fields to plow them, but water buffalos are more effective because they can also plow through deep mud, which is not possible for less strong cattle.

The megalithic statues of Bada Valley are indicative of the early Shiva mining activities of those who sought out gold in the land of Suvarnabhumi—the land of gold. How did they reach this remote valley in central Sulawesi many thousands of years ago? Did they come in boats and then trek inland to this remote mountain paradise to carve megalithic statues and mine for gold? Or, did they come by airship—a vimana of ancient Hindu literature—to scout out the mining and agricultural promise of Bada Valley?

In the empire of Shiva, this is a definite possibility. Let us look at the many areas that stretch out of India and Mount Kailash—Shiva's home in southern Tibet—to the west in the Middle East, Europe, Africa and Madagascar and then to the east into the Pacific and the Americas. We will also look at the astonishing technology of this trans-continental civilization that achieved great heights that are written in ancient books that have survived over the millennia. There is also the megalithic stone evidence that has been left in full view of the historian. This stone evidence made out of granite and basalt is virtually indestructible and will last for hundreds and even thousands of years. The empire of Shiva has left us that.

This Bada Valley sculpture looks similar to Olmec work.

Chapter 3

Göbekli Tepe and Shiva

Everyone is waiting, just anticipating on you
Won't you make a showing, everybody knows what to do
Take a dive from your ivory tower
And fall on everyone—we'll catch you
— *Love of the Common Man*, Todd Rundgren

I first visited Göbekli Tepe in 2010 with my wife Jennifer. At the time we flew from London to Istanbul and then to Sanliurfa in southern Turkey, a town near the Syrian border. This town, formerly known simply as Urfa, is mentioned in the Bible as a place where the ancient patriarch Abraham lived for a time. His name is a curious one, essentially "A-Brahmin" and a Brahmin is well known as a person of the Hindu priestly caste. Brahmins devoted their time to studying, teaching, performing sacrifices, and officiating religious services. It seemed that there was already a connection to Shiva and India right here in Sanliurfa.

Just east of Sanliurfa are the ruins of Göbekli Tepe, now said to be among the oldest archeological ruins in the world, built in approximately 9500 BC. A nearby site which has just begun to be excavated, Karahan Tepe, is thought to be slightly older.

Sanliurfa is an ancient city that has a history dating back 9,000 years. Urfa, as it was known then, is where the Prophet Abraham, the genetic father of Judaism, Christianity and Islam, resided and is also where the Prophet Job lived. In a park in the center of the old city is the sacred Balikli Lake plus a cave (now a holy shrine) where Abraham was said to have been born. According to local legend, King Nemrut of the region had the Prophet Abraham thrown into a big fire lit at the spot, but water emerging from the fire saved the Prophet Abraham from burning. The water became the lake that can be seen today, and

the pieces of wood from the fire were transformed into fish that now inhabit the shallow lake and pools at the Halil Rahman and Rizvaniye Mosques.

On our first day in Sanliurfa we visited the old city and its mosques, sacred lake and cave. It was delightfully pleasant to walk along the green park with its grass, trees and pools, in sight of the citadel of the old Roman fortress that looms above the city.

The next day we visited the museum in Sanliurfa and then took a bus to the ancient Biblical town of Harran to the south. Harran is also mentioned in the Old Testament and is only a few kilometers from the modern Syrian border. According to the ancient texts, the Prophet Abraham stayed in Harran when he was migrating southward from Urfa and his father, Terah, died there. We toured the ruins of a massive caravanserai that would have accommodated travelers in Abraham's time, and might have walked in the very footsteps of the great prophet. Many scholars believe that the foundations of the three religions of Moses, Jesus and Mohammed were laid in Harran. The first University of Islam was located there and the old city still has the remains of a 40-meter observation tower among these ruins from the early Islamic age. Archaeological excavations in the city are continuing and much of the area was fenced off to keep all visitors out.

The Ancient Temple of Göbekli Tepe

The third day, we hired a taxi and went northeast to the archeological dig of Göbekli Tepe, said by mainstream archeologists to be the secondoldest human structures yet discovered. German archeologists involved with the site say that it was built approximately 9500 BC, or about 11,500 years ago. Other estimates are that it was built between 12,000 and 13,000 years ago, giving it a date of 10500 BC. No matter what the exact date, it is generally agreed that this is the oldest temple that mainstream archeologists acknowledge as authentic. And, like any good lost temple, it is megalithic—built out of a combination of finely cut megalithic pillars and walls of smaller stones.

A reconstruction of Gobekli Tepe.

The site is called by the local Kurds "potbelly hill," hence "Göbekli Tepe" in Turkish. Göbekli Tepe was first noted in 1964 by an American survey, but nothing was done to investigate the partially man-made hill at the time. Now excavations are being conducted by the German Archaeological Institute (Istanbul branch) and the Sanliurfa Museum. Though only a portion of the hill has been exposed, it is still being excavated by the Turkish and German archeologists, who began work in 1994. The project was conducted under the direction of the German archaeologist Klaus Schmidt until his death in 2014. No digging was happening the day we were there, and the site was virtually deserted.

The site has absolutely stunned the archeological community who now say that they were "completely wrong" about man's past. One of the best accounts of the site was published in a *Newsweek* article by Patrick Symmes in the March 1, 2010 issue; it called Göbekli Tepe a "temple complex in Turkey that …is rewriting the story of human evolution."

Says the article:

> After a dozen years of patient work, Schmidt has uncovered what he thinks is definitive proof that a huge ceremonial site flourished here, a "Rome of the Ice Age," as he puts it, where hunter-gatherers met to build a complex religious community. Across the hill, he has found carved and polished circles of stone, with terrazzo flooring and double benches. All the circles feature massive T-shaped pillars that evoke the monoliths of Easter Island.
>
> Though not as large as Stonehenge—the biggest circle is 30 yards across, the tallest pillars 17 feet high—the ruins

> are astonishing in number. Last year Schmidt found his third and fourth examples of the temples. Ground-penetrating radar indicates that another 15 to 20 such monumental ruins lie under the surface. Schmidt's German-Turkish team has also uncovered some 50 of the huge pillars, including two found in his most recent dig season that are not just the biggest yet, but, according to carbon dating, are the oldest monumental artworks in the world.
>
> The new discoveries are finally beginning to reshape the slow-moving consensus of archeology. Göbekli Tepe is "unbelievably big and amazing, at a ridiculously early date," according to Ian Hodder, director of Stanford's archeology program. Enthusing over the "huge great stones and fantastic, highly refined art" at Göbekli, Hodder—who has spent decades on rival Neolithic sites—says: "Many people think that it changes everything... It overturns the whole apple cart. All our theories were wrong."

Indeed, the apple cart has been turned upside down, and suddenly civilization is much older than the "experts" told us for years. They were wrong, and now they admit it. But, unfortunately, they don't admit much more than that. In fact, Schmidt, the leading authority on Göbekli Tepe and main "theorist" on the site is said to be a staunch Catholic and tends towards the conservative side of archeology. Says the *Newsweek* article about Schmidt and this theories on Göbekli Tepe:

> Schmidt's thesis is simple and bold: it was the urge to worship that brought mankind together in the very first urban conglomerations. The need to build and maintain this temple, he says, drove the builders to seek stable food sources, like grains and animals that could be domesticated, and then to settle down to guard their new way of life. The temple begat the city.

A view of part of Gobekli Tepe.

Civilization that is 10,000 Years Old Changes History

Up until the discoveries at Göbekli Tepe and nearby Nevali Cori and Karahan Tepe, it was thought that primitive man went through a "Neolithic revolution" 10,000 to 12,000 years ago wherein the hunter-gathers gradually settled down and developed the tools of civilization. But Schmidt thinks that nomads created a cult center at Göbekli Tepe first, and civilization arose later. It doesn't quite make sense. Says the *Newsweek* article:

> In the old model, shepherds and farmers appeared first, and then created pottery, villages, cities, specialized labor, kings, writing, art, and—somewhere on the way to the airplane—organized religion. As far back as Jean-Jacques Rousseau, thinkers have argued that the social compact of cities came first, and only then the "high" religions with their great temples, a paradigm still taught in American high schools.
>
> Religion now appears so early in civilized life—earlier than civilized life, if Schmidt is correct—that some think it may be less a product of culture than a cause of it, less a revelation than a genetic inheritance. The archeologist Jacques Cauvin once posited that "the beginning of the gods was the beginning of agriculture," and Göbekli may prove his case.
>
> The builders of Göbekli Tepe could not write or leave other explanations of their work. Schmidt speculates that nomadic bands from hundreds of miles in every direction were already gathering here for rituals, feasting, and initiation rites before the first stones were cut. The religious purpose of the site is implicit in its size and location. "You don't move 10-ton stones for no reason," Schmidt observes. "Temples like to be on high sites," he adds, waving an arm over the stony, round hilltop. "Sanctuaries like to be away from the mundane world."

So, which came first: knowledge of engineering, stone work, ceramics, animal husbandry, agricultural cultivation and such, or the cult center of Göbekli Tepe? According to Schmidt, Göbekli Tepe came first. Civilization came later. However, as well shall see, it seems likely that the level of civilization

Some of the monoliths at Gobekli Tepe.

necessary to create what has so far been found at Göbekli Tepe and other nearby sites was quite high, and must have come from an older lineage of scientific knowledge—just as ancient books such as the Old Testament, the Mahabharata, Plato's Timaeus, etc., tell us.

Curiously, Göbekli Tepe was discovered completely intact, and it is thought that the site was purposely buried. Perhaps this would have been done to conserve the site for future generations, or perhaps to safeguard it from destruction by others.

The pillars at Göbekli Tepe are carved in excellent detail with depictions of cattle and wild boar, as well as totem-type animals like lions, foxes and leopards. There are some abstract symbols, but the site is mainly covered with graceful, naturalistic sculptures and bas-reliefs of the animals that were central to the "imagination of hunter-gatherers." There is also human symbolism at the site. Says the *Newsweek* article:

> Many of the biggest pillars are carved with arms, including shoulders, elbows, and jointed fingers. The T shapes appear to be towering humanoids but have no faces, hinting at the worship of ancestors or humanlike deities. "In the Bible it talks about how God created man in his image," says Johns Hopkins archeologist Glenn Schwartz. Göbekli Tepe "is the first time you can see humans with that idea, that they resemble gods."
>
> The temples thus offer unexpected proof that mankind emerged from the 140,000-year reign of hunter-gatherers with a ready vocabulary of spiritual imagery, and capable

of huge logistical, economic, and political efforts. A Catholic born in Franconia, Germany, Schmidt wanders the site in a white turban, pointing out the evidence of that transition. "The people here invented agriculture. They were the inventors of cultivated plants, of domestic architecture," he says.

Ancient India, Zoroastrians and Asia Minor

So, here we have a megalithic site with a number of 10-ton granite T-megaliths that are typically carved with spiders, scorpions, snakes, triple-fanged monsters, and, most common of all, carrion birds such as vultures. It is curious that depictions of carrion birds outnumber those of any other animal at Göbekli Tepe. The single largest carving on a pillar shows a vulture poised over a headless human. A similar depiction was found at Catal Huyuk, further west. This gives rise to the fascinating theory that sky burials were taking place here—a practice that continues to this day in some parts of the world.

Sky burials were apparently an ancient Zoroastrian custom, practiced in Persia, Turkey, and throughout the Middle East at one time. Tibetans are known to carry out sky burials as well. So did some Native Americans. The Parsis of ancient Persia, who migrated to the area of Mumbai, India, continue their practice of sky burials to this day. They place dead bodies on platforms high above their temples so that carrion birds may pick the skeletons clean, and then they crush the bones. This may have been an ancient Hindu custom, though cremation is now the norm in that religion.

At nearby Nevali Cori the local limestone was

A monolith at Gobekli Tepe.

A portion of the ancient site of Nevali Cori.

carved into numerous statues and smaller sculptures, including a more than life-sized bare human head with a snake or sikha-like tuft. As we have discussed a "sikha" is a tuft of hair on the back of an otherwise shaven head, often worn by Hindu priests. Many people recognize this tonsorial style because Hari Krishna devotees wear the sikha-tuft.

I first learned about the Nevali Cori site from reading Andrew Collins' 1998 book *The Gods of Eden,*[19] He discusses Nevali Cori in one chapter and mentions how the discoveries there in the 1990s had made it the oldest human habitation site of the time—until Göbekli Tepe came along a few years later with its earlier dates. Dates at Nevali Cori are to the 9th and 10th millennia BC, with carbon dates of 8400 BC and earlier being reported. Collins says the temple found at Nevali Cori is very similar to the sunken temple of Kalasaya at Tiwanaku in Bolivia, especially the pillars with human hands on their sides.

Statue with sikha from Nevali Cori.

Nevali Cori is not far from Göbekli Tepe, about 30 miles to the north, but the site is now under water because of the ambitious agricultural programs underway in central Turkey.

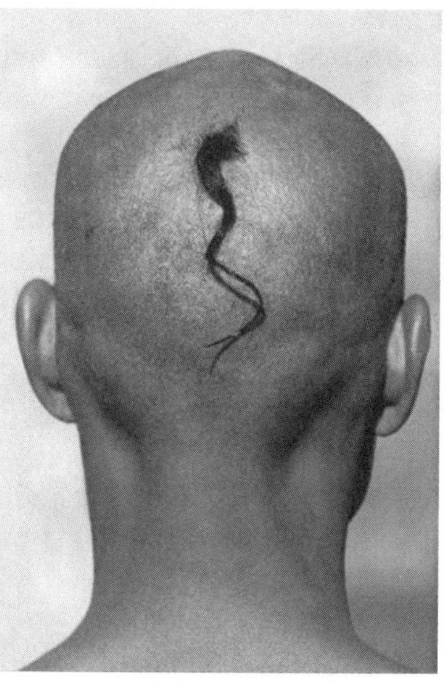

Modern sikha on a Hindu male.

The site was examined in 1993 in the context of rescue excavations during the erection of the Atatürk Dam below Samsat. Excavations at the site were conducted by a team from the University of Heidelberg under the direction of Professor Harald Hauptmann. Along with a number of other archaeological sites in the vicinity, Nevali Cori has now been submerged by the dammed waters of the Euphrates. Therefore, the site is essentially permanently lost. We now have only a few photographs of the site (there are not many to be found) and some artifacts now kept at the Sanliurfa Museum.

Also found at Nevali Cori were several hundred small clay figurines (about five cm high), most of them depicting humans, which have been interpreted as votive offerings. It has been determined that they were fired at temperatures between 500 and 600°C, which suggests the development of ceramic firing technology before the advent of pottery proper. Are they possibly images of Shiva?

So, we have ceramics that are fired at a high temperature, indicating advanced knowledge of ceramics; we have people, possibly priests, having a shaved head with a Hindu sikha-tuft; and we have sky burials, which continue in India today. Could it be that this area was already a Hindu kingdom in 10,000 BC and practiced many of the Hindu-like customs that are still in use today, 12,000 years later? It would seem so. I would even say that these customs are many thousands of years older than Göbekli Tepe, and may have come from an area of the world that is now under water, such as the inundated continental shelves that were flooded in the last ice age. Nevali Cori is apparently the town that supported the ceremonial activities at Göbekli Tepe.

Says the 2010 *Newsweek* article:

> Schmidt theorizes that human corpses were exposed here on the hilltop for consumption by birds—what a Tibetan would call a sky burial. Sifting the tons of dirt removed from the site has produced very few human bones, however, perhaps because they were removed to distant homes for ancestor worship. Absence is the source of Schmidt's great theoretical claim. "There are no traces of daily life," he explains. "No fire pits. No trash heaps. There is no water here." Everything from food to flint had to be imported, so the site "was not a village," Schmidt says. Since the temples predate any known settlement anywhere, Schmidt concludes that man's first house was a house of worship: "First the temple, then the city," he insists.
>
> Some archeologists, like Hodder, the Neolithic specialist, wonder if Schmidt has simply missed evidence of a village or if his dating of the site is too precise. But the real reason the ruins at Göbekli remain almost unknown, not yet incorporated in textbooks, is that the evidence is too strong, not too weak. "The problem with this discovery," as Schwartz of Johns Hopkins puts it, "is that it is unique." No other monumental sites from the era have been found. Before Göbekli, humans drew stick figures on cave walls, shaped clay into tiny dolls, and perhaps piled up small stones for shelter or worship. Even after Göbekli, there is little evidence of sophisticated building. Dating of ancient sites is highly contested, but Çatalhöyük is probably about 1,500 years younger than Göbekli, and features no carvings or grand constructions. The walls of Jericho, thought until now to be the oldest monumental construction by man, were probably started more than a thousand years after Göbekli. Huge temples did emerge again—but the next unambiguous example dates from 5,000 years later, in southern Iraq.

It is interesting that the site was not a village. Schmidt says that there is no water there. As I looked around the rocky soil and grass hills, it seemed fairly green in the area, but the nearest stream or river must have been some miles away. This therefore poses the problem of bringing water to the site. Was it done with large ceramic amphora on auroch carts or such? I am reminded of some of the clay seals that were found at Indus Valley sites such as Harappa and Mohenjo Daro that depict a type of cattle that is unknown to us, brahma cattle with a distinct hump. Were those cattle first domesticated here at Göbekli Tepe and its environs?

Indeed, mainstream archeologists contend that genetic mapping shows that the first domestication of wheat was in the immediate area of Göbekli Tepe, and that animal husbandry also began near here—the first domesticated pigs came from the surrounding area in about 8000 BC, and cattle were domesticated in Turkey before 6500 BC.

Schmidt believed that whatever mysterious rituals were conducted in the temples, they ended abruptly before 8000 BC. At that time the entire site was buried, deliberately and all at once, he determined. A decline in the temples' use followed by a sudden burial marked "the end of a very strange culture," Schmidt said, but then a new, settled civilization began. The hilltops of the hunters were exchanged for the valleys of farmers and shepherds. He suggested that the temples simply moved to the valley areas and the priests had the hilltop temples buried.

We may never know why Göbekli Tepe was abandoned, but it is changing history—ever so slowly. The Greek philosopher Plato famously reported that Egyptian priests maintained that civilization was over 10,000 years old, and that ancient Greece and a lost civilization called Atlantis had fought a war in the eastern Mediterranean. Mainstream archeologists—the professors at universities and the writers of textbooks—said that this was impossible because civilization wasn't that old. But now, civilization is getting that old.

Did these people who lived over 10,000 years ago have tools to carve their megaliths? Certainly. Did they have boats? Were they capable of building bridges, houses and harbors? I would say they were, and we know that they had knowledge of high temperature ceramics.

Whenever megaliths are involved, there is always the question of quarrying and transporting such large and heavy stones, and the "reason" for wanting to attempt something that would seem so exceptionally difficult. Not only would some sort of engineering be involved—and often very clever solutions—but some mysterious desire to build with giant stones that would take a lot of organization to move. Where did these hunter-gatherers get the skills to quarry and move 10-ton blocks of stone and then chisel fine reliefs into them? According to Schmidt, they didn't really have these skills, they were to come later.

Indeed, it seems to me that the organization of Göbekli Tepe came from an earlier civilization still unseen by mainstream archeologists such as Dr. Schmidt. It would seem to be a Hindu civilization that already existed in Asia Minor, the Persian Gulf and India, and probably other areas such as Malaysia and Indonesia. We can be sure that mainstream archeologists won't be saying the "A-word" (Atlantis) any time soon when discussing Göbekli Tepe, but this find may pave the way for the acceptance of even older sites that are proven to be 12,000 to 15,000 years old. With such firm dates, and the proven seafaring ability of mankind, the legends of Atlantis won't seem so scientifically impossible any more!

The Latest Discovery: Karahan Tepe

Another similar ancient hilltop is Karahan Tepe (formerly called *Keçili Tepe*) which lies approximately 23 miles southeast of Göbekli Tepe, and was apparently built a few hundred years earlier. Karahan Tepe has been dated to 11,400-10,200 years old, with over 250 monoliths recorded at the site, mostly T-pillars, as well as many unique stone carvings and statues recently unearthed. As at Göbekli Tepe, this site is covered with many strange depictions of humans, symbols, and animals, but also with a sunken pit containing phallic-shaped pillars and a 3D portrayal of a human head with a serpentine neck. The artifacts from the excavation are now on display at the Şanlıurfa Archaeology Museum.

Karahan Tepe is a unique Pre-Pottery Neolithic complex built upon a large limestone hill. When viewing the horizon from its peak, it feels like it is in the middle of nowhere. There are several sites of a similar age and style being excavated right now in a zone called "Tas Tepeler," meaning "Stone Hills/Mounds." This covers an area 124 miles in width. Karahan Tepe is one of 11 sites under investigation. Göbekli Tepe being the primary site, it is the only one currently open to the public. At the time of writing, Karahan Tepe is yet to officially open, but visitors are welcome.

British researcher and author Hugh Newman first explored the un-excavated site of Karahan Tepe in 2014 with Andrew Collins, making further visits in 2015 and 2018. During these visits only the tops of T-pillars on the surface of the hill, an 18-foot-long

Two statues at Karahan Tepe inclduing one with an erect penis. Shiva?

unfinished T-shaped monolith below the hill on the western edge, and some relief carvings on a few stones were visible. For many years it was an enduring mystery as to what was going to be found underneath.

In 2019 excavation finally began, led by archaeologist Prof. Necmi Karul, associate professor in the Prehistory Department of Istanbul University. As his team slowly uncovered the northern slopes of the stone hill, some astonishing discoveries began to be made. One of the most fascinating elements of the excavation was the "hypogeum" style chambers and pits, and the way the western side of the main 75-foot-wide enclosure (Structure AD) has what appeared to be T-Pillars carved out of solid bedrock, whilst others in the circle were freestanding. The site looks like it was damaged (or decommissioned) before it was deliberately, and very carefully, covered over. Having said that, only one percent of Karahan Tepe has been opened up so far.

Necmi Karul wrote a paper examining the techniques and implications of the burying process suggesting this was a very important facet of the complex. He focused on the AB Pit (also called the Pillar Shrine), a 7m by 6m shaft with 10 bedrock pillars, a freestanding monolith and a protruding carved head on the western wall. Its elongated neck has serpent scales etched into it and a V-shape under the chin. On the southeast edge of the pit is a 70-cm-wide porthole that leads out to the main 75-foot-wide enclosure. Like at Göbekli Tepe, numerous holed stones have been unearthed at Karahan Tepe, but why was this one, which is carved from the natural bedrock, in this exact position in relation to the Pillar Shrine?

The Pillar Shrine has a trapezoidal plan with rounded corners. The 11th pillar is the only one not carved directly out of the bedrock; rather it is inserted into a carved socket at its base. All pillars are conical, perfectly upright, and all except one are shaped like an erect phallus. Below the porthole are worn steps, which may have been where people would climb down after entering through the hole from Structure AD.

It would seem that Karahan Tepe and Göbekli Tepe were hilltop funeral sites for a city that was Nevali Cori. Nevali Cori was a city with water, wheat fields, houses and streets. It came first, before the funeral hills nearby. We know from the sikha on the statue found at Nevali Cori that the population were Hindus—some of whom were worshippers of Shiva—in 10,000 BC!

The Mystery of the Druze

The Druze population in Syria, Lebanon and Israel is another curious mystery when it comes to ancient Shiva worship in Arabia. The Druze, who are thought to have immigrated to Egypt and the Levant from somewhere in southern Arabia, may be the last of the ancient Shaivite religions of Arabia that preceded the advent of Mohammed and his armies.

The Druze call themselves al-Muwaḥḥidūn which means "the monotheists" or "the Unitarians." They are a secretive Arab esoteric religious group from Arabia who adhere to the Druze faith, an Abrahamic, monotheistic religion whose main tenets assert the unity of God, reincarnation, and the eternity of the soul.

Although the Druze faith developed from Isma'ilism, Druze do not identify as Muslims. Muslims, generally, do not believe in reincarnation. Sunni Muslims particularly do not believe in reincarnation—a Hindu concept—but some Sufis of the Shia branch of Islam do accept the idea of rebirth. Druze identify themselves as Arabs and maintain the Arabic language and culture as integral parts of their identity.

Although it is known that the Druze teach reincarnation, most Druze religious practices are kept secret, and conversion to their religion is not permitted. The only new Druze people are those that are born to Druze families. Marriage is only allowed within the Druze community which exists today in Syria, Lebanon and

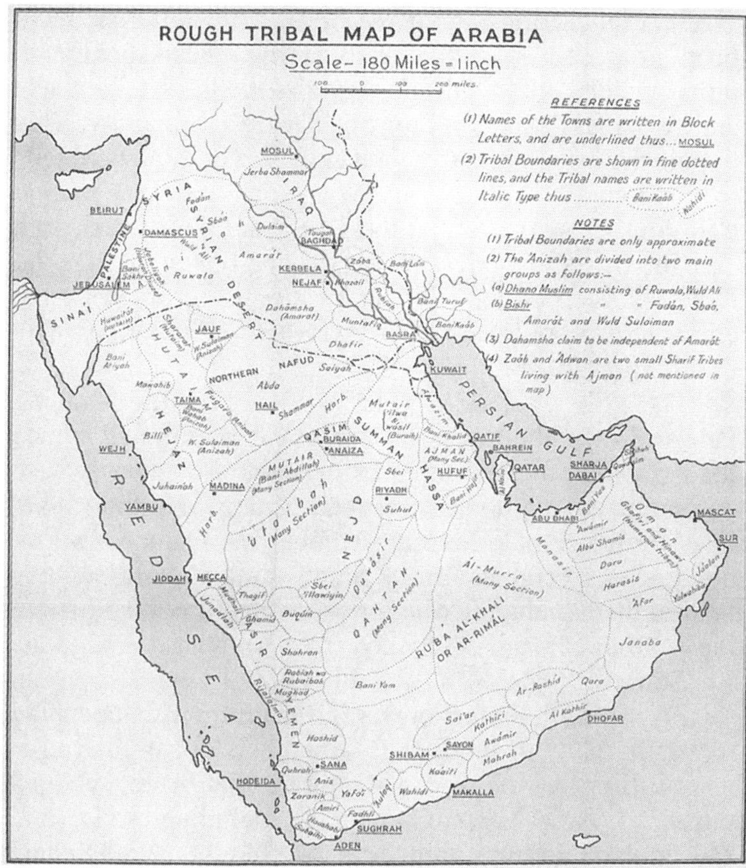

A 1914 map of the tribes of Arabia.

Israel (and a small section of northern Jordan near Syria). The oldest and most densely populated Druze communities exist in Mount Lebanon and in the south of Syria around Jabal al-Druze ("Mountain of the Druze").

The Druze hold the early prophet Shuaib of the Quran in high regard, believing him to be the reincarnation of the biblical Jethro, father of Moses. They regard Adam, Noah, Abraham, Moses, Jesus, Muhammad, and the Isma'ili Imam Muhammad ibn Isma'il as prophets who have also reincarnated. Additionally, Druze tradition honors figures such as Salman the Persian, al-Khidr (whom they identify with Elijah, John the Baptist and Saint George), Job, Luke the Evangelist, and others as "mentors" and "prophets" that have reincarnated at various times.

Wikipedia says this about the origin of the Druze:

> Several theories about the origins of the Druze have been proposed, with the Arabian hypothesis being the most widely accepted among historians, intellectuals, and religious leaders within the Druze community. This hypothesis significantly influences the Druze's self-perception, cultural identity, and both oral and written traditions. It suggests that the Druze are descended from 12 Arab tribes that migrated to Syria before and during the early Islamic period. This perspective is accepted by the entire Druze communities in Syria and Lebanon, as well as by most Druze in Israel.
>
> The tribes of Arabia have inhabited the Arabian Peninsula for thousands of years and traditionally trace their ancestry to one of two forefathers: Adnan, whose descendants originate from West Arabia, North Arabia, East Arabia, and Central Arabia; or Qahtan, whose descendants originate from South Arabia. Further, it is held in the Abrahamic religions—particularly Islam—that the Arab people are descended from Abraham through his son Ishmael.
>
> From the 7th century onward, concurrent with the spread of Islam, many of these tribes' members began migrating and settling in the various regions that were subdued during the early Muslim conquests, including the Levant, Mesopotamia, Egypt, Khuzestan, the Maghreb, and Sudan. This phenomenon triggered a process of Arabization that significantly influenced demographic shifts across most of West Asia and North Africa, culminating in the growth of the Arab population far beyond the Arabian Peninsula.

The story of the creation of the Druze faith between 1017 and 1018 is dominated by two men and their struggle for influence. Both of these men were Ismaili mystics from an area of eastern Persia known as Khorasan. They each came to Fatimid Egypt to preach their version of Sufism which included reincarnation.

Hamza ibn Ali ibn Ahmad was an Ismaili mystic and scholar from Khorasan who arrived in Cairo in 1014 or 1016 and began to preach a Muwaḥḥidūn ("Unitarian") doctrine. One of his early adherents was the sixth Fatimid caliph al-Hakim bi-Amr Allah.

Then Muhammad bin Ismail Nashtakin ad-Darazi arrived in Cairo from the same area of eastern Persia around the year 1017.

A Druze male with beard and mustache.

He joined the movement and became an important preacher.

By 1018, al-Darazi had gathered around him partisans—"Darazites"—who believed that universal reason became incarnated in Adam at the beginning of the world, was then passed to the prophets, then into Ali, the cousin and son-in-law of the Islamic prophet Muhammad (and the first Shia Imam), and then into his descendants, the Fatimid Caliphs. Al-Darazi wrote a book laying out this doctrine, but when he read from his book in the principal mosque in Cairo, it caused riots and protests against his claims and many of his followers were killed.

Hamza ibn Ali rejected al-Darazi's ideology, calling him "the insolent one and Satan." The controversy led Caliph al-Hakim to suspend the Druze charter in 1018.

In an attempt to gain the support of al-Hakim, al-Darazi started preaching that al-Hakim and his ancestors were the incarnation of God. An inherently modest man, al-Hakim did not believe that he was God, and felt al-Darazi was trying to depict himself as a new prophet. In 1018 Al-Hakim had al-Darazi executed, leaving Hamza the sole leader of the new faith.

Years later in 1043, Baha al-Din al-Muqtana declared that the sect would no longer accept new pledges, and since that time proselytism has been prohibited awaiting al-Hakim's return at the Last Judgment to usher in a new Golden Age.

The sect, while no longer admitting new adherents, must have been many thousands of people strong, and they moved out of the Cairo area of Egypt to the Jabal al-Druze area of Syria, the nearby Golan Heights (now part of Israel), and the Mount Hermon area of Lebanon. They were a mountain people, secretive, and known for the thick mustaches worn by the men. They were also known to be warriors. In this way they are similar to the Sikhs of northern India who became a fierce warrior class who believed in reincarnation and refused to accept the traditional Muslim religion. Might we call the Druze and the Sikhs "warriors for Shiva"?

It was during the period of Crusader rule in the Levant (1099–1291) that the Druze first emerged into the full light of history in the Gharb region of the Chouf, which included the area around Beirut. As powerful warriors serving the leaders in Damascus against the Crusaders, the Druze were given the task of keeping watch over the Crusaders in the seaport of Beirut, to prevent them from making any encroachments inland. Subsequently, the Druze chiefs of the Gharb placed their considerable military experience at the disposal of the Mamluk sultans in Egypt (1250–1516); first, to assist them in putting an end to what remained of Crusader rule in the coastal Levant, and later to help them safeguard the Lebanese coast against Crusader retaliation by sea.

The Strange Druze Religion

The Druze have a number of curious beliefs, although reincarnation—for everyone—is paramount. The Druze are very secretive about their beliefs but we can learn a few things from the various saints and prophets that they admire and the areas of Arabia or Hindustan that they were from.

Complicating their identification is the custom of taqiyya—concealing or disguising their beliefs when necessary. The Druze adopted this from Ismailism, in which many teachings of a sect are kept secret. This is done in order to keep the religion from those who are not yet prepared to accept the teachings and therefore could misunderstand it, as well as to protect the community when it is in danger. Some Druze claim to be Muslim or Christian in order to avoid persecution; some do not.

As we have mentioned, the Druze hold the early prophet Shuaib of the Quran in high regard, believing him to be the reincarnation of the biblical Jethro, who was Moses's father-in-law. Shuaib is mentioned in the Quran 11 times. He is believed to have lived after Abraham and Muslims believe that he was sent as a prophet to the Midianites of northwest Saudi Arabia, who are also known as the Aṣḥāb al-Aykah ("Companions of the Wood") for their worship of a large tree. To the Midianites, Shuaib proclaimed the "straight path," warning them to end their fraudulent ways. When the community did not repent, God destroyed it.

In Druze tradition, it is believed that towards the end of his life, Shuaib took refuge in a cave outside Hittin (a village just west of Tiberias in Israel), where he would die in old age. His followers buried him at the site and placed a tombstone at his grave.

Another Druze tradition holds that the Ayyubid sultan Saladin had a dream the night prior to the Battle of Hittin in which an angel promised him victory on the condition that after the battle, he would ride his horse westward; then, where the horse would stop, the angel said he would find the burial site of Shuaib. The tradition holds that when Saladin's dream was realized, the Druze built a shrine for Shuaib at the site.

Alongside Hud, Saleh, and Muhammad, Shuaib is understood by Muslims as one of the four Arabian prophets sent by God as mentioned in the Quran. It is said that Shuaib was known as "the eloquent preacher amongst the prophets" because he was, according to tradition, granted talent and eloquence in his language.

The Druze honor Shuaib as their principal prophet and hold an annual pilgrimage to Nabi Shu'ayb—a site in the Lower Galilee in Israel believed by Druze to be his tomb—from April 25 to 28, known as Ziyara.

The Prophets Saleh and Hud and the Land of Ad

Saleh is a prophet mentioned in the Quran who preached to the tribe of Thamud in ancient Arabia, before the lifetime of the Islamic prophet Muhammad. It is thought that many of the early Druze had come from this part of Arabia.

According to the Quran, the city that Saleh was sent to was called Al-Ḥijr (Arabic: "The Stonetown"), which corresponds to the Nabataean city of Hegra which today is called Mada'in Saleh. The ancient city, whose origin is unknown, was a major stop on the caravan route along the western side of Arabia. This route has been used for thousands of years; it was used by the Queen of Sheba circa 1000 BC and by Moses before that.

Saleh reminded his people of the castles and palaces they built out of stone, and of their technological superiority over neighboring communities. Furthermore, he told them about their ancestors, the Ad tribe, and how they were destroyed for their sins. Some of the people of Thamud believed Saleh's words, but the tribal leaders refused to listen to him and continued to demand that he demonstrate a miracle to prove his prophethood.

According to the Quran, in response, God gave the Thamud a blessed she-camel as both a means of sustenance and a test. The tribe was told to allow the camel to graze peacefully and avoid harming her. But in defiance of Saleh's warning, the people of

A portion of the rock carved buildings at Mada'in Saleh.

the tribe hamstrung the camel. Saleh informed them that they had only three more days to live before the wrath of God descended upon them. The people of the city were remorseful, but their crime could not be undone, and all the disbelieving people in the city were killed in an earthquake. Al-Hijr was rendered uninhabited and remained in ruins for all time thereafter. Saleh himself and the few believers who followed him survived.

Adjacent to the city were large, decorated rock-cut tombs used by members of various religious groups. The site has been referred to as Mada'in Saleh (Arabic: lit. "the cities of Saleh"), referring to the prophet mentioned by Muhammad. For many years the Saudi government denied tourists permission to visit this strange site of large carved rock tombs but has recently decided to explore its tourism potential.

According to the Quran, the Thamudis were punished by God for their idolatry and were struck by an earthquake and blasts of lightning. Thus, the site has earned a reputation as a cursed place—an image which the national government is attempting to overcome.

The Land of Ad in southern Arabia is where the prophet Hud lived and preached. Hud is believed by the Druze to be an incarnation of Eber. In the Old Testament Eber was a great-grandson of Noah's son Shem and the father of Peleg, born when Eber was 34 years old. He was the son of Shelah, a distant ancestor

A portion of the rock carved buildings at Mada'in Saleh.

of Abraham. According to the Hebrew Bible, Eber died at the age of 464. Eber is repeatedly mentioned in the Quran, whose eleventh chapter is also named after him.

Wikipedia says that the 13th-century Muslim historian Abu al-Fida relates a story that the patriarch Eber refused to help with the building of the Tower of Babel. As a result, his language was not confused when the tower was abandoned. He and his family alone retained the original Adamic language, which al-Fida identified as Hebrew, a language named after Eber.

The Quran says that the people of Ad were extremely powerful and wealthy and they built countless buildings and monuments to show their power. However, the Ad people's wealth ultimately proved to be a source of pride, and they became arrogant and forsook God and began to adopt idols for worship, including three named Samd, Samud and Hara.

Hud, even in childhood, was a consistent prayer to God. It is related in the Quran that Hud's mother, a pious woman who had seen great visions at her son's birth, was the only person who encouraged Hud in his worship. Thus, the Lord raised up Hud as a prophet for the Ad people. According to a tafsir of the whole Surah Hud by scholars, the Ad were a powerful empire that preceded the era of Abraham and Nimrod, and they were tyrannically oppressive towards other civilizations at that time.

When Hud started preaching and invited them to the worship of the only true God, and when he told them to repent for their past sins and ask for mercy and forgiveness, the Ad people began to revile him and wickedly began to mock God's message. Hud's story epitomizes the prophetic cycle common to the early prophets mentioned in the Quran: the prophet is sent to his people to tell them to worship the one God and tells them to acknowledge that it is God who is the provider of their blessings.

The destruction of the Ad is described in the Quran:

> Then when they saw the torment as a dense cloud approaching their valleys, they said happily, "This is a cloud bringing us rain." But Hud replied, "No, it is what you sought to hasten: a fierce wind carrying a painful punishment!" It destroyed everything by the command of its Lord, leaving nothing visible except their ruins. This is how We reward the wicked people.
>
> — Surah Al-Ahqaf 46:24-25

A photo from 1873 of two Lebanese Christians and a Druze (on right).

Several sites in southern Arabia are revered as the tomb of Hud. The most noted site, Qabr Hud, is located in a village in Hadhramaut, Yemen, and is a place of frequent Muslim pilgrimage.

This ancient land of Ad and the strange city of Mada'in Saleh would seem to have been Hindu-Shiva states prior to Islam and their destruction. In fact, this whole area of southern Arabia, the ancient home of Sinbad the Sailor, was connected intricately to ancient Hindustan. The dhows from the Hadhramaut and Oman sailed from India and Sri Lanka across the Indian Ocean to Zanzibar and East Africa.

The many idols that the prophet Saleh would speak about are the many idols used in Hinduism. As in Egyptian, Greek and Scandinavian religions, the Hindus have many confusing gods and accompanying idols. The name Mohammed is actually a Hindu name and is mentioned as such in ancient Hindu texts.

For the Druze these areas of southern Arabia are part of their strong religious beliefs which include reincarnation. For the Druze, all of these people including the prophets have been reincarnated and continue to be reincarnated. Everyone continues to be reincarnated until they reach "unity" with god.

Yet today the Druze live in the mountains of Jabal al-Druze, the Golan Heights, and Mount Hermon. They are a secretive warrior class who often served as mercenaries for various Muslim caliphs. Now they serve in the Israeli military and are proud of their heritage and independence. Their most holy shrine lies in Israel while their most holy mountain, Jabal al Druze, is in Syria near the Golan Heights. The northern border of Jordan is basically Jabal al Druze as this area was clearly independent from the Kingdom of Jordan. The Druze have always been well-armed and have their own security in areas in which they live.

The Druze religion is essentially a Hindu-Shiva offshoot in the middle of Arabia that is respected by the various governments of the area. While being Arabs who speak Arabic and consider the Quran one of their holy books, they have a very different spiritual outlook from the larger Muslim population.

The Druze continue to prosper and grow even though they do not allow any new adherents to their religion. They are indeed a rather unique community. One has to wonder if their innermost secret is about Shiva and perhaps the trinity with Vishnu and Brahma. This same trinity appears in Christianity as "the Father, Son and Holy Ghost." Who is this Holy Ghost? The Druze would say that it is the many prophets who have come to us continually through reincarnation.

Chapter 4

The Indian Ocean and Shiva

Have you seen the little pieces of the people we have been?
Little pieces blowing' gently on the wind...
Little pieces slowly settling on the waves
I'm one of a million pieces fallen on the ground
—*Come Around*, Counting Crows

That ancient India had numerous ports on what we now call the Indian Ocean cannot be doubted. These ports and voyages from them probably go back many thousands of years. Ports along the west coast of India were very active as were ports in what is now Pakistan. Ports on the east coast were just as active, but we will leave that for another chapter.

Countries with ports in Arabia, especially Oman, were constantly trading with India, a rich source of spices, nuts, gems, cloth, metal items and more. In fact, the name Mohammed is a Hindu name originally used in southern India, especially among the Tamils. Of the hundreds of idols that were once at the Kabah in Mecca many were probably Hindu idols. Mohammed removed them all from this early temple, leaving only a black meteorite to be worshipped.

Oman was also the home of the legendary sailor named Sinbad. Sinbad sailed his dhow to India, Sri Lanka and Indonesia in the east and to the Red Sea, East Africa and Madagascar to the west and south. It is also believed that India had a strong connection to Ethiopia and the churches at Axum and Lalibela.

The eleven rock-hewn churches of Lalibela are monolithic churches located in the western Ethiopian Highlands near the town of Lalibela. They are said to have been built during the Zagwe dynasty, under the rule of King Gebre Mesqel Lalibela (r. ca. 1181–1221 AD). However, it is more likely that they evolved into

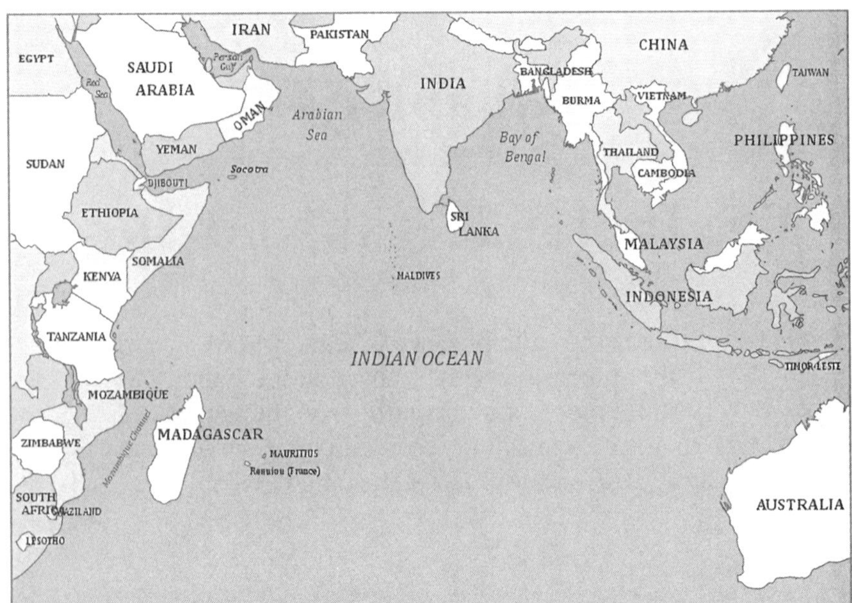

their current form over the course of several phases of construction and alteration of preexisting structures. These rock-hewn churches are very similar to the rock-hewn caverns of Elora, Ajanta and Elephanta in western India. Indeed, it seems that iron tools were brought from India to carve the churches out of red granite.

Legend says that the churches were cut at night by angels. Local tradition says that Lalibela (traditionally known as Roha) was founded by the Zagwe family. Tradition holds that prior to his accession to the throne, Gebre Meskel Lalibela was guided by Christ on a tour of Jerusalem, and was instructed to build a second Jerusalem in Ethiopia. This was apparently accomplished with the amazing churches at Lalibela. The site remains in use by the Ethiopian Orthodox Christian Church to this day, and it remains an important place of pilgrimage for Ethiopian Orthodox worshipers.

It is interesting to note that Ethiopians are in fact racially categorized as Semites, like Arabs and the Israelites. A lost tribe of Israelites was revealed in the 1980s living in central Ethiopia and many of them were flown to Israel as modern Jewish immigrants to the small state. Similarly, Moses spent time in Ethiopia and one of his wives was Ethiopian. Most Ethiopians today believe that the biblical Ark of the Covenant is being kept in a small church in Axum in the northern part of the country.

During its many thousands of years of history, starting with the Queen of Sheba in 900 BC or so, the Red Sea port of Adulis was the main commercial center for goods being exported and imported from Ethiopia. Traders from India, Persia, Oman, East Africa, Israel and Egypt all visited Adulis and brought spices, silks, iron tools and dried coconut. Adulis exported ivory and exotic animals, dried fruit and coffee (the coffee bean is originally from Ethiopia). The modern donkey or ass also originated in the highlands of Ethiopia and was exported to India and China as well as the Middle East. Horses arrived later from Central Asia. The modern domestic cat was apparently bred in Egypt from an Ethiopian wild cat about 5,000 years ago and spread throughout the Mediterranean and India from Egyptian ports.

During all of this time the religions at these many ports—before Christianity—were Hinduism, Mithraism, Isis worship, the veneration of Greek and Roman gods, plus Judaism. The worship of Baal and other gods should be included. However, the biggest migration to Africa came not from India but from Indonesia and the Malay peninsula. This came as several waves of Shaivites from Borneo, Java and Sumatra starting around 300 AD to the island of Madagascar. There were several large waves of Indonesian-Polynesians who came directly across the Indian Ocean rather than following coastlines. After the advent of Islam, many of these areas became Muslim, including Malaysia and Indonesia. Madagascar began as a Buddhist-Shaivite country but lost its religion over the centuries. Eventually it became a nominally Christian island.

Shiva and Madagascar

Madagascar is an island country that includes the island of Madagascar and numerous smaller peripheral islands. Lying off the southeastern coast of Africa, it is the world's fourth largest island, the second-largest island country and the 46th largest country overall. Its capital and largest city is Antananarivo which is in the highlands near the center of the island.

In the Malagasy language, the island of Madagascar is called Madagasikara and its people are referred to as Malagasy. The origin of the name relates Madagascar to the word Malay, referring to the Austronesian origin of the Malagasy people in the archipelago now known as Indonesia. Wikipedia says that in a map by Muhammad al-Idrisi dating from the year 1154, the island is named Gesira Malai, or "Malay Island" in Arabic. The inversion of this name to Malai Gesira, as it was known by the Greeks, is

An 1865 photo of Ambohimanga Hill in central Madagascar.

thought to be the precursor of the modern name of the island.

The name Malagasikara, or Malagascar, was also used in the past. Wikipedia says that a British state paper in 1699 records the arrival of eighty to ninety passengers from "Malagaskar" to what eventually became New York City. An 1882 edition of the British newspaper *The Graphic* referred to "Malagascar" as the name of the island, stating that it is etymologically a word of Malay origin, and may be related to the name of Malacca. In 1891, Saleh bin Osman, a Zanzibari traveler and English author, refers to the island as "Malagaskar" when recounting his journeys.

It is thought that Madagascar was uninhabited until about 300 BC when Austronesian-Malay people arrived by ship from present-day Indonesia. Traditional archaeologists have estimated that the earliest settlers arrived in successive waves in outrigger canoes from South Borneo, possibly throughout the period between 350 BC and 550 AD. These dates make Madagascar one of the most recent major landmasses on Earth to be settled by humans, predating the settlement of Iceland and New Zealand.

The Malagasy language shares many of the same words as the Ma'anyan people of Borneo. The Malagasy language also uses a number of Javanese and Malay loan words. One speculation is that the Ma'anyan people were brought as laborers and slaves by Malay and Javanese in their trading fleets, reaching Madagascar circa 300 BC. It is thought that the island was uninhabited by humans at the time, although early Malagasy folklore speaks of the Vazimba, the original inhabitants of this strange island. It should be noted that Wikipedia says that archaeological finds such as cut marks on bones have been found in the northwest of Madagascar as well as stone tools in the northeast which indicate that Madagascar was visited by foragers around 2000 BC. Such foragers must have arrived in boats.

Upon arrival, the early Malay settlers practiced slash-and-burn agriculture to clear the coastal rainforests for cultivation. These first settlers encountered Madagascar's abundance of megafauna, including the large flightless elephant birds (including probably the largest bird to ever exist, Aepyornis maximus), 17 species of giant lemurs, the giant fossa (a sort of giant mongoose), and several species of Malagasy hippopotamus, which have since become extinct because of hunting and habitat destruction. By 600 AD, groups of these early settlers had begun clearing the forests of the central highlands.

It is believed that the Malays were joined around the ninth century AD by Bantu groups crossing the Mozambique Channel from East Africa. They settled along the northwest coast and other groups continued to settle on the island over time, each one making lasting contributions to Malagasy cultural life. Consequently, there are 18 or more classified peoples of Madagascar, the most numerous being the Merina of the central highlands, of Malay

Old photo of the excavation of a massive tomb at the Ambohimanga Palace.

ancestry.

In October 2024 it was reported by *Archeology* magazine (Jan/Feb 2025) that ancient stone architecture and rock-cut niches at the site of Teniky in southern Madagascar have long baffled archeologists as they are unlike anything produced by the local Malagasy culture. Located 125 miles inland and 12 miles from the nearest modern road Teniky has been difficult to study. However, says *Archeology* magazine, a "new analysis suggests that the site contains similarities to some Zoroastrian necropolises in Iran, and researchers now believe it may have been used as a burial ground by Zoroastrian settlers who arrived on the island between the 10th and 12th centuries."

Archeologist Guido Schreurs said:

> During field prospecting on this hill we discovered niches, cut in the walls of a rock shelter, that had not been described before. Excavations at this rock shelter revealed more archaeological structures, including carved sandstone walls and a large stone basin. Radiocarbon dating of charcoal samples from the site dated to the late 10th to mid-12th centuries AD. Pieces of ceramic items of southeast Asian and Chinese origin found there have been dated by a specialist to the 11th to 14th centuries AD. We also found sandstone quarries from which the stones used to build the walls at the rock shelters were extracted. And we found more stone basins on terraces.

This curious theory has these Zoroastrians arriving in the southern portion of Madagascar and going inland at a time when the Malagasy had already colonized the island. Yet, like Sinbad the Sailor who ranged from Oman to Ceylon and Zanzibar, a number of Arab and Persian explorers may have come across the island and even encountered the giant flightless bird Aepyornis maximus. Such a gigantic elephant bird was probably the inspiration for the legendary Roc, a giant bird that Sinbad encountered.

The Vazimba

According to popular belief, the Vazimba were the first inhabitants of Madagascar. While descriptions of the physical appearance of the Vazimba reflect regional variation, they are generally described as smaller in stature than the average person, leading some scientists to speculate that the Vazimba may have been a pygmy people (and therefore a separate Malagasy ethnic group) who migrated from the islands that constitute modern-day Indonesia in the first wave of two major waves of migration. Tales of a pygmy race, often with dark skin, also exist on Pacific Islands, especially in Hawaii with its stories of the Menehune.

A Malagasy book on the Vazimba.

According to this theory, the waves of migrants originated from the same region of Southeast Asia, spoke the same language and shared the same culture. When the second wave arrived, they found the island sparsely populated by descendants of the first wave whose culture and way of life had evolved from the first settlers' way of life, reflecting centuries of adaptation to local surroundings in total isolation from outside threats.

The oral histories of the Merina people, who arrived in the central highlands around 1000 AD, describe encountering an established population they called the Vazimba. The Vazimba were assimilated or expelled from the highlands by the Merina kings Andriamanelo, Ralambo, and Andrianjaka in the 16th and early 17th centuries. Today, the spirits of the Vazimba are revered as tompontany (ancestral masters of the land) by many traditional Malagasy communities. Among some Malagasy, the Vazimba are not believed to be human at all, but rather a form of supernatural creature possessing magical powers (mahery).

According to folklore, the Vazimba did not possess knowledge of metallurgy or rice farming and used weapons made of clay. The Vazimba were said to have herded their zebu cattle without eating them for meat. This is clearly a Hindu practice and it is said that the early inhabitants of Madagascar did not eat cattle; some legends say that the people did not know that cattle were edible. In some ways the Vazimba seem to be similar to the Tamils of southern India, known for their dark skin and sometimes frizzy hair.

A Mohenjo Daro seal depicting a Zebu with writing similar to Rongorongo.

The zebu, sometimes known as humped cattle, is a species or subspecies of domestic cattle originating in South Asia. Zebus differ from taurine cattle by a fatty hump on their shoulders, a large dewlap, and sometimes drooping ears. They are well adapted to withstanding high temperatures and are farmed throughout the tropics. Zebus are used as draught and riding animals, dairy cattle and beef cattle, as well as for byproducts such as hides and dung for fuel and manure. Zebu are found throughout India, Southeast Asia, Madagascar and East Africa. Zebu were imported from India to Egypt around 4000 BC, but did not appear in Subsaharan Africa until about 700 AD, except in Madagascar, apparently.

Zebus are venerated in Hinduism in India. In the historical Vedic religion they were a symbol of plenty. In later times they gradually acquired their present status. According to the Mahabharata, they are to be treated with the same respect "as one's mother." In the middle of the first millennium, the consumption of beef began to be disfavored by lawgivers. Zebus are very important to the economy of Madagascar and must have been brought by ship from Indonesia in the early migrations.

Says Wikipedia about the early wave of Malagasy to the island:

> If the multi-wave settlement theory is correct, the indigenous (first-wave) population that the more technologically advanced second-wave settlers would have encountered upon arrival in Madagascar would provide the historic basis for stories of the primitive nature of the Vazimba societies they are said to have encountered there.
>
> Archaeological research and oral histories have provided some indication of how these early inhabitants of the highlands might have lived. Upon their arrival in those ancient tropical highland forests, the Vazimba practiced tavy (swidden, slash-and-burn agriculture) to clear the land for cultivating bananas, tubers, ginger and other staples.

It may be the Malagasy who brought the banana to Africa. The banana is known to have originated in the area of northern Australia and New Guinea. It was then spread throughout Southeast Asia and the Pacific. Eventually it was found throughout Africa and South America. The banana probably came from Indonesia to Madagascar in the first wave around 350 BC and then spread to East and Central Africa shortly afterwards.

The Vazimba gathered honey, fruits and edible seeds and hunted small game in the forests. As their population increased, villages were established and ruled by chiefs and later kings. Wikipedia says that rulers are believed to have reddened their hair using a local mushroom; the association of the color red with royalty is found in many parts of Madagascar to this day.

Oral history classifies the Vazimba according to the parts of the island where they are believed to have settled. The vazimba andrano ("Vazimba of the Water") settled along rivers and lakes. The vazimba antety ("Vazimba of the Soil") were believed to be the most numerous and were reportedly clustered around the valley of Betsiriry in the central Highlands. The vazimba antsingy ("Vazimba of the Tsingy") lived in the caves around the limestone formations (tsingy) of Bemaraha in western Madagascar and were believed to scavenge fruit and other forest products to live. Says Wikipedia:

> The first period of Malagasy oral history is known as the Vazimba period (faha vazimba), beginning with the initial population of the island by the Vazimba and their

> establishment of kingdoms—often ruled by Queens—in the central Highlands region of Madagascar. According to some accounts, the first Vazimba sovereign of the central highlands was named Andriandravindravina. The second period in the oral history of the Highlands begins with the conquest of the Vazimba Highland kingdoms by Merina sovereigns in what would come to be known as Imerina in their honor. Andriamanelo (1540–1575)—who was himself half-Vazimba through his antecedents Queen Rangita and Queen Rafohy—is credited (along with his successors, Ralambo and Andrianjaka) with successfully forcing the Vazimba out of the Highlands and into the western part of the island.
>
> It is commonly believed that the last of the Vazimba were annihilated during the reign of Andrianjaka (1610–1630). However, dismissing the stories of distinctive Vazimba physical appearance, Jean-Pierre Domenichini has theorized that the term Vazimba may have been more of a statement of cultural than ethnic difference and that many who had been considered Vazimba in this period did not die out, but instead may have simply chosen to become assimilated into the vanquishing Merina culture. The oral history of many Merina and Betsileo families speaks of intermarriage between Merina and Vazimba ancestors, and some Malagasy speculate that the hunter-gatherer Mikea peoples and the Vezo fishing tribe, both concentrated along the coastline of western and southern Madagascar, may be descended from Vazimba.

The Merina people were farming rice on the eastern side of the island and moved into the highlands where they continued to create rice paddies as in Indonesia and had herds of zebu. Beginning in the early 19th century, most of the island was united and ruled as the Kingdom of Madagascar by a series of Merina nobles. The monarchy was ended in 1897 by the annexation by France, from which Madagascar gained independence in 1960.

Madagascar and European Contact

Historians say that Arab traders first reached the island between the 7th and 9th centuries AD. A wave of Bantu-speaking migrants from southeastern Africa arrived in the northwest around the year

1000. The Arabs established trading posts along the northwest coast by at least the 10th century and introduced Islam, the Arabic script (used to transcribe the Malagasy language in a form of writing known as sorabe), Arab astrology, and other cultural elements.

European contact began in 1500, when the Portuguese sea captain Diogo Dias sighted the island while participating in the 2nd Armada of the Portuguese India Armadas. The Portuguese then created a settlement on the south coast called Matatana. In 1508, settlers there built a tower, a small village, and a stone column. This settlement was established in 1513 at the behest of the viceroy of Portuguese India, Jeronimo de Azevedo.

The French established trading posts along the east coast in the late 17th century. From about 1774 to 1824, Madagascar gained prominence among pirates and European traders, particularly those involved in the transatlantic slave trade. The small island of Nosy Boroha off the northeastern coast of Madagascar has been proposed by some historians as the site of the legendary pirate utopia of Libertalia.

Many European sailors were shipwrecked on the coasts of the island, among them Robert Drury, whose journal is one of the few written depictions of life in southern Madagascar during the 18th century. European accounts until the early 20th century identified Malagasy people as being of Jewish origin. Therefore they were

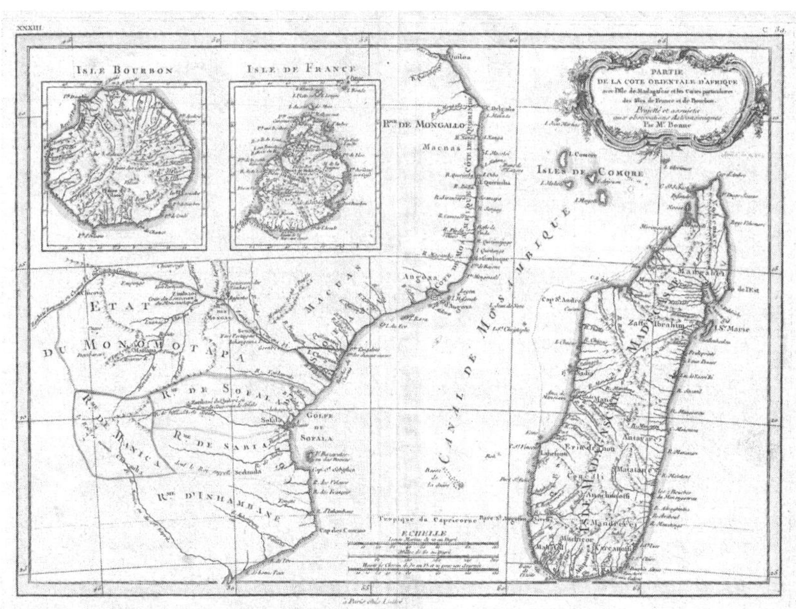

The 1770 Bonne Map of East Africa and Madagascar.

thought to be one of the lost tribes of Israel.

The wealth generated by maritime trade spurred the rise of organized kingdoms on the island, some of which had grown quite powerful by the 17th century. Among these were the Betsimisaraka alliance of the eastern coast and the Sakalava chiefdoms of Menabe and Boina on the west coast. The Kingdom of Imerina, located in the central highlands with its capital at the royal palace of Antananarivo, emerged at around the same time under the leadership of King Andriamanelo.

With its emergence in the early 17th century, the highland kingdom of Imerina was initially a minor power relative to the larger coastal kingdoms and grew even weaker in the early 18th century when King Andriamasinavalona divided it among his four sons. Following almost a century of warring and famine, Imerina was reunited in 1793 by King Andrianampoinimerina (r.1787–1810). From his initial capital Ambohimanga, and later from the Rova of Antananarivo, this Merina king rapidly expanded his rule over neighboring principalities. His ambition to bring the entire island under his control was largely achieved by his son and successor, King Radama I (r.1810–28), who was recognized as King of Madagascar by the British government.

Radama concluded a treaty in 1817 with the British governor of Mauritius to abolish the lucrative slave trade in return for British military and financial assistance. Artisan missionary envoys from the London Missionary Society began arriving in 1818 who established schools, transcribed the Malagasy language using the Roman alphabet, translated the Bible, and introduced a variety of new technologies to the island.

Radama's successor, Queen Ranavalona I (1828–61), responded to increasing political and cultural encroachment from Britain and France by issuing a royal edict prohibiting the practice of Christianity in Madagascar and pressuring most foreigners to leave the territory. The Queen made heavy use of the traditional practice of fanompoana (forced labor as tax payment) to complete public works projects and develop a standing army of between 20,000 and 30,000 Merina soldiers, whom she deployed to pacify outlying regions of the island and further expand the Kingdom of Merina to encompass most of Madagascar.

The combination of regular warfare, disease, difficult forced labor, and harsh measures of justice resulted in a high mortality rate among soldiers and civilians alike during her 33-year reign;

the population of Madagascar is estimated to have declined from around 5 million to 2.5 million during her rule.

Among those foreigners who continued to reside in Imerina were Jean Laborde, an entrepreneur who developed munitions and other industries on behalf of the monarchy, and Joseph-François Lambert, a French adventurer and slave trader, with whom then-Prince Radama II signed a controversial trade agreement termed the Lambert Charter. Succeeding his mother, Radama II attempted to relax the queen's stringent policies but was overthrown two years later by Prime Minister Rainivoninahitriniony and an alliance of Andriana (noble) and Hova (commoner) courtiers, who sought to end the absolute power of the monarch.

Following the coup, the courtiers offered Radama's queen, Rasoherina, the opportunity to rule, if she would accept a power-sharing arrangement with the Prime Minister: a new social contract that would be sealed by a political marriage between them. Queen Rasoherina accepted, first marrying Rainivoninahitriniony, then later deposing him and marrying his brother, Prime Minister Rainilaiarivony, who would go on to marry Queen Ranavalona II and Queen Ranavalona III in succession. Over the course of Rainilaiarivony's 31-year tenure as prime minister, numerous policies were adopted to modernize and consolidate the power of the central government. Schools were constructed throughout the island and attendance was made mandatory. Army organization was improved and British consultants were employed to train and professionalize soldiers. In 1869 polygamy was outlawed and Christianity was declared the official religion of the court and was adopted alongside traditional beliefs among a growing portion of the populace. Legal codes were reformed on the basis of British common law and three European-style courts were established in the capital city.

In 1883 France invaded Madagascar primarily on the basis that the Lambert Charter had not been respected, in what became known as the first Franco-Hova War, Hova being another name for the Merina language. At the end of the war, Madagascar ceded the northern port town of Antsiranana (Diego Suarez) to France and paid 560,000 francs to Lambert's heirs. This began the acquisition of Madagascar by France. In 1890, the British accepted the full formal imposition of a French protectorate on the island, however this authority was not acknowledged by the Merina royalty. To force capitulation, the French bombarded and occupied the harbor of Toamasina on the east coast in December 1894, and Mahajanga on the west coast in January 1895.

A French military column then marched toward Antananarivo in the center of the island. Upon reaching the city in September 1895, the column bombarded the royal palace with heavy artillery, causing heavy casualties and leading Queen Ranavalona III to surrender. France annexed Madagascar in 1896 and declared the island a colony the following year, dissolving the Merina monarchy and sending the royal family into exile on Réunion Island and to Algeria.

Under colonial rule, plantations were established for a variety of export crops. Slavery was abolished in 1896 and approximately 500,000 slaves were freed; many remained at their former masters' homes as servants or as sharecroppers. Wide paved boulevards and gathering places were constructed in the capital city of Antananarivo and the Rova palace compound was turned into a museum. Additional schools were built, particularly in rural and coastal areas where the schools of the Merina had not reached. Education became free and mandatory between the ages of 6 and 13, focused primarily on the French language and practical skills.

Malagasy troops fought for France in World War I. In the 1930s, Nazi political thinkers developed the Madagascar Plan that had identified the island as a potential site for the deportation of Europe's Jews. During World War II, the island was the site of the Battle of Madagascar between the Vichy French administrators and an Allied expeditionary force.

The occupation of France by the Nazis during World War II tarnished the prestige of the colonial administration in Madagascar and galvanized the growing independence movement, leading to the Malagasy Uprising of 1947. This movement led the French to establish reformed institutions in 1956 and Madagascar moved peacefully toward independence. The Malagasy Republic was proclaimed on 14 October 1958, and gained full independence on June 26, 1960.

Genetics and Food Culture

Genetic studies of the population show that all Malagasy have a mixture of Malay and Bantu genes. The highland Merina people are about 45% Bantu with coastal populations having a higher concentration of Bantu blood.

Due to Madagascar's proximity to Africa, the connection with

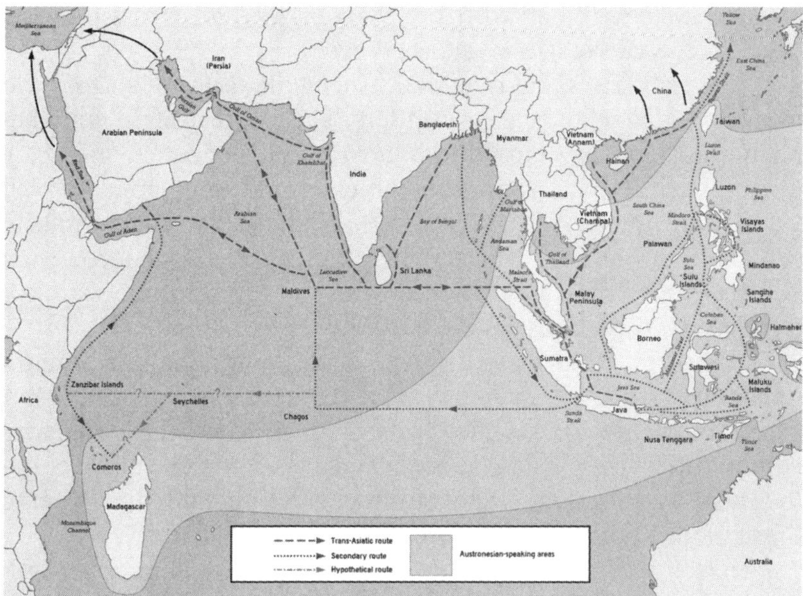

A map of the many routes around the Indian Ocean.

Asian populations aroused the most curiosity. Around 1996, a study was launched in an attempt to identify the presence of the Polynesian motif in the Malagasy population (mtDNA haplotype B4a1a1a). A more recent study identified two additional mutations (1473 and 3423A) found in all Polynesian motif carriers of Madagascar, hence was named the Malagasy motif. The frequency varied among three ethnic groups: 50% in Merina, 22% in Vezo, and 13% in Mikea.

The closest Asian parental population of the Malagasy are found in what is now Indonesia, among the Banjar and other South Kalimantan Dayak people of southeast Borneo. Language footprints of their ancestors from Southeastern Asia can be traced by the many shared words of basic vocabulary with Ma'anyan, a language from the region of the Barito River in southern Borneo. This seems to be a region of Indonesia that has not had a lot of external genetic impute over the last few thousand years, while areas of Sumatra, Java and other islands have had a lot of genetic influx.

Wikipedia says that the Malagasy language is the westernmost member of the Malayo-Polynesian branch of the Austronesian language family, a grouping that includes languages from Indonesia, Malaysia, the Philippines and the Pacific Islands. There are some Sanskrit loan words in Malagasy, which are said to have been borrowed via Malay and Javanese.

Wikipedia says that rice, the cornerstone of the Malagasy diet, was cultivated by the earliest settlers. They also brought with them plantains (bananas), taro, and water yam plus coconut, sugarcane, ginger, sweet potatoes, pigs and chickens. At some point the zebu cattle were introduced as well. While many historians think the zebu came from East Africa, where they were introduced around 1000 AD, they may have arrived from Java and Borneo with even the earliest migrations, as we have discussed.

This plentiful diet was supplemented by foraging and hunting wild game, which contributed to the extinction of the island's bird and mammal megafauna such as the elephant birds. Early Malagasy communities may have eaten the eggs and—less commonly—the meat of the world's largest bird, which remained widespread throughout Madagascar as recently as the 17th century.

These elephant birds must have been a frightening vision at nearly 12 feet tall, and they were dangerous and not that easy to kill. But a large hunting group with spears could do it and then have quite the drumstick feast. While several theories have been proposed to explain the decline and eventual extinction of Malagasy megafauna, clear evidence suggests that hunting by humans and destruction of habitats through slash-and-burn agricultural practices were key factors.

Foods were commonly prepared by boiling in water (at first using green bamboo as a vessel, and later clay or iron pots), roasting over a fire or grilling over hot stones or coals. Fermentation was

A comparison of the elephant bird, an ostrich, a man and a chicken.

also used to create curds from milk, develop the flavor of certain dried or fresh tubers or produce alcoholic beverages from honey, sugarcane juice or other local plants.

In the colonial period estates were established for the production of crops exported to foreign markets such as England and France. Cloves were imported and planted in 1803, and coconuts were cultivated on plantations for the production of oil. Similarly, coffee had been grown on family plots of four to five trees until the early 19th-century, when more intensive cultivation for export began.

Vanilla, later to become one of Madagascar's premier export crops, was introduced by French entrepreneurs in 1840 and planted in eastern coastal rainforests. The technique of hand pollination, critical to higher vanilla yields, was introduced 30 years later. The vanilla bean comes from the vanilla orchid in the Veracruz, Mexico area and was an early Aztec and Totonac spice.

The Early Indian Ocean was Dominated by Hindus

It is known that Hinduism and Shiva worship were the combined religion of Sumatra, Java, Bali, most of the other Indonesian islands and Southeast Asia starting in 2000 BC if not earlier. Buddhism came to the Indian Subcontinent, Ceylon and Southeast Asia around 300 BC. The people of Thailand, Cambodia, Southern Vietnam and the southern area of the Philippines were also Hindu-Buddhist-Shaivites.

Therefore these voyages from Borneo and Java would have been of Hindu seafarers who were colonizing both east and west of Java and all the coastal areas of the central islands of Indonesia. They spread north to the southern Philippines. This early Hindu religion from Java and Borneo was lost over the many centuries but the basic caste system and beliefs in these places remained the same and, as in all cultures, ancestors were honored and semi-worshipped.

Meanwhile the Indonesian Hindus were voyaging from Java across the Indian Ocean to Madagascar, a new land to be colonized. They must have had scouting voyages to locate new lands such as Madagascar. When the scouts returned to Java and other islands, they were able to organize a larger migration across the Indian Ocean.

The Indian Ocean is not called that without reason. That Hindu traders sailed throughout the Indian Ocean, along the southern coast of Arabia and up the Red Sea is not doubted. They also ranged along the coasts of Somalia, Kenya, Tanzania and Mozambique. The island of Zanzibar off the coast of Tanzania is said to be one of the homes of the Omani sailor Sinbad. As we have mentioned, is famously said to have encountered giant birds on his adventures which may have been in Madagascar.

These scouts of Shiva would not just go west across the Indian Ocean but they would also go east into the vast Pacific with its many islands. The Pacific Ocean is one-third of the surface of the earth. It is a huge area, but these scouts of Shiva would not only explore the thousands of islands in the central Pacific, they would go beyond to the North and South American continents as well.

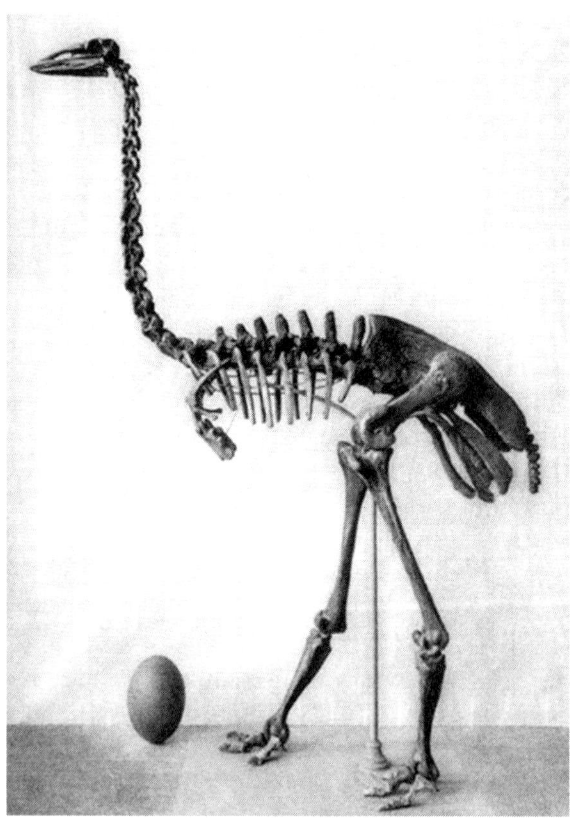

A 1913 photo of an elephant bird skeleton and egg.

Chapter 5

The Lost Land of Hiva-Shiva

Limitless, undying love
Which shines around me like a million suns
It calls me on and on across the universe
—*Across the Universe*, The Beatles

I have been to Easter Island three times, once in 1988, in 1999, and in the spring of 2013. Every voyage left me amazed at the fine stone carving and construction and wondered what the mainstream had to say about the local history. As I suspected, they maintained that the making of the statues was fairly recent and that most of the mysteries associated with the island had been solved. Had they?

I wondered about a few things that seemed to need explaining:

1. When and why did the islanders excavate and move such gigantic statues when smaller ones would have presumably served the same purpose? How were they moved? Why go through such a monumental task of quarrying and moving the statues?
2. Why are the statues buried with up to 30 feet of soil? Was this done on purpose or has the soil built up over thousands of years?
3. Why did the islanders think that putting statues facing inward around the island would keep it from sinking into the ocean like their lost land of Hiva? Who were the statues of?
4. How did they make fine drill holes and saw cuts on some of the stone walls?
5. Why would a small remote island population invent its own written language called rongorongo? Could such a script be related to other ancient forms of writing?
6. Could a remote island like Rapa Nui be related to

thousands of years of transpacific contact that spanned Asia, Oceania and the Americas?

The Strange Rongorongo Script

Little is known of this strange script which includes pictographic and geometric shapes; often the figures are of a birdman with his arms and legs in various positions. The script was written in the unusual boustrophedon pattern of writing where the successive lines are read ("as the ox plows") alternately left to right and then right to left. According to the Encyclopedia Britannica and Wikipedia, certain older forms of Greek, such as Doric Greek, were written in the boustrophedon pattern, as were Etruscan, Sabaean, Safaitic, Hittite and possibly Indus Valley writing such as that from Harrapa or Mohenjo Daro.

The writing was first reported by Eugene Eyraud, a French missionary on the island, in 1864. Eyraud sent some specimens to the Archbishop of Tahiti, since he recognized the significance of a written language being developed on a tiny, remote island in the South Pacific—it was against all accepted theories of the time. It was generally thought that only peoples with contact with different cultures could rise to a high level of civilization that included written communication. But here on Easter Island, it was then surmised, was a culture that had independently of the rest of the world developed writing, art, megalithic construction and more. The notion that a few hundred people should create all that without the aid of the outside world was astounding, and still is. This is still the accepted anthropological theory on the island's development.

A sample of rongorongo script.

At the time of Eyraud, a few of the island "royalty" were still able to read the rongorongo tablets. These few people were quickly dying out, and some had been taken to the guano islands in Peru. The French author and archeologist Franis Maziere claimed in his book *The Mysteries of Easter Island*[14] that the last initiate of the rongorongo tablets

Indus Valley	Easter Island	Indus Valley	Easter Island	Indus Valley	Easter Island	Indus Valley	Easter Island
I	II	III	IV	V	VI	VII	VIII

A comparison of a few of the many Easter Island written symbols with similar Indus Valley signs.

A rongorongo book photographed by Francis Maziere.

died of leprosy and had once told him: "The first race invented the rongorongo writing. They wrote it in stone. Of the four parts of the world that were inhabited by the first race it is only in Asia that the writing still exists." The native was apparently speaking of the Indus Valley culture and the writing at Mohenjo Daro and other cities.

Rongorongo has eluded translation, as have many ancient languages, but similarities have been noted, starting in the 1960s, between it and the undeciphered Indus Valley script. A Hungarian scholar named de Hevseg made a comparison of the writing on Easter Island and that found at the Indus Valley civilization cities of Mohenjo Daro and Harappa. These cities existed about 1500 BC if not earlier, and the culture literally vanished about 1300 BC. That rongorongo writing is very similar, if not identical, to this ancient, undeciphered language, is extraordinary. They are precisely on opposite sides of the earth: Mohenjo Daro is located at 27°23' North and about 69° East; Easter Island is at 27°08' South and 109°23' West. No other land area could be farther away from the Indus Valley cities as Easter Island.

The script at Mohenjo Daro is now believed to be related to ancient Dravidian; the fragments of this language still exist in southern India in the language of Tamil. An article in *Scientific American* (vol. 248, No. 3, March 1983) by Walter Fairservis, Jr. entitled "The Script of the Indus Valley Civilization" describes the author's attempts to decipher the writing. A fairly dry article, it makes no reference to the similarity with rongorongo

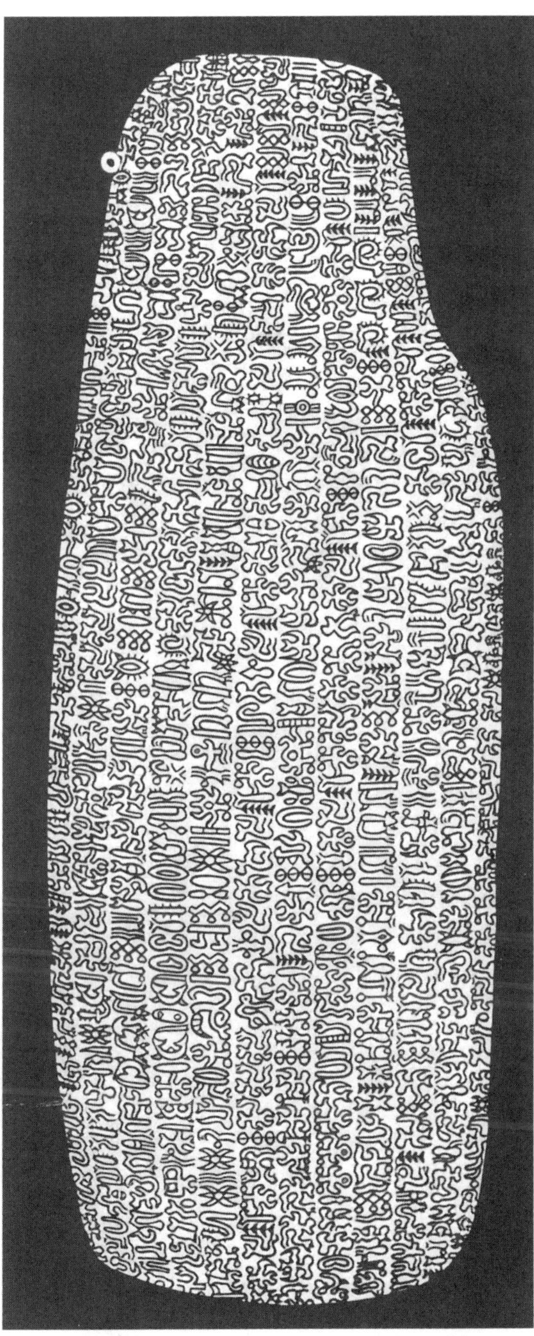

A drawing of rongorongo on a wooden tablet.

script, but does say the author believes that a form of Dravidian was the spoken language of the valley. Significantly, Fairservis does say that there are 419 "signs" and that the script is neither alphabetic (as in Sanskrit or English) or logographic (as in Chinese) but rather logo-syllabic, meaning that some signs represent words and others serve purely for their symbolic value or sounds. The author says that other examples of such writing are Egyptian hieroglyphs, early Sumerian ideographs and modern Japanese. It has also been noted that some early Shang Dynasty symbols found in "oracle bone script" are also similar to rongorongo.

Were Sumerians and Indus Valley seafarers making transpacific voyages starting sometime around 3000 BC? As I have already stated, I believe so. Did they bring with them a complicated form of writing that came down through history on a small island on wooden tablets with rongorongo writing on them? What sort of cataclysm stopped the ancient seafarers from returning to tiny Easter Island in the middle of the South Pacific?

The islanders patiently waited year after year for the big ships to come back, but they never did. Or maybe some did. Polynesians on great epic voyages, such as the ones to Hawaii, must have managed to arrive at Easter Island. Pitcairn Island, the nearest island to the north, was uninhabited when the *Bounty* mutineers settled there, but there was evidence of statues on that island as well. Pitcairn may have been a stopover island between Tahiti and Easter Island. Easter Island is also associated with the Marquesas Islands, which are not the closest Polynesian Islands to it—and the big question is whether there was contact with South America. The mainstream says no, but scholars such as Thor Heyerdahl say yes!

Old print of a reed surfer with a top knot, a reed surfboard and bananas.

The Shaivites and the Bird Men

One thing that archeologists have grappled with is the purpose of the red topknots that were separately quarried and then placed on top of some of the statues. Not all of the statues had these topknots, made from a red volcanic tuff that is lighter and easier to carve than the granite that makes up most of the statues. The statues that are found on the slopes of Rano Raraku never had a red topknot on their heads, only statues that had been moved from the quarries and walked to their spots on the coast where they would sit on a stone platform and face inland. These statues had the red topknots on them, as well as inlaid eyes of obsidian and ivory from which the powerful mana (magical force) could emanate and keep the island from sinking like the homeland of Hiva. It was these statues that got this special topknot. What was the importance of the red topknot? Was it the hairstyle that the men in ancient ships had worn? Was the red color of importance? We do not really see this with other statues in Polynesia or South America. However, with the Olmecs we do have statues that show men, sometimes in a quizuo position, that have very long hair tied in a big bun on the top of their heads.

No, they are not women who have tied their hair in a bun; these are men who chose to wear their hair long, probably for a religious-spiritual reason. In many ancient cultures it was common for men to have long hair, though in more advanced cultures this hair was cut into various styles and lengths and often worn beneath a turban or other elaborate headgear.

The Shaivites often feature the third eye as part of their imagery and the depiction of Shiva with his long hair in a topknot and a third eye in his forehead is very common. This is a common theme in Champa art and essentially any Shivite who is wearing his hair in this manner is imitating the god Shiva. Shaivites are allowed to engage in sex with very little restriction. There is no call for celibacy as there is for Buddhist monks or nuns, for instance.

The god Shiva also carries a trident. He smokes marijuana and has tantric sex with goddesses. In a similar way Shaivites also practice yoga, wear their long hair in a topknot, sometimes put ash on their faces and carry a trident with them—even on the remote mountainsides of the Himalayas. At some Shaivite shrines in the Himalayas, such as the one near the sacred mountain Gauri Shankar in Nepal, hundreds of tridents are left in enclosed shrines as they complete their Shaivite pilgrimage. Don't we view the trident as a symbol of gods like Neptune and the sea?

So is Shiva also a god of the sea, the patron of sailors who wear long hair in topknots and carry a trident for fishing? It would seem

A photo of a Shiva statue showing the top knot, third eye and long ears of Shiva.

so. As the Wikipedia entry notes, Shaivites were notable in the area that I am calling the Cham Empire: Java, Bali and Cambodia. We can add Vietnam and Sumatra to that list, and probably such islands as Borneo, Sulawesi and the Sulu Islands of the southern Philippines.

The question now is: are the statues at Easter Island meant to be

An old print of a long-eared man from Easter Island-Rapa Nui.

statues of longhaired Shaivites who wore their hair in a topknot? It would also be interesting to speculate whether the red topknot that was placed on the heads of the grey granite statues symbolized red hair. If this was the case we can imagine red-haired Vikings with their hair tied up on top of their heads. When Dutch explorer Roggveen landed on Easter Island in 1722, he found that some of the population looked European with red hair and light skin.

Easter Island would appear to be the far southern portion of empire of Shiva that extended from Southeast Asia into the Pacific to Mexico and western South America. New Zealand was probably part of the empire of Shiva as well. In the west the empire of

Shiva, centered on India and Tibet, spanned Pakistan, Afghanistan, Persia, Iraq and Turkey. This is empire is approximately five times the size of Alexander the Great's. It is about three times the size of Genghis Khan's. It would seem that only the British Empire was larger than that of Shiva.

Easter Island undeniably was a culture in decline at the time of European discovery. When the first explorers reached the island the natives were living in reed huts. Yet, someone had constructed megalithic stone blocks of incredible perfection as witnessed at Vinapu. Was the precision stonework at Vinapu the result of power tools as some surmise were used at Tiwanaku and Puma Punku? Was the written language of the Rama Empire the same written language called rongorongo? It seems fantastic!

What of the great cataclysm that had affected Rapa Nui? Had some tsunami hit the island, burying the statues in many meters of mud and muck? Had it struck thousands of years ago, or only a few hundred years ago?

It seems that Easter Island had two cataclysms. One was a natural disaster that halted the quarrying of the statues at Rano Raraku. The other was a cultural disaster marked by the sudden halt of large ships arriving on the island and going elsewhere, either to Tahiti or on to Southeast Asia. When large ships arrived on the island there would have been festivals that included sex

Some of the many giant statues half buried at the Rano Raraku crater quarry.

with the sailors to bring new blood into the island gene pool, plus there would have been opportunities for men and women to leave the island and go elsewhere. Similarly, sometimes one or more of the ships' crew might stay on the island to serve as a priest, architect or physician.

Once the islanders became isolated they tried to preserve their history by the continual copying of the rongorongo tablets, yet most of their history was irretrievably lost. All that we get today are confusing tales of Hiva and a world that is gone, or the strange tale of the war of the long ears and the short ears. It should be pointed out here that Buddha and Shiva are typically depicted as having very long ear lobes, particularly in the case of Buddha. The Inca royalty were also depicted as having very long ear lobes. This was also the style of the Cham.

Rapa Nui is an island of enduring mysteries and the connection with Shiva, Shaivites and the Cham is strong. Even for these ancient voyagers, Rapa Nui was a remote island at the end of the world—but back then it was part of the empire of Shiva.

Recently a major study of Polynesian DNA was published in the British journal *Nature*, volume 597, on September 22, 2021 and it contained information that "No one could have predicted." The article was entitled "Paths and timings of the peopling of Polynesia inferred from genomic networks" and was authored by a number of scientists and researchers including Alexander G. Ioannidis, Javier Blanco-Portillo, Andrés Moreno-Estrada and more.

The article essentially said that the dispersion of Polynesian DNA centered on the islands of Samoa in the central Pacific. Said the beginning of the article:

> Polynesia was settled in a series of extraordinary voyages across an ocean spanning one third of the Earth, but the sequences of islands settled remain unknown and their timings disputed. Currently, several centuries separate the dates suggested by different archaeological surveys.
>
> Here, using genome-wide data from merely 430 modern individuals from 21 key Pacific island populations and novel ancestry-specific computational analyses, we unravel the detailed genetic history of this vast, dispersed island network. Our reconstruction of the branching Polynesian migration sequence reveals a serial founder

> expansion, characterized by directional loss of variants, that originated in Samoa and spread first through the Cook Islands (Rarotonga), then to the Society (Tōtaiete mā) Islands (11th century), the western Austral (Tuha'a Pae) Islands and Tuāmotu Archipelago (12th century), and finally to the widely separated, but genetically connected, megalithic statue-building cultures of the Marquesas (Te Henua 'Enana) Islands in the north, Raivavae in the south, and Easter Island (Rapa Nui), the easternmost of the Polynesian islands, settled in approximately ad 1200 via Mangareva.

It is known that other islands in the vicinity such as Tonga and Fiji were settled at an earlier date than the 11th century AD, but this is not mentioned in the article. This article is only concerned with DNA distribution from Samoa starting around 900-1000 AD. Another article published by Science.org on the same day referring to the *Nature* article was entitled: "'No one could have predicted.' DNA offers surprises on how Polynesia was settled Early explorers island hopped to discover islands thousands of kilometers apart." The article went on to say:

> The peopling of Polynesia was a stunning achievement: Beginning around 800 CE, audacious Polynesian navigators in double-hulled sailing canoes used the stars and their knowledge of the waves to discover specks of land separated by thousands of kilometers of open ocean. Within just a few centuries, they had populated most of the Pacific Ocean's far-flung islands. Now, researchers have used modern DNA samples to trace the exploration in detail, working out what order the islands were settled in and dating each new landfall to within a few decades.
>
> Archaeologists already had hints of how this great exploration took place. Studying the styles of stone tools and carvings, as well as languages, of the people on the various islands had suggested the original ancestors traced back to Samoa and that the expansion ended halfway across the ocean in Rapa Nui, or Easter Island. But they disagreed on whether it happened in a few centuries, beginning around 900 C.E., or started much earlier and lasted 1 millennium or more.

One of the giant statues half buried at the Rano Raraku crater quarry.

To learn more, Stanford University computational geneticist Alexander Ioannidis and Andrés Moreno Estrada, a population geneticist at Mexico's National Laboratory of Genetics for Biodiversity, compared the DNA of 430 modern individuals from all across Polynesia (most collected for previous studies), and then eliminated later genetic input from European people. Because the researchers knew Polynesians had journeyed stepwise from island to island, their genetic analysis utilized a genetic phenomenon known as a population bottleneck. When a few dozen to a few hundred individuals from already-isolated island populations settled a new island, and then a subset of that group left to settle an additional island, and so forth, their genetic diversity would have shrunk with each voyage—like a telescope in reverse.

The analysis suggests canoes set sail from the shores

The Polynesian migration from India and Southeast Asia to Polynesia.

of Samoa—more than 2000 kilometers north of New Zealand—around 800 CE. The explorers arrived first on Rarotonga, the largest island in a chain now called the Cook Islands. Successive explorers moved in all directions, island hopping over the course of centuries and eventually reaching all the way to Rapa Nui, 6500 kilometers from Samoa and 3700 kilometers off the coast of Chile, by 1210 CE.

And because the genetic evidence allowed the researchers to reconstruct the order in which the islands were settled, they could spot connections between islands that might not seem intuitive based on the geography. For example, they argue that three island cultures known for carving massive stone statues—Rapa Nui, Raivavae, and the North and South Marquesas—shared a common founder population in the Tuamotu Islands, even though they are thousands of kilometers apart and geographically closer to other parts of the Pacific.

Those three islands also hold the earliest genetic traces of Native American ancestry among Polynesians. That suggests ancient Polynesians first contacted the Americas around 1100 CE, when the seafarers were beginning their last, and longest, expeditions. "That's something no one could have predicted through archaeology or oral history," Moreno Estrada says.

Voyages from Samoa to the Outer Pacific

This article on DNA dispersal is essentially saying three things. One: that Samoa was the hub for DNA dispersal into the outlying islands of Polynesia around 900 AD. It should be noted that people are known to have lived in Samoa and Tonga for thousands of years because Lapita pottery has been found there. The 900 AD dispersal is a later series of voyages for the Polynesians, who were Shaivites. Two: that this DNA dispersal went in waves to the remoter islands of the Marquesas, Mangareva, the Tuamotus and Easter Island. Three: DNA from the Americas was found in three major island groups: Rapa Nui, Raivavae, and the North and South Marquesas. These island groups apparently had a significant amount of American Indian DNA within the Polynesian population. It would seem that the closer the DNA search comes to the core islands of Samoa and Tonga that the American Indian

An old print of oceangoing canoes in Tahiti, 1768.

DNA is quite diluted.

Apparently, the thing that "no one could have predicted" was that American Indian DNA would be found in the Polynesian population. This indeed is a game changer for mainstream anthropology, as the consensus at universities has been that there was not any contact by sea with the Americas. This is now proven false.

That the central area for the distribution of Polynesian DNA should be Samoa is not surprising at all. This makes perfect sense given the location of the Samoan Islands. The Samoans have long believed that they are the "Hawaiki" of ancient Polynesian legends regarding the peoples' ancient homeland. They say that their largest island, Savaii, was originally Hawaiki. This island has a pyramid on it, made of small stones. We will discuss Hawaiki in more detail later.

Another of Samoa's islands, this one rather small, Manua, claimed to be the central island of Samoa and that its chief, the Tu'i Manu'a, was the chief, or king, of the entire Polynesian realm. It was said that the Tu'i Manu'a of Manua had special powers and could fly from island to island. The last Tu'i Manu'a, Chris Young, was photographed around 1910. Much of his family apparently became Mormons and moved to Utah.

One of the interesting things about the island of Manua, now part of American Samoa, is that it is the site of an obsidian field.

This field of glass-like obsidian yields very sharp blades that can be used as knives and spearheads. In ancient times obsidian was highly prized and traded over great distances. In a similar manner to salt mines, anyone who could control an obsidian source would have essentially an endless stream of wealth. Such was the island of Manua, and the chief of this small island would naturally be very powerful. Other sources of obsidian in the Pacific were Hawaii, the Solomon Islands, the island of Tafahi in northern Tonga and Easter Island. Indeed, Easter Island, or Rapa Nui, has a number of obsidian sites and these would have been very important to the development of the island. Indeed, the obsidian sites on Easter Island may have been key to its occupation by Polynesians. New Zealand also has numerous obsidian sites. Obsidian needles were used in tattooing which was widespread throughout the Pacific. Recent studies in the Solomon Islands have confirmed this.

Samoans have always believed that they were the central hub of the Polynesian world, although this belief is also held in Tonga and the island of Raitea in Tahiti. The islanders of the Marquesas has said that they would make a voyage to Samoa every few years and return to their islands. This probably would have involved trade in obsidian.

The central theme of Havaiiki being a lost homeland of the Polynesians also fits in with the central Polynesian islands of Samoa, Tonga and Tahiti. These islands are clearly the heart of

An old print of Fijian chiefs with their turbans.

Polynesia. It is known that Fiji was early on a Polynesian island but wars with Melanesian islands ultimately turned Fiji from a Polynesian island into a Melanesian one. Wars between Tonga and Fiji went on for hundreds of years.

Another lost land of the Polynesians concerns the lost homeland of the Easter Islanders, the land of Hiva, or I might say, Shiva.

The Lost Land of Hiva-Shiva

Back in 1988 I visited Easter Island and one of the first things that I acquired when I got there was the Chilean government tourist brochure. This English brochure related the legends of Easter Island and the tradition of a lost land of Hiva:

> According to one legend going back 1,500 years, a group of courageous Polynesian seafarers, making use of primitive boats, guided by the stars, currents and winds, were the first to set foot on Easter Island.
>
> Others believe that the first boats to arrive drifted away from the coast of South America, right out into the Pacific Ocean. After a long solitary voyage, they reached an island of extinguished volcanoes, today transformed into green and grassy hillsides.
>
> The natives, however, say that in the 15th Century Hotu Matu'a, leading a memorable expedition from Marae Renga Island, set foot on Easter Island. His voyage from Hiva—Maori land—denoted the beginning of this cultural treat: Easter Island.

The next section, called "The Legend of Hotu Matu'a," was about how Hotu Matu'a escaped a big cataclysm:

> One day, starting from far-distant lands, enraged Uoke stirred up the bottom of the Polynesian seas, destroying islands and rousing storms and earthquakes. Using a gigantic lever he lifted chunks of earth and later dropped them back into the sea. But the lever broke just before reaching the shores of Rapa Nui, and Easter Island was thus saved from destruction. At the same time, warned by a certain Hau Maka's dreams, King Hotu Matu'a, together with his wife Vakai, relatives and many friends were running away from this cataclysm in two boats. One early

> morning they found themselves sailing in the calm waters surrounding the small island of Motu Nui. While looking for a good landing place, they reached the beautiful beach of Hanga Morie Roa [on Rapa Nui]. Today known as Anakena, its clear waters are ideal for swimming. Wearing their multicolored robes and feather capes, they leapt with delight from their hundred-foot boats onto the white sand of the beach. Singing and dancing, they carried with them tools, household goods, and baskets full of plants like taro, ti, sweet potatoes, bananas and sugar cane. They also brought flowers and fowl.

This is an interesting story, indicating that the Easter Islanders were coming from a lost land of Hiva. Was Hiva the central island of Samoa as the DNA detectives are telling us? Also, is this lost land of Hiva really the lost land of Shiva, the Hindu god?

At the end of the first passage above it says that the Easter Islanders came from "Hiva—Maori land." Some anthropologists believe that Easter Islanders (Rapa Nuians) are from New Zealand, where the modern Maori live. Yet, in the next section quoted speaks of a cataclysmic reapportionment and sinking of a beloved homeland. In Easter Island mythology, this sunken continent and

Easter Island statues of Shiva with topnots at Anakena Beach.

homeland is called Hiva. Hiva is a land now gone, a lost land beneath the Pacific Ocean, according to Easter Islanders and their legends. New Zealand is very much above the ocean, however, and tradition seems to place Hiva elsewhere. The DNA detectives are telling us that the Easter Islanders came from Samoa.

Old photo of the megalithic arch in Tonga.

In his fascinating and important work, *Mysteries of Easter Island*,[34] Francis Maziere explores the legends of the lost land of Hiva. Maziere was able to talk with a dying leper named Gabriel Veriveri who was allegedly the last initiate of the secrets of Easter Island. Said Veriveri to Maziere, "King Hotu-Matua came to Easter Island in two canoes. He landed at Hangaroa, but he gave the bay the name of Anakena, because it was the month of July." Maziere notes that the winds from Polynesia to Easter Island blow in July and August. Says Maziere:

> King Hotu-Matua's country was called Maori (in the Maori dialect of New Zealand, the word maori means "ordinary people"), and it was on the continent of Hiva. The place where he lived was called Marae-Rena... the king saw that the land was slowly sinking in the sea. The king therefore called all his people together, men, women, children and the aged, and he put them into two great canoes. The king saw that the disaster was at hand, and when the two canoes had reached the horizon he observed that the whole of the land had sunk, except for a small part called Maori.

Continues Maziere about Hiva:

> The tradition is clear: there was a cataclysm; and it appears that this continent lay in the vast hinterland that reaches to the Tuamotu archipelago (what is today in French Polynesia) to the north-west of Easter Island.
>
> Another legend, handed on by Aure Auviri Porotu, the last of the island's learned men, says this: 'Easter Island

> was a much larger country, but because of the sins of its people Uoke tipped it up and broke it with a crowbar...' Here too we have a cataclysm.
>
> A more important point is that according to tradition Sala-y-Gomez, an islet some hundred miles from Easter Island, was formerly part of it, and its name, Motu Motiro Hiva, means 'small island near Hiva.'
>
> We have three signs pointing to this cataclysm. Yet generally accepted geology does not acknowledge any vast upheaval in this part of the world, at least not within the period of human existence. However, there are two recently discovered facts that make the possibility of a sunken continent seem reasonable. When the American submarine *Nautilus* made her voyage round the world she called attention to the presence of an exceedingly lofty and still unidentified underwater peak close to Easter Island. And secondly, during his recent studies carried out for the Institute of Marine Resources and the University of California, Professor H.W. Menard not only speaks of an exceedingly important fracture-zone in the neighborhood of Easter Island, a zone parallel to that of the Marquesas archipelago, but also of the discovery of an immense bank or ridge of sediment.[34]

Maziere's book came out in 1965 in France, four years before the revolutionary geological theory of tectonic plates changed geology forever. Maziere favored the existence of an archipelago and even a long, thin "continent" extending south and north of Easter Island between the Marquesas Islands and the Galapagos Islands. Easter Island was the last peak (along with Sala-y-Gomez) of this former continent "wrent beneath the sea by Uoke's crowbar":

> Apart from preserving the memory of these upheavals, tradition also states that King Hotu-Matua came from the west. Now in Easter Island on the Ahu A'Tiu there are seven statues and they are the only ones on the island that look towards the sea, and more exactly, the western sea.
>
> Their precise placing might well fix the area of the cataclysm, which would thus lie between the Marquesas and the Gambier islands. It seems probable that during

Two statuettes of the Egyptian god Bes, having a tiki motif on the left.

> one of those sub-oceanic upheavals still so frequent in the zone between the Cordillera of the Andes and the New Hebrides, an archipelago—I do not presume to say a continent—may have sunk or been altered. Moreover, according to Professor Metraux's findings, it seems possible that King Hotu-Matua's men emigrated from this area of the Marquesas; the reasons for believing this are based on linguistics—the use of Hiva is an example—and many points of ethnological agreement. The date of this migration, according to the genealogies that we collected, would be towards the end of the twelfth century.

Maziere then goes on to discuss the legend of seven explorers first sent out to find "the navel of the world," who would then return and guide the two giant canoes to safety on Rapa Nui. He finds it odd that in the Marquesas, where some of the islands actually have the name Hiva in them, there is really no legend of a sunken continent. He then says that the footless, handless old leper Veriveri told him of a legend he had learned that the island was inhabited already when Hotu-Matua came by "very big men, but not giants, who lived on the island well before the coming of

Hotu-Matua."

Indeed, the name Hiva shows up in such islands as Nuku Hiva, Fatu Hiva and Hiva 'Oa in the Marquesas Islands to the northeast of Tahiti. The Marquesas are among the largest island groups in French Polynesia. One of the islands in the group, Nuku Hiva, is the second-largest island in the entire territory (after Tahiti) and the largest of the Marquesas Islands.

The Marquesas Islands group is one of the most remote in the world. It lies about 852 miles (1,370 km) northeast of Tahiti and about 3,000 miles (4,800 km) west of Mexico (the nearest continental land mass). The Marquesas are the closest of all the Polynesian Islands to North America while Easter Island is further south and eastward; its nearest landmass is Peru and Chile.

The Marquesas Islands fall naturally into two geographical divisions. There is the northern group, consisting of Eiao, Hatutu, Motu One, and the islands surrounding the large island of Nuku Hiva: Motu Iti, Ua Pou, Motu Oa, and Ua Huka. And there is the southern group, consisting of Fatu Uku, Tahuata, Moho Tani, Terihi, Fatu Hiva, and Motu Nao which are clustered around the main island of Hiva 'Oa.

The islands were discovered by Europeans on July 21, 1595 when the Spanish explorer Álvaro de Mendaña de Neira stopped at Fatu Iva and called the islands Los Marquesas after the wife of the Viceroy of Peru. The Spanish kept note of the location of the islands for several hundred years, but did not return to them. The British Captain James Cook visited the south in 1774, and the French Solide expedition visited the islands in 1791.

A gigantic block of stone at one of the pyramids in Tonga.

An old print of a double-hulled Tongaraki canoe used in Tonga.

Herman Melville wrote his book *Typee* based on his experiences in the Taipivai valley in the eastern part of Nuku Hiva. Robert Louis Stevenson's first landfall on his voyage on the *Casco* was at Hatihe'u, on the north side of the island, in 1888. There are numerous megaliths and large statues on the islands. The men and women were heavily and artfully tattooed, just as they are in Samoa—famous for its tattoo art.

So the obvious question is: are the Marquesas Islands, with all of their "Hiva" names the land of Hiva that the Easter Islanders were talking about? This is what Francis Maziere considered but ultimately rejected because he was looking for a sunken land and the Marquesas Islanders had no such legends.

Is the real lost land of Hiva the Samoan Islands as the DNA detectives assert? The Marquesas Islanders say themselves that they journeyed to Samoa every year or few years. Was this the central Shiva-Hiva hub from whence the powerful Shaivite shamans began their voyages?

As I detail in my book *The Lost World of Cham*,[8] these Hindu Shiva worshippers controlled all of Southeast Asia from 1000 BC until about the 9th century AD when their vast sea kingdom collapsed due to internal wars. This vast empire of Shiva worshippers included what is today southern Vietnam, Cambodia, Thailand, Malaysia, and most of present-day Indonesia including Sumatra, Java, and Bali. This oceanic empire even extended to Madagascar and out into the Pacific.

As I outline in my book, the southern Philippines were also part of the Cham or Champa empire and it was a route between the southern Philippines and the northern coast of Borneo that the ships took into the Central Pacific. They would have passed through Micronesia and the northern coast of New Guinea, past the Solomon Islands and Vanuatu and into the central Pacific islands of Fiji, Tonga and Samoa. From here, according to the DNA detectives, the Polynesians—men of Shiva with their long hair tied in a topknot on their head—went north to the Marquesas and Hawai'i; east to Tahiti and the Tuamotu Islands; and southeast to such remote islands as Rapa Iti, Ravavae, and Rapa Nui (Easter Island). They also went directly south to Rarotonga and New Zealand.

These Hindu-Shiva voyages went on for thousands of years throughout Southeast Asia and the sailors even settled Madagascar during this period with ships from Sumatra and Java. The megalith culture of Madagascar is poorly understood today, but it is acknowledged that these megalith builders and the current population of Madagascar came from Indonesia and Malaysia in pre-history.

What ultimately happened was that the Cham-Champa empire began to crumble from within as fighting began between the Champa cities in southern Vietnam and the Cham kingdom of Srivijaya in Sumatra and western Java. At about the same time, the Champa cities in Vietnam were attacked by Chinese naval forces, eager to sack these cities for the huge amounts of gold that they collected. This gold came from sources within the islands of Indonesia but also on transpacific voyages that the Cham made to southern Mexico, Colombia and Peru.

In fact, on mainland India where the worship of Shiva continues to this day, the region of Southeast Asia—which begins at Sumatra—was known in Sanskrit as "Suvarnabhumi" which means "Land of Gold."

As this maritime empire collapsed, it stopped sending ships out to the central Pacific and transpacific trade came to a complete halt, circa 900 AD. This affected cultures in Peru and Mexico, such as the Maya. Essentially, the long ocean voyages—except in the central Pacific—came to a halt. There was still considerable traffic around Sumatra and the Gulf of Siam where Islamic sailors began spreading their doctrine throughout the region. Certain areas like the island of Bali and the Buddhist areas of Cambodia and Thailand held out, however the religion of Islam went all the way to the southern Philippines.

Voyages within the central Pacific continued for hundreds of years, right up until the time of European contact. In fact, while these men of Shiva were now cut off from the big ships and the homeland of Shiva—any of the ports or monuments in Indonesia, Cambodia or Vietnam such as Borobadur, Angkor Wat, or My Son—they still had fairly large ships that could go between island groups. In this way ritual raiding and invasion began in Melanesia and Fiji, with the Fijians attacking the Tongans to the east. Many voyages were made from Tonga and Samoa to the islands to the east and southeast, including Tahiti and the many islands surrounding it. While the remote Marquesas Islands remained in contact with the central Polynesian islands, such islands as New Zealand, Hawaii and Easter Island became isolated from the core islands of Hiva-Shiva, which the DNA detectives have identified as Samoa.

Kon Tiki, Hawaiki, and Shiva-Hiva

At Anakena Beach on Easter Island is a solitary moai with a plaque commemorating Thor Heyerdahl's visit in 1956. Born in Larvik, Norway in 1914, Thor Heyerdahl was to become an adventurer and explorer whose theories would rock the scientific world and ultimately make him rich. Shortly after finishing his studies in zoology at the University of Oslo he fled from civilization with his wife to live on an isolated island in the Marquesas. From 1936 to 1937 they lived on the remote island of Fatu Hiva where an old man called Tei Teua told them a legend of how the first inhabitants of those islands had come from a land to the east, on the other edge of the sea, under the command of a divine king called Tiki. Heyerdahl then set off on a ten-year study of American Indian and Pacific literature for some evidence of New World-Pacific contacts.

Among Peruvian legends dating from before the Inca Empire, he found an account of a certain Kon Tiki, a name that signified "Tiki of the Sun," who ruled a domain in the vicinity of Lake

Titicaca. Kon Tiki was defeated in battle and fled with some loyal companions to the Peruvian coast. There he built a raft and sailed west. Heyerdahl believed that this might be the same Tiki as in the Marquesan legend. He then found evidence that peoples in the central Andean coastal region had been capable of making oceangoing rafts.

The Kon Tiki statue at Tiwanaku.

Heyerdahl and four companions set off to Ecuador after World War II to build a raft using ancient techniques and sail it to Polynesia. They cut balsa logs from the interior, floated them to the coast and constructed a raft with a large square sail and peculiar Peruvian centerboards made of vertical planks passed downward between the logs.

He named the vessel *Kon-Tiki* and on April 28, 1947, he and his companions sailed westward from Lima. Using the prevailing southeasterly winds and the westward drift of the Humboldt current, they arrived at Raroia in the Tuamotu Archipelago after 101 days. Being unable to maneuver the raft to an opening in the reef, they ran it over the sharp coral, destroying the ship.

There is a statue at Tiwanaku (pre-Inca ruins near Lake Titicaca in Bolivia) that is situated in the middle of the Sunken Temple that is called Kon Tiki. It is a standing stone about 12 feet high depicting a bearded man with his hands over his heart and stomach in the manner of the tiki art of the Pacific.

The early transpacific voyages began in Vietnam, Sumatra, Malaysia and Java and traversed the Pacific to lands rich in gold on the other side of this vast ocean. Yet, there are many islands throughout the Pacific and most of them are inhabited. At one point there were literally thousands of ships coming from Southeast Asia into the Central Pacific and they were going to all of the islands that they could. They might eventually go to southern Mexico and Peru before the long journey back through the islands. These voyages would take many years, probably three or four, or even more.

The lost Polynesian homeland of Hawaiki features in with the tiki statues and the lost land of Hiva. For many Polynesians, Hawaiki is their original homeland, but where is Hawaiki?

According to Wikipedia:

> On several island groups, including New Zealand and the Marquesas, the term has been recorded as associated with the mythical underworld and death. William Wyatt Gill wrote at length in the nineteenth century recounting the legends about ‘Avaiki as the underworld or Hades of Mangaia in the Cook Islands. …There is no real contradiction in Hawaiki being both the ancestral homeland (that is, the dwelling place of the ancestors) and the underworld, which is also the dwelling place of ancestors and the spirits.
>
> Other possible cognates of the word Hawaiki include sauali‘i (“spirits” in Sāmoan) and hou‘eiki (“chiefs” in Tongan). This has led some scholars to hypothesize that the word Hawaiki, and, by extension, Savai‘i and Hawai‘i, may not, in fact, have originally referred to a geographical place, but rather to chiefly ancestors and the chief-based social structure that pre-colonial Polynesia typically exhibited.
>
> …According to various oral traditions, the Polynesians migrated from Hawaiki to the islands of the Pacific Ocean in open canoes, little different from the traditional craft found in Polynesia today. The Māori people of New Zealand trace their ancestry to groups of people who reportedly travelled from Hawaiki… Polynesian oral traditions say that the spirits of Polynesian people return to Hawaiki after death. In the New Zealand context, such return-journeys take place via Spirits Bay, Cape Reinga and the Three Kings Islands at the extreme north of the North Island of New Zealand. This may indicate the direction in which Hawaiki may lie.

It is said that Havai'i is the old name for Raiatea. Anthropologists have thought over the years that Raiatea, an important ceremonial island just north of the main island of Tahiti and east of Bora Bora, is a good candidate for being Hawaiki. This core island group in what is today French Polynesia was important in the settling of the Marquesas Islands and Hawaii.

A drawing of Viracocha at Tiwanaku.

It seems that there is one level of Hawaiki being an allegory for a spirit world where one goes upon transition like that of Hiva. On the other hand, the legend seems to be of a physical place, an ancient homeland that went down in a catastrophe. Is this event then the actual sinking of some part of the Pacific thousands of years ago? Perhaps the final subsidence of a large area that remained above the surface, something of a lost continent, such as James Churchward's Mu?

The Pacific is a very active geological area with many volcanoes, earthquakes, tsunamis and tidal waves. That some region of the Pacific was decimated in the past, perhaps near Samoa, is entirely possible. It may be the ancient Hawaiki and lost Hiva are the original homeland in Southeast Asia and India. Shiva, from whence the name Hiva derives, I maintain, is a maritime god, complete with a trident as has the Greek god Posiedon, but he actually lives in Tibet. Mainstream historians today admit that the Cham and Champa and Southeast Asians were Shiva worshippers and wore their hair long and tied as a topknot on their head.

These are the same statues of Easter Island, stoic statues of a god with a topknot of hair upon his head. This is the god Shiva. He is the lord of the land of Hiva-Shiva. While this land is in Tibet and Southeast Asia, it is also by extension that core area of Polynesia.

This land may not have disappeared in a cataclysmic sense but more of a figurative sense. The big ships just stopped coming. The annual trade that came from Southeast Asia completely stopped. The outer islands like Easter Island became isolated over time. They lacked the large ships to make the long ocean voyages that were required to get to Tahiti, Tonga or Samoa.

In fact, at the time of European contact it was only the Tongans with their large Tongaraki double canoes that could make the journey between island groups with a large number of people. Other canoes were similar to the war canoes used by the Maoris, Hawaiians and Marquesan Islanders.

Perhaps the lost land of Hiva (Shiva) was beneath the waves as the Easter Islanders believed. Perhaps the lost land of Hiva was the core Polynesian area of Tonga, Samoa and Raiatea (Tahiti). This was the core island group of Shiva. Hawaiki was then a land to the west, the land of Suvarnabhumi, the land of gold. A land dominated by Shiva and infiltrated by other Hindu gods and goddesses. A land of temples, great ships, fantastic monuments like Borobadur, and long-haired Shiva worshippers, going to temples and working on the ships. This was the vast, little-known world of ancient Southeast Asia and its megalith builders.

Chapter 6

The Cham-Khmer Shaivites

Like a star that guides a ship across an ocean
That's how your love can take me home back to you
And if I wish upon that star—that someday I'll be where you are
I know that day is coming soon—I'm coming back to you
—*Back to You*, Bryan Adams

My journeys in search of lost cities and ancient mysteries have taken me around the world, from the mountain peaks of the Andes to beneath the waters of the oceans. My search for the answers to such enduring mysteries as the building of megalithic walls in prehistory and evidence for ancient transoceanic contact was to take me to an unlikely place: Vietnam.

In central Vietnam, a few miles south of the famous DMZ of the Vietnam War (called in Vietnam the "American War") was the mysterious capital of the Cham Civilization. The Cham, or Champa, were a Hindu maritime people, apparently related to the Hindus of ancient Indonesia, whose influence can still be seen on the island of Bali, the last bastion of Hinduism in a predominantly Muslim country.

The Cham (pronounced "Kom" or "Kam") peoples inhabited much of central Vietnam and a group of islands off the coast called the Cu Lao Cham, or Cham Islands. This island base, as well as cities up several rivers in the area, were once the center of an accomplished maritime trading empire—an empire that not only traded with China to the north and Indonesia to the south, but also with nations across the vast Pacific!

Having apparently arrived from India via Malaysia and Indonesia, the Champa kingdom was a federation of several smaller states called Mandala and comprised several ethnic groups. This included Caucasian Hindus from western India, dark skinned Tamils, and dark skinned Khmer or Cambodian-Malaysian-Javan

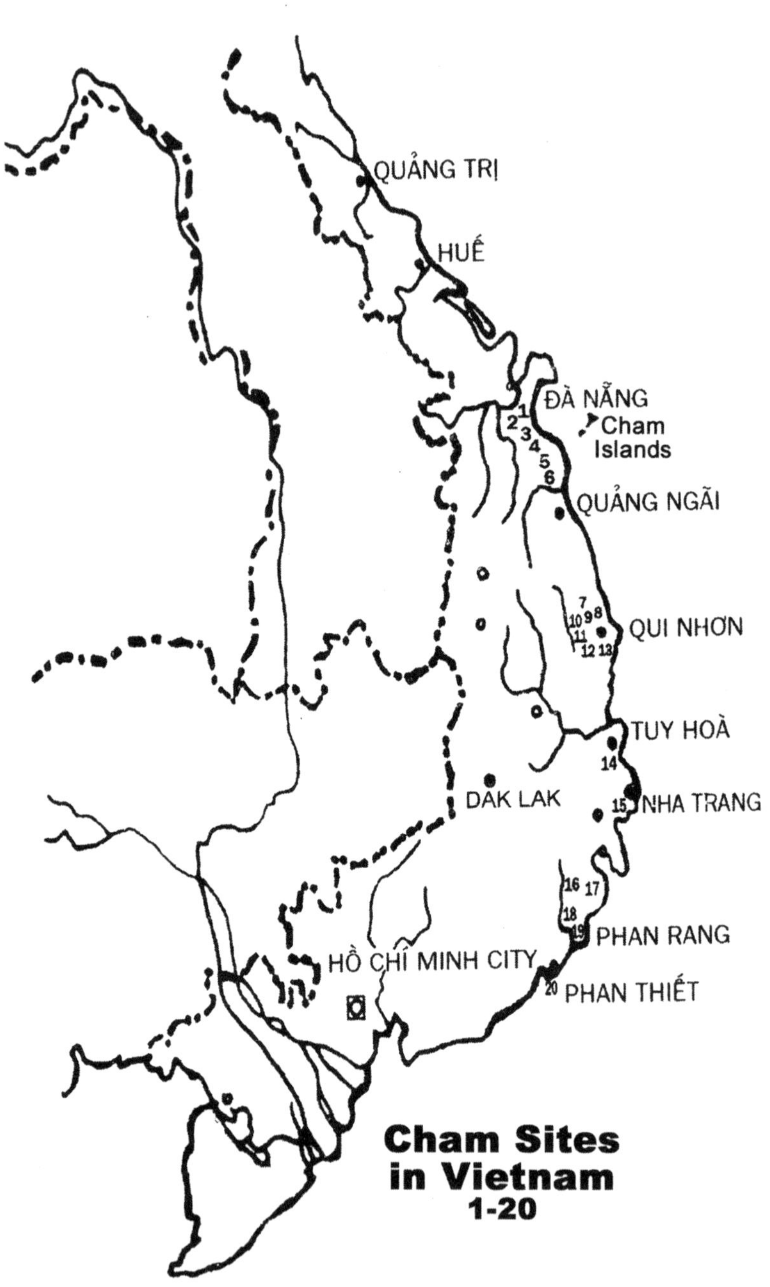

A map showing 20 important Cham sites in the southern portion of Vietnam.

people. The light-skinned Dai Viet lived in North Vietnam and began moving south in the early 1800s. They eventually conquered the entire Vietnam coastline and created modern Vietnam as it is today. Prior to about 1850 Vietnam was quite different ethnically.

According Ivan Van Sertima and Runoko Rashidi in their book *African Presence in Early Asia,*[15] Chinese records from as early as 192 AD reference a kingdom in what is now central Vietnam known as Lin-yi, which meant the "land of black men." Its inhabitants possessed "black skin, eyes deep in the orbit, nose turned up, hair frizzy." The kingdom of Lin-yi was known in Sanskrit documents as Champa, a substantially Indianized kingdom (Buddhist and Brahmin) with close contacts with India and China.

Other states had names such as Huang-Wang and Chang-Chen. The Cham territories stretched from south of the Ngang Pass in Quang Binh Province to the delta area of the Dong Nai River in Binh Thuan Province. It included the coastal plains, highlands and mountain ranges. This area of Vietnam is very mountainous, with cliffs often coming right up to the coast. Occasional rivers and hidden bays are found along the coast, making it a rugged area best traversed by boat. An army marching through this territory would not get very far, thereby making the Cham harbors something of a naturally protected territory. The Cham Islands off the coast were even more protected, and these islands were probably the central base for what is assumed to be a very large navy of the Cham.

The Cham built mostly out of stone and brick. Many of their early buildings were quasi-megalithic with keystone cuts and clamps used to hold large blocks together, often basalt—similar to those seen in Egypt, Greece, Java and Tiwanaku in Bolivia. The most important legacy of the Cham are the brick temples and

A street in the megalithic Cham city of My Son.

towers that are scattered over the coastal lowlands and highlands. The structures date from between the 7th and 8th centuries to the 16th and 17th centuries and are concentrated in Quang Nam, Danang, Binh Dinh, Khanh Hoa, Ninh Thuan and Binh Thuan.

The brickwork in Cham temples is so incredibly sophisticated and durable that a number of legends have sprung up about them. Ngo Van Doahn says in his book, *Champa: Ancient Towers—Reality & Legend*,[1] that the construction method of these buildings remains a mystery to modern architects and archeologists. He mentions an old Vietnamese legend that the Cham people built their towers from air-dried bricks, then shaped them, and finally heated the whole structure in a gigantic furnace. He mentions that at the beginning of the 20th century the French archeologist H. Parmentier commented on the "foolish" idea of this legend. Parmentier could not figure out how air-dried brick could withstand the tremendous weight of a structure that was 20 or 30 meters high before baking.

Since this seemed impossible, Parmentier surmised that the bricks must have been fired separately and were very hard. Yet, the structures were so finely built with the bricks so perfectly fitted together that it appeared that the structure had been fired all at once in a huge kiln. Fieldwork on the structures showed that mortar was used between the bricks, but that in the outermost layers of bricks,

A square in the megalithic Cham city of My Son.

the mortar was "so thin that the bricks look stuck together."

The other mystery of the Cham brick construction is the elegant carvings found on the brick faces of many of the temples. The Vietnamese surveying these Cham structures wondered how it was possible to carve out bricks like stones, as they would normally crumble. This was one of the reasons for the legend of the towers being fired as a whole, rather than being built one brick at a time. Modern archeologists surmise that the motifs may have been carved on each brick as part of a larger pattern while still soft, and then fired individually and each brick placed in its artistically appointed spot.

Two basalt blocks with keystone cuts found at My Son.

In December of 2007, I visited the most important of the Cham cities, the site known as My Son with my wife, Jennifer. My Son is situated in Quang Nam Province about 60 kilometers from the historic cities of Danang and Hue. It was an all day bus and boat ride, highlighted by a tour of the main group of monumental complexes scattered over an area of about 10 hectares.

My Son is the impressive remains of the holy city built over the centuries around the sanctuary of Bhadresvara (Shiva), which was thought to be founded in the 4th century AD. Today, there are some seventy brick buildings still visible, constructed by the Cham kings to commemorate the great events of their reigns and to perpetuate their legacy. Building at My Son continued until the 13th century. The majority of the temples were dedicated to the Cham Kings who, after their death, were associated with divinities of the Hindu pantheon, especially Shiva, who was considered the founder of the Cham Dynasty.

We were quite impressed by the stone and brick structures, and the fine decorations. I pointed out to our guide the use of keystone cuts on basalt blocks, and the metal clamps that were evident on some stone walls that had been partially demolished. He had never seen or heard of keystone cuts and clamps before, and was genuinely amazed at the discovery of these unusual construction

T-shaped keystone cuts on stone blocks found at My Son, identical to Tiwanaku.

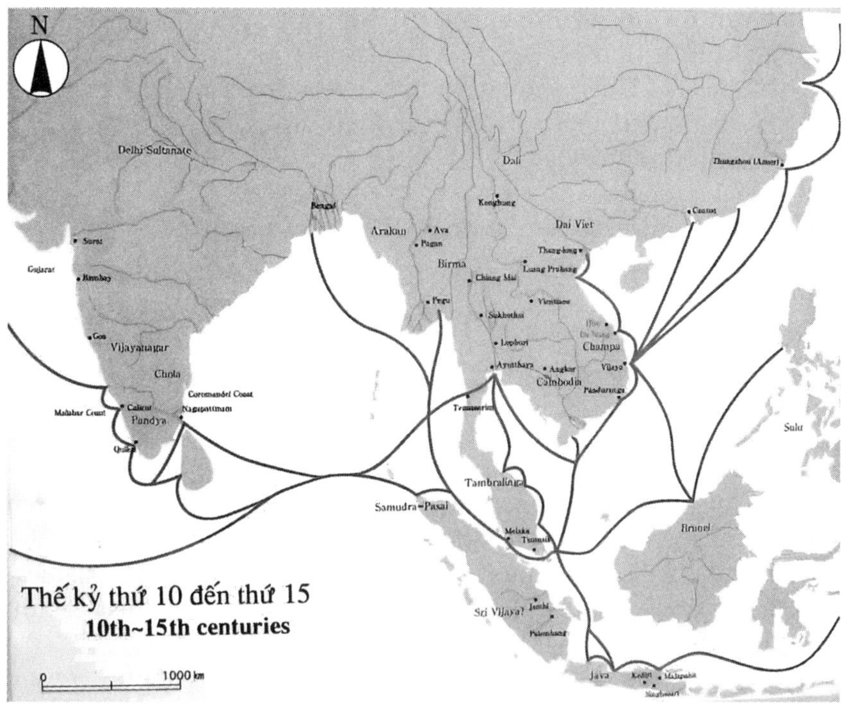

A map showing the trading routes of the Cham throughout Southeast Asia.

techniques at the site. For that moment, I became the guide and he the tourist.

Cham architecture is characterized by high shrine towers, with doors facing the east and false doors on the other sides. The doorways feature carved sandstone, which is similar to Khmer temples in Cambodia. The tower is crowned with four stories of decreasing size. The temples and towers themselves are considered to be sculptural artifacts. They are decorated on the exterior of their brick walls with bas-relief columns, flowers and leaves and worshipping figures between brick pillars. The tympana, lintels and ornamental corner pieces are of sandstone carved with the figures of gods, the holy animals of the Hindus and more flowers and leaves. The greatest piece of architecture at My Son was an enormous, 70-foot-high tower that was destroyed by United States Army commandos in August of 1969. Unfortunately, the temple site is just a few miles to the south of the Demilitarized Zone and hence was considered "fair game."

We learned an interesting story of lost treasure: when the Cham were forced to withdraw towards the south of the country in the face of incessant raids by the Vietnamese and Javanese, and exhausted by their wars against the Khmers, the Cham at the end entrusted to a number of mountain tribes jewelry and precious metal objects. This became known as the treasure hoard of the Cham kings, and these tribes still faithfully guard the treasures today. Or so the story goes.

A Mayan Statue at the Cham Museum in Danang?

After our amazing visit to My Son, we visited the Cham Museum in Danang. Our taxi driver let us off at the gate to the museum, and upon entering I was immediately impressed by the quality of the statuary.

Built in 1915, the museum displays an intensive and diverse collection of Champa sculpture dating from the 7th to the 15th centuries. The museum was established at the end of the 19th century by the Ecole Francaise d'Extreme Orient with a collection of artifacts gathered in central Vietnam, from Quang Binh to Binh Dinh. Today, the museum displays a trove of altars, statues and decorative works collected from Hindu and Buddhist Cham temples and towers.

Cham sculpture displays various styles, and the museum

A stone portrait called Nam Than at the Danang Museum that looks very Mayan.

divides the statues and other art into two categories, those made before the year 1000 AD and those made thereafter. Little, if any, statuary has survived from the earliest periods of Cham art (thought to have originated sometime BC, though the earliest records are from 192 AD) and most of earliest art discovered is from 600 AD to 800 AD.

Among the masterpieces of this period on display at the museum is the Tra Kieu Altar. The altar was used for the worship of Shiva, the creator and destroyer of the universe, and the symbols of his creative ability, the Lingam and Yoni, are present on it. The four scenes carved around the base of the altar tell part of the story of Prince Rama, the subject of the famous *Ramayana*. In that epic, he went to the citadel of Videha to try to break the sacred bow of Rudra so that he could marry Princess Sita. Prince Rama broke the bow, a task that had been tried by many before him, and he and the princess were wed in the beginning of the epic. Later Sita runs off with—or is kidnapped by—the Prince of Lanka. After some years of penance and meditation, Rama goes to get her in his flying machine called in Sanskrit a vimana.

Museum literature says:

> Artifacts in the Dong Duong room (the 9th and 10th centuries) create a deep impression with their vigorous, lively and exaggerated style and represent the climax of the development of Champa art. These statues of the first Champa kings, with the characteristic big eyes and noses and thick lips of the native people, show their vitality and imposing appearance. These carvings show the absolute belief that a supernatural force was supporting the rule of the Champa kings during the period when Buddhism was the dominant force.
>
> The second period lasted from the 11th to the 15th centuries. The devastating wars from the end of the 10th century onwards took the Champa kingdom into decline, and the relocation of the capital from Tra Kieu (Quang Nam) to Tra Ban (Binh Ding) in about the year 1,000 brought about a new direction in their art. Artifacts discovered at Thap Mam (style of the 12th-14th centuries) are monumental sculptures of large animals such as elephants, makara (sea monsters) and garudas (the birds of the gods, much like the American Thunderbird) which

served as protectors of the temples and towers.

After the Thap Mam period Champa art declined. The Shiva statue displayed in the Kontum room has an exhausted appearance. This was one of the last artifacts of the Champa sculptors. By the end of the 17th century the Cham dynasties came to an end.

By this time, like many Malaysians and Indonesians, the Cham had become Muslims, and embraced the religion of Islam.

Several pieces of art caught my eye as unusual and significant. One was a stone plaque that looked amazingly Mayan and Olmec to me. The Cham were said to appear African in some of their features, which is also an important factor in Olmec art. The sign with the statue said that it was "Nam Tham," a "forest spirit." I showed the statue to Jennifer, who agreed that it looked remarkably Mayan and Olmec.

Was there a connection between the Cham and the Olmecs? The Olmecs are now known to have been the predecessors of the Maya in Mesoamerica, and many of their statues depict people with the African features of thick lips and wide noses, distinctly non-American Indian traits. We do not think of the Vietnamese or Chinese as looking African, but it is admitted that the Cham had these features.

The African-Cham-Mesoamerican Connection

Anthropologist Runoko Rahshidi, coauthor of *The African Presence in Early Asia* with Ivan Van Sertima (Rutgers University,1988), maintains that the Cham were, in fact, Africans who had come to Vietnam from the Indian subcontinent.

Rahshidi visited Vietnam in 2001 and says on his website (http://www.cwo.com/~lucumi/vietnam.html):

> The Cham Museum has many of the finest objects of Cham art in the world and is just magnificent. It is an open air museum holding about three-hundred artifacts. Many of the objects, superb sandstone Buddhist and Hindu works, I had previously only seen in books, and so in many ways the visit was a dream come true. Many of the pieces are as Africoid (dark skin, full lips, broad noses) as any art that you will ever see. The Cham Museum has to be one of the finest museums in all of Southeast Asia and is a must

see for any African who goes to Vietnam.

My initial interest in the African presence in Southeast Asia started almost thirty years ago, stimulated by the reports that I received from numerous friends, acquaintances and family members who had served in the United States military during the Vietnamese War. I remember, beginning even back then around the age of sixteen, how fascinated I was when I heard their descriptions of the different Black people that they had encountered. They referred to these Black folks as *Montagnards*. I was later to find out that these so-called *Montagnards* were not recent arrivals to Vietnam. Nor were they the offspring of African-American soldiers and Vietnamese women, but,

A statue at the Danang Museum that looks very Negroid.

rather, these were people who had been in Vietnam for a very long time.

...The Cham seem to have possessed what appears to have been a strong Melanesian element and are believed to have settled along the coastal plains of mid-southern Vietnam more than two millennia ago. Another view is that the Cham were actually Black colonists from south-central India. Either way, it is clear that the Cham dominated the region for centuries.

According to one account the kingdom of Champa was born of a victory by the Blacks "over the Chinese province of Je-Nan... later, it frequently demonstrated its unruliness and the spirit of conquest, including against China." Early records further note that, "For the complexion of men, they consider black the most beautiful. In all the kingdoms of the southern region, it is the same." Chinese scribes added that the people of Champa adorned themselves "in a single piece of cotton or silk wrapped about the body... They are very clean; they wash themselves several times each day, wear perfume, and rub their bodies with a lotion compounded with camphor and musk."

H. Otley Beyer believed that between 900 and 1200 C.E. a group of sea-farers made their exodus from central Vietnam and found their way to the Philippines. These sea-farers, noted Beyer, were called the "*Orang Dampuans* or Men of Champa." During this same period Cham ships, known to the Chinese by the appellation *kun-lun-bo* (the "vessels of Black men") were navigating the currents of the Indian Ocean ranging from Southeast Asia to Madagascar.

According to Leonard Cottrell, "The term *k'un-lun* found in Chinese texts relating to south-east Asia, is an ethnic term which seems to apply to a number of peoples who are characterized by black skin and frizzy hair... Their geographical location and their maritime skills made them important contributors to the cultural history of Southeast Asia and south China. There are also pointers to a connection with the Kao-li of Korea. By association, and as a conventional Chinese transcription, the term k'un-lun is also applied to the Khmer. Later, by extension, because of physical resemblances, the term was used by Chinese writers for African Negroes. The connection with the

Right: Shiva giving the Sudarsana Chakra to Vishnu. *Below*: A Champa bust of Shiva made of the gold-silver-copper alloy of electrum. Note the third eye and topknot.

Right: Shiva meditating on Mount Kailash in Tibet,

Top: A photo of the megalithic city of My Son in central Vietnam. *Left and Above*: The stone blocks with their unusual and complicated articulation and keystone cuts are very similar to those found at Tiwanaku and Puma Punku.

Above: The amazing and mysterious Buddhist stupa known as Borobudur. *Left*: Borobudur is built as a gigantic mandala that is to be walked in a certain pattern to the top. Did the Cham build Borobudur?

Left: A stone vat in Bada Valley probably used as a crucible melt gold ore. *Below*: The large tiki statue in Bada Valley with an erect penis. This is apparently a statue of Shiva.

ɔove: A dolmen with a
ɪnged Shiva flanked by two
ɪardians with clubs. *Right*:
statue at San Agustin
ʼ the Bhairava aspect of
ɪiva with fangs. Note the
nilarity to the statue in
ɪda Valley and the opposite
.ge.

Above Left: The mysterious precision-cut monument on Sumba Island called Kampung Paronabaroro. *Above Right*: Hug slab dolmens on Sumba Island. *L* More slab dolmens on Sumba Is *Below Left*: Two stone tiki faces northern Sumatra. *Below Right*: Toraja megaliths on the island of Sulawesi

Above: A photo of the south side of Mount Kailash with the swasika visible.
Below: A Tibetan painting of the land Tag-Zig Olmo Lung Ring.

Above: A photo of a disk-shaped flying object in eastern Tibet on February 20, 2011. The inset in the upper left is a blow-up of the object. *Below*: A photo of the "Robot-like figure" apparently flying at the Ladakh site of Samudra Tapu in 2004.

Khmer was justified because of the parallel between the mythical K'un-lun Mountain of Chinese cosmology and the mountain cult, assimilated with the Indian Meru, of the Khmer kingdoms."

The Mystery of the Cham Islands

It is fascinating that the Cham were these amazing Hindu-Buddhist seafarers who were ranging from Madagascar to Indonesia, Vietnam and beyond. They were well situated in central Vietnam, and especially the Cham Islands, to voyage out into the Pacific—to the Philippines and even further afield. By passing between Borneo and the Philippines, they could have sailed along the north coast of New Guinea and into the Melanesian islands of the Western Pacific, possibly even populating them! The people of Melanesia are Black and do not resemble the Polynesians of the central Pacific Island groups.

From Melanesia it would have been an easy trip to Tonga, Samoa, the Marquesas Islands and the Americas. This is essentially one of the transpacific routes that I suggest in my book, *The Mystery of the Olmecs*.[22] In that book I show that Shang Chinese were in contact with the Olmecs as early as 1300 BC. The Cham are from

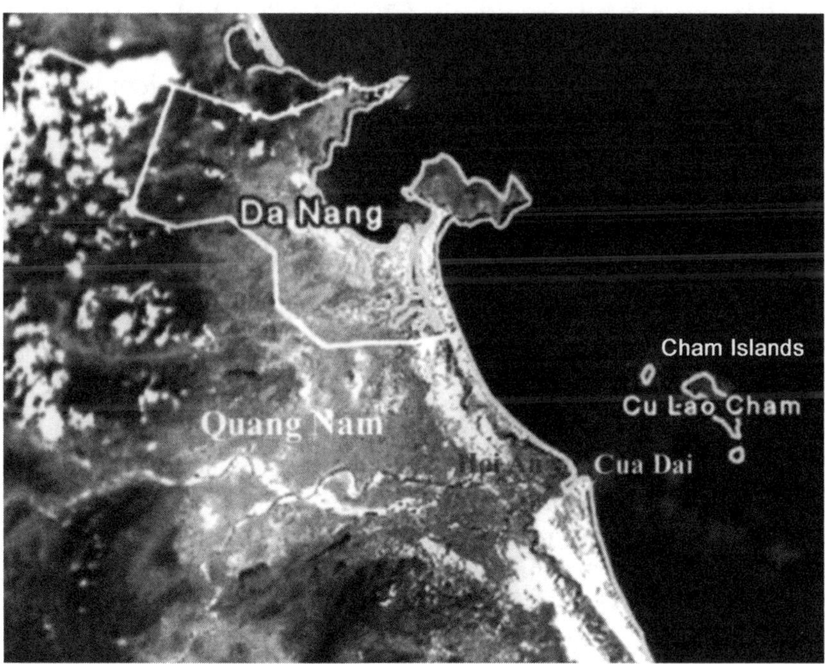

A satellite photo of the Da Nang area and the Cham Islands.

a later period, but they may have been making transpacific contact during the period of around 200 BC to 800 AD. Perhaps they had inherited from the Shang Chinese the long distance sea routes that went beyond the Philippines and New Guinea to even New Zealand and Australia.

From a balcony on the second story of the museum I looked out to the Pacific Ocean in the distance. Only 25 kilometers off shore were the Cu Lao Cham, or Cham Islands, that must have been the Cham's main naval base. The main island of the seven, Lao, has a deep and protected cove on the western side that is a very good shelter for ships during storms and even typhoons. It would seem that the sizable Cham fleet of presumably gigantic ships must have been based here.

Reached from the mainland in a few hours by boat, the Cham Islands were first settled some 3,000 years ago according to archeologists. If the Cham were the first settlers, then we could extend the reign of the Cham people back to 1000 BC, which puts them within the time frame of the early Olmecs.

Today there are about 3,000 people living on the Cham Islands in small fishing villages. Some curious features on Lao include a rock-cut, square well that, amazingly, provides clear fresh water all year round, while most wells have salty, brackish water. There are many good beaches that are ideal for dragging ships up onto, plus cliffs with millions of swallows and several ancient temples including the Ong temple where a "giant fish" is buried and "worshipped." Could this possibly be one of the giant Cham ships, now buried on the island?

In 2007, races were held at the Cham Islands to swim the channel between the islands and the mainland. It was won by Rudy van Bork, a Dutch athlete, who did the 25 km stretch in just six hours and seven minutes. Van Bork is actually the second person to complete the channel swim, as Akkiko Izawa, a female swimmer from Japan, performed the feat in 2002. The Dutch swimmer competed with ten Japanese and two Vietnamese rivals. About 20 volunteers on boats, kayaks and speedboats accompanied the swimmers to ensure safety.

"It was a great race," said Van Bork in the local tourist publication. "It is strange to swim in a direction with only seawater on the horizon. After several hours I started seeing some land and structures. Then I knew I could finish the adventure."

As the moon began to rise over the ocean, I thought of the

adventurous Cham and their far-flung journeys. Where did they originate? Well, Cham, or Kam, is a familiar name in many places, including Kampuchea and Cambodia. Also, Kam is the name of ancient Egypt. Even today, Egypt is called in Arabic "Kam-et," or "Kem-it." Were the Cham of Vietnam the same as the Kam of Egypt? Egypt-Kam is located in northeast Africa, and many Egyptians were Black Africans, including a number of the Pharaohs. The famous Giza Sphinx is thought to depict a Black African with thick lips and a wide nose.

Egypt-Kam had the advantage of having ports on both the Mediterranean Sea and the Red Sea. From the Red Sea ports, the Kam seafarers could journey to the Maldives, Sri Lanka, India, Indonesia, Vietnam and beyond. As they settled parts of Southeast Asia they became Hindus who worshipped Shiva. The ancient Kam seafarers could continue across the Pacific to the Pacific coasts of North and South America. Easter Island would have been used as a stopover on return voyages from South America.

Starting around 1000 BC or earlier Hinduism and Shiva worship was the religion from India to Sri Lanka, Sumatra, Java, Malaysia, Thailand, Cambodia and Vietnam. Even the Philippines and islands in Micronesia had Shiva worshippers. Over time there were invasions of Thailand and Vietnam from southern China. Champa had a war with Srivijaya, a Hindu kingdom in southeastern Sumatra, in the 7th century AD and the long voyages into the Pacific stopped occurring. The fleets no longer assembled at the Cham Islands. This ultimately cut off the many islands of Micronesia and Polynesia from the large homeports in Southeast Asia. Then the Muslim religion swept into Sumatra, Java, Malaysia as well as southern Vietnam and the southern Philippines.

At the museum in Da Nang I took one last look at a statue of Shiva, his third eye distinct on his forehead. He was no doubt content on his mountaintop home in the Himalayas. Yet his calm and reassuring smile reached the world over, to Champa and the Pacific Islands beyond.

A 13th c. gold statue of Shiva's wife Parvati found in the southern Philippines.

Chapter 7

Shiva and North America

I'm a thousand miles from nowhere
Time don't matter to me
'Cause I'm a thousand miles from nowhere
And there's no place I want to be
—*A Thousand Miles from Nowhere*, Dwight Yokum

It is not necessary to understand things
in order to argue about them.
—*Pierre Beaumarchais* (1732 - 1799)

The Mysterious Hohokam

One of the mysterious cultures of the Southwest is the Hohokam of Arizona, Sonora and New Mexico. The word Hohokam (Ho-Ho-Kam) is borrowed from the O'odham language. The name Kam or Cham is explicitly part of the name. It would seem that they are related to the oceangoing Champa of Vietnam and Indonesia. The Hohokam emerged around 300 BC and flourished from 300 AD to 1500 AD. According to local oral tradition, Hohokam societies may be the ancestors of the historic Akimel and Tohono O'odham in Southern Arizona.

No one knows where the Hohokam came from or where they went. We do not know much about their civilization except that it lasted over a thousand years. It was very extensive. No doubt the Hohokam used large canoes to move up and down the large rivers and canals distributing the wealth of the land including corn

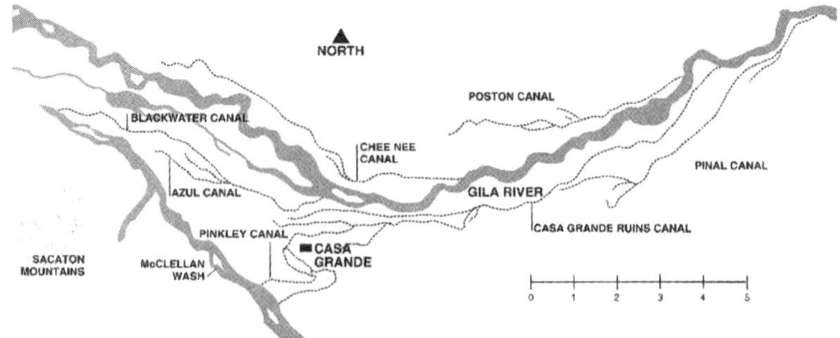

A map of Hohokam canals in the Phoenix area.

(maize), beans, squash, melons, tomatoes, peppers and other foods. Especially in the heartland around modern-day Phoenix, it was a land of plenty. Rabbits and ducks were hunted with boomerangs, much as was done in ancient Egypt. People kept domesticated dogs, and games were held at the ballcourts.

Hohokam settlements were located on trade routes that extended past the Hohokam base area, east to the Great Plains and west to the Pacific coast. Hohokam societies had a considerable amount of long distance trade and some communities established significant markets, such as that in Snaketown and other areas north and south of Phoenix. One of the things that was traded extensively was Hohokam pottery which was of good quality; they made many large jars. The Hohokam had ballcourts at nearly all of their settlements which went to southern Utah and Colorado and included such large ruins in New Mexico as the Aztec and Salmon ruins plus the extensive buildings at Chaco Canyon.

The Hohokam are recognized for their large-scale irrigation networks located in modern-day Phoenix,. Their canal network in the Phoenix metropolitan area was the most complex in the pre-contact Western Hemisphere. A portion of the ancient canal system has been renovated for the Salt River Project and helps to supply the city's water. The original canals were dirt ditches and required routine maintenance. When Hohokam society collapsed around 1500 AD, the dirt canals fell into disrepair. Those currently in use are lined with concrete.

The Hohokam core group were located along rivers, and as such inhabited a prime trade position for territory that spread into

New Mexico and beyond. This area included port communities at the Sea of Cortez, where the powerful Colorado River emptied into the Pacific. The trade in dried fish and sea shells was brought inland to the central cities of the Hohokam.

Trade occurred between the Hohokam and the Patayan, who were situated along the Lower Colorado River and in southern California; the Trincheras of Sonora, Mexico; the Mogollon culture in Eastern Arizona; the people of Southwest New Mexico and Northwest Chihuahua, Mexico; and the Ancestral Puebloans in Northern Arizona.

From 900 to 1150 CE, neighboring Chaco society encouraged trade throughout northern Arizona and into southwest Colorado and southern Utah. These trade networks increased hand-to-hand trade throughout the region, with goods traveling across the Colorado Plateau, northern Arizona, and the Phoenix area.

Hohokam irrigation systems supported the largest population in the Southwest by 1300 AD. Archaeologists working at a major archaeological dig in the 1990s in the Tucson Basin, along the Santa Cruz River, identified a culture and people that may have been the ancestors of the Hohokam. This prehistoric group may have occupied southern Arizona as early as 2000 BCE, and in the

An artist's conception of the abundant farming done by the Hohokam.

Part of the Hohokam site known as Casa Grande.

Early Agricultural Period grew corn, lived year-round in sedentary villages, and developed sophisticated irrigation canals.

Wikipedia says that the Hohokam used the waters of the Salt and Gila rivers to build an assortment of simple canals with weirs for agriculture. From 800 to 1400 CE, their irrigation networks rivaled the complexity of those of the ancient Near East, Egypt, and China. They were constructed using relatively simple tools and engineering technology, yet achieved drops of a few feet per mile, balancing erosion and siltation. The Hohokam cultivated varieties of cotton, tobacco, maize, beans, and squash, and harvested a vast variety of wild plants. Late in the Hohokam Chronological Sequence, they also used extensive dry-farming systems, mainly to grow agave for food and fiber. Their agricultural strategies were vital in the inhospitable desert, and allowed the aggregation of rural populations into complex urban centers.

Many features of earlier Hohokam domestic architecture, such as rectangular pithouses, were apparently transplanted relatively intact from the Tucson basin during the early Formative Period. Throughout the Hohokam Chronological Sequence, individual homes were usually excavated approximately 16 inches below ground level, had plastered or compacted floors of 12 to 35 square feet, and had a bowl-shaped, clay-lined hearth near the wall-entry.

Wikipedia says that by 600 AD, a distinct Hohokam architectural tradition emerged that had similarities with Mesoamerica, such

An artist's conception of a Hohokam community.

as ballcourts that also served as neighborhood gathering and trade spaces. By 1150 AD, pithouses were replaced by above-ground structures in the compound style with central courtyards. By 1200 AD, rectangular platforms mounds were being constructed.

Wikipedia says that Hohokam burial practices varied over time, but cremation was a defining cultural characteristic of the Hohokam core. Cremation has been used by archaeologists to suggest cultural interaction through trade or immigration with neighboring communities. By the late Formative and Preclassic periods, the Hohokam cremated their dead, very similar to the traditions documented among the historic Patayan culture to the west along the Lower Colorado River. Although the particulars of the practice changed somewhat, cremation remained the main practice in Hohokam until around 1300 AD. This is an obvious Hindu and Buddhist custom.

While modern archeologists like to confine the Hohokam culture to southern Arizona and northern Mexico, they were not just affiliated with the Anasazi and Chaco cultures, they were the Anasazi and Chaco cultures. They are also the "Sinagua" (no-water) people of Tuzigoot and Montezuma's Castle near Cottonwood and Camp Verde, Arizona.

All of these sites, several days' walk north of Phoenix, were formerly Hohokam and all of these sites, going as far north as Utah and Colorado, had the same ballcourts that the Hohokam used. Ballcourts were used as far south in Central America as Panama.

It is surmised by historians that climatic change combined with an invasion from Oklahoma of the Apache-Dene peoples into New Mexico and Arizona around the year 1200 AD sped the decline of the Hohokam. Around the year 1300 the Anasazi and the Hohokam abandoned their cities and essentially vanished. Some historians surmise the Hohokam may have moved south to the Lake Texcoco and become the Aztecs.

A photo of a Hohokam canal in Phoenix.

How did the Cham get to the American Southwest? They would have had to cross the Pacific, stopping at such island groups as Samoa and the Marquesas. They would need to enter the Sea of Cortez at the southern tip of the Baja Peninsula and sail up to the northern shores where they could have built a port that was connected to the river systems of the American Southwest and Sonora. It is known that cities on the northern edges of the Sea of Cortez were part of the Hohokam area, and seashells were traded and used in jewelry far inland.

California and Hindu-Chinese

In Hemet, California is the Hemet Maze Stone. Now an official California Historical Landmark, it is said to have designs of the Buddhist-Hindu swastika on it and is traced back, typically, to ancient transpacific people who were apparently exploring inland from the coast around Long Beach. Going east from Hemet, the California desert becomes particularly stark and barren. Plants are few and far between. This barren desert continues for hundreds of miles until you reach the Colorado River and the border with Arizona.

The very name of California is a mystery, the actual source of the name being unknown. In tracing the roots of the word, the California Historical Society has only been able to discover that it is first mentioned in a Spanish book *Las Sergas de Esplandián* by the conquistador Garcia Ordóñez de Montalvo circa the year 1500. It has not been traced to either Indian or European sources.

According to Chaman Lal, a University of Bombay archaeologist and author of *Hindu America?,*[31] the name California comes from ancient Hindu and the land is so named because of the profusion of Kali Temples built there by early Hindu explorers. Kali Temples have been found as far into the Pacific as Hawaii. We might call it Kalifornia, land of Kali.

Chaman Lal's whole thesis that ancient Hindu sailors and settlers formed the basis of many current Native American tribes is one shared by Thor Heyerdahl, Barry Fell, the Epigraphic Society, and many other practicing archaeologists. Ancient Hindu exploration and trading well into the Pacific is evidenced by the existence of Bali and many other parts of Indonesia that are still Hindu in their culture and religion. The rest of Indonesia was forcibly converted to Islam by the Moslem expansion a thousand years ago.

The constant use of betle nut and Indian Pepper Root (*Kava* in Fiji, *Sakau* in Pohnpei and Yap) throughout Micronesia shows the ancient Hindu influence into the western Pacific. Curiously, the strange and undeciphered Rongorongo writing at Easter Island has been shown to be similar to ancient Indus Valley writing of three thousand BC!

Not long ago, popular and well-reviewed books came out that champion the historical facts of early Chinese voyages, literally, around the world. In his best-selling book *1421: The Year China Discovered the World*, author Gavin Menzies maintains that a massive fleet of junks that were nearly 500 feet long was launched on March 8 of that year. This fleet was under the command of eunuch admirals loyal to the Emperor Zhu Di and they were to sail to the ends of the earth to collect tribute from the barbarians. They were to go 'beyond the seas' and thereby unite the world in Confucian harmony. The journey of this fleet would take two years and circumnavigate the world, Menzies claims.

In another book about China's pre-Columbian explorations,

When China Ruled the Seas by Louise Levathes,[10] the author maintains that Shang Chinese were sailing to the Americas circa 1000 BC. I believe that they were accompanied by the Cham. Although she does not specifically maintain that Olmecs were part of the Shang Chinese contact with Mexico, other archeologists and historians have done so, including some linked to the prestigious Smithsonian Institution.

The Smithsonian Institution published a monograph in 1974 entitled "The Transpacific Origin of Mesoamerican Civilization" by Betty J. Meggers. Meggers was a career archeologist employed by the Smithsonian Institution until her death in 2012. In her monograph, Meggers says:

> Anthropologists generally assume that civilization developed independently in the eastern and western hemispheres. Review of the features that distinguish the Olmec culture of Mesoamerica from preceding village farming groups shows, however, that many are present in the earlier Shang civilization of China. If Olmec civilization originated from a transpacific stimulus, this has important implications both for reconstruction of New World cultural development and for formulation of a valid theory of the evolution of civilization.

In her Smithsonian paper Meggers gives archaeological evidence of the Olmec as the earliest civilization in Mesoamerica, discussing their pyramids, monuments, art, calendars, trade, and religion. She then discusses the various characteristics of Shang civilization. Among the similarities between these two societies, she says, are their writing styles, the esteemed use of and long-distance trade in jade, the use of batons as symbols of rank, their settlement patterns as well as architectural styles, the long-range acquisition of luxury goods, worship of feline deities, and the use of cranial deformation.

While she admits the difficulty of the task, Meggers concludes that the Shang-Olmec similarities can be used to prove either independent development or cultural diffusion. The basic difficulty we face, she notes, is that a search for cultural origins is handicapped by both unrecognized biases and limitations of data.

In his 1923 book *The Children of the Sun,*[24] University of Manchester archeologist W. J. Perry attempted to demonstrate how a dual system of Egyptians and Hindu Indians ventured out into the Pacific and colonized such places as Tonga, Tahiti, Hawaii and Easter Island. Perry presented evidence that envoys of the ancient Sun Kingdoms of Egypt and India traveled into Indonesia and the Pacific circa 1500 BC, spreading their sophisticated culture. Perry traces the expansion of megalithic building from its origin in Egypt through Indonesia and across the Pacific all the way to the Americas. These early mariners searched for gold, obsidian, and pearls in their incredible explorations from island to island—Perry says they were known as the Children of the Sun!

Lapita pottery that is found throughout the Solomons, New Caledonia, Vanuatu and as far as Fiji, Tonga and Samoa, is only dated to 4,000 years before present. Still, the obvious network of trade, mining and commerce of 2,000 BC may well be connected with Egyptian traders and their far-flung voyages to the distant land they called Punt. It is believed by historians such as Harvard's Barry Fell that the island of Sumatra played a major role in the long sea voyages of antiquity.

Fell has claimed that voyages beginning in the Red Sea and the Horn of Africa went to Sri Lanka, Sumatra, Eastern Indonesia, New Guinea and out into the Pacific. Manning these ships were Caucasians and Negroes. Fell thinks that these voyagers, on a one-year trip to the Isthmus of Tehuantepec in southern Mexico (or alternately Peru), would pass into the Pacific on either the north or south side of New Guinea and then continue past such islands as New Britain, New Ireland, the Solomons, Vanuatu and ultimately arrive at Fiji, Tonga and Samoa. Indeed, Fell is talking about a culture very much like the Cham who were also traversing this part of the Pacific.

Pyramids and other megalithic structures found on these islands, like the Ha'amonga stone arch on Tonga, lend credence to this idea. The traders brought Lapita pottery with them. Later, Tahiti and Hawaii were settled and Rai'tea near Tahiti became the eastern capital. From here such islands as the Marquesas, Rapa Iti and Easter Island (Rapa Nui) were settled. Fell surmises that the ancient seafarers voyaged to Mexico, Central America, Ecuador and Peru from these island bases. Throughout the Pacific, many of the islands' names include "Ra," the Egyptian name of the sun god.

Since there is a connection between the Egyptian sailors of Khem and the Hindu sailors of Cham, we might surmise that the Egyptian sailors ventured through the Red Sea to the Indian Ocean and crossed eastward to India and Sri Lanka. From southern India and Sri Lanka they proceeded further east to the Cham-held lands of Sumatra, Java and the coastal areas around the Gulf of Siam, including Cambodia and Vietnam.

Did these Egyptian (Khem) sailors team up with the Cham fleets and cross the Pacific in conjunction with Cham sailors? Had some of the blacks that are featured in Cham statuary originally come from Africa as sailors on the Egyptian boats? This is what Barry Fell and Ivan van Sertima clearly believed.

There is a cave painting in the Prince Regent River Valley in the Kimberleys of Western Australia that includes a man with a beard and tall hat, looking very Middle Eastern or Egyptian in origin. Around him are three women with long hair that is tied at the end. These women have been identified as Egyptian dancers with weights at the end of their hair. Their long, weighted hair played an intricate part in their show.

While Australian aboriginals are famous for using boomerangs, it is not well known that Egyptians used them, too. The Egyptians frequently hunted ducks in the marshes of the Nile with boomerangs, and also played games with them. It is an archaeological fact (though not well publicized) that a trunk full of boomerangs was discovered in 1924 when King Tutankhamun's tomb was opened by the archaeologist Howard Carter. Many of these boomerangs, inlaid with gold and lapis lazuli, are on display in the Tutankhamun exhibit at the Egyptian Museum in Cairo.

Next to them is an Australian boomerang for comparison.

Boomerangs were also used in southern Mexico, Texas, Arizona, and California. It is likely that the Olmecs used boomerangs as well, and boomerangs can be seen on display in Mexico City's Anthropology Museum. It is an interesting thought that the Australian Aboriginals, as well as tribes in the American Southwest, learned the use of the simple but ingenious boomerang from the Egyptians!

The anthropologist Elizabeth Gould Davis says in her book *The First Sex* (G.P. Putnam's Sons, 1971), "In Australia was found a pendant amulet of greenstone, carved in the shape of the Celtic cross, an exact duplicate of an amulet found in Egypt at Tel el Amarna, the site of the ancient city where Nefertiti and the Pharaoh Akhenaten held court thirty-five hundred years ago."

The timeframe of Akhenaten and Nefertiti (circa 1200 BC) is also the time frame for Lapita pottery (circa 1000-2000 BC) and of the Shang Dynasty of China (1600-1028 BC). This is also the timeframe often given for the beginning of the Olmecs, and I believe it might have been the beginning of the Cham.

One clear link between Australia and Egypt is that the Torres Straits Islanders, between New Guinea and Northern Queensland, use the curious practice of mummification of the dead. The Macleay Museum at Sydney University has a mummified corpse of a Darnley Islander (Torres Strait), prepared in a fashion that has been compared to that practiced in Egypt between 1090 and 945 BC.

Another similarity with the Torres Strait Islanders (as well as people in the Solomon Islands, Fiji and Polynesia) is the use at nighttime of a wooden headrest. This carved headrest was used to slightly elevate the head, while the subject slept on his back. This custom is unusual to ancient Egypt, China, and certain Pacific Islands around New Guinea.

As I have said, the Cham—and the Olmec—were a mixed group that included bearded and mustachioed Caucasians, and people with African, Oriental and classic "Chinese" features. They sailed the Pacific with large, diverse clues. Along for the ride were dwarves and hunchbacks (both considered good luck), who often served as musicians and storytellers to amuse the crew and keep them entertained. No one was a slave on the ship, though there was a strict hierarchy. All were welcomed heartily in the festivities that were had at the many ports of call, and all shared in the booty. For the sailor who had made a few voyages, it would be a fulfilling and profitable life.

On board, beside the captain and his close mates, there would have been a priest of sorts, a shaman and magician. He would deal with the local plant experts and obtain the correct herbs and psychedelics. These priests apparently even wore pointed hats and otherwise acted as we might expect some ancient wizard to act.

The Pacific City of Izapa

One of Meggers's students, Vincent H. Malmstrom, writes in his monograph "Izapa: Cultural Hearth of the Olmecs," published by Dartmouth College (available online at: www.dartmouth.edu/~izapa/M-6.pdf) that the ancient city of Izapa, near the Pacific Coast in the Isthmus of Tehuantepec was a major seaport with contacts with Ecuador, and probably Shang China. It also had knowledge of magnetism. Izapa is inland but it is near the Pacific port city of Paso de la Amada.

The settlement at Izapa extended over 1.4 miles, making it the largest site in Chiapas. The site reached its apogee between 850

A photo of the overall site of Izapa.

BC and 100 BC; several archaeologists have theorized that Izapa may have been settled as early as 1500 BC, making it as old as the Olmec sites of San Lorenzo Tenochtitlán and La Venta. Izapa remained occupied through the Early Postclassic period, until approximately 1200 AD.

After showing that Izapa was probably the place the Olmec calendar was invented, Malmstrom says:

> …Had Izapa served solely as the birthplace of Mesoamerican calendrics that would have been reason enough to regard it as a major cultural hearth amongst the Olmecs. However, in at least one other field of knowledge Izapa seems to have been in the vanguard of Olmec learning as well, namely terrestrial magnetism. For some time, researchers have believed that the Mayas were aware of magnetism, apparently using it to align the structures in their major ceremonial centers (Fuson, 1969, 494).
>
> Then, in 1973, Coe discovered a small bar of polished hematite at San Lorenzo that he assumed may have been used as part of a compass. Found in a layer dated to approximately 1000 BC, this suggests that the Olmecs were aware of magnetism about a millenium before the Chinese (Carlson, 1975, 753). However, during field work at Izapa in January, 1975, the author discovered evidence that the inhabitants of this site not only knew about magnetism but that they also seem to have associated it with the homing instinct in the sea-turtle. Such a conclusion stems from the fact that a large sculpture of a turtle head, located about thirty meters to the southeast of the main pyramid, has been carved from a

An Izapa stele depicting a dragon.

basaltic boulder rich in magnetic iron and executed with such precision that all the magnetic lines of force come to focus in the turtle's snout. Although no other magnetic stones have been found at Izapa, there are at least two other representations of the turtle present at the site.

One of these is a sculpture near the east wall of the main pyramid which has the shape of an upturned turtle shell and which, when filled with water during the rainy season, may have provided a frictionless surface on which to float a needle or sliver of lodestone. The other is a large altar in the form of a turtle at the west end of the ceremonial ball court, in whose north wall is embedded a carving of a bearded man standing in a boat moving across the waves. That the Izapans were a sea-faring people and maintained relatively regular contacts with places as far distant as Ecuador over a long period of time has been shown by the similarities in ceramics found in the two areas (Coe, 1966, 45; Badner, 1972, 24).

That they should have failed to observe the great migrations of east Pacific Ridleys moving between Baja California and Ecuador or of the black turtle which migrates between the Guatemalan coast and the Galápagos Islands while on such voyages is quite inconceivable (Carr, 1967, 136, 216). And that they should have been impressed by the sureness of the turtle's navigational ability and compared this to the direction-finding property of the lodestone would have taken no great leap of imagination. Whether Izapa's maritime connections included trans-Pacific contacts cannot be demonstrated at this point, though Meggers, among others, has presented striking evidence of similarities between the Olmecs and the Shang-dynasty Chinese (Meggers, 1975, 17). In any event, it would appear that Izapa served as a major center of cultural innovation in Mesoamerica, whether as a trans-Pacific bridgehead or as a hearth in its own right.

Therefore, Izapa may have been a major Olmec-Shang port on the Pacific. As such, many of the overland roads from Oaxaca and other areas would have converged at Izapa or nearby. Goods from the Atlantic side of the isthmus would have been brought overland as well, and it may well be the case that tons of jade, gold, hallucinogenic mushrooms, chocolate and other valuable trade items were shipped out of Izapa across the Pacific—some of it no doubt getting back to China and Champa. Later, Spain ran this lucrative trade through their ports in Manila and Acapulco.

In a *US News & World Report* story published November 4, 1996, it was reported that a Chinese language scholar named Han Ping Chen examined the famous Olmec figures and accompanying jade celts found at La Venta which are now at the National Museum of Anthropology. According to the news magazine he declared after examining some "writing" on the celts that, "Clearly, these are Chinese characters." Meggers became involved in this important discovery, as well.

So, it is fairly obvious that the Olmecs were in contact with the Shang Chinese. I think that it is fairly likely that the Shang Chinese were in contact with the Cham and that these dark-skinned master sailors went on Shang voyages to the Pacific and beyond. Maybe

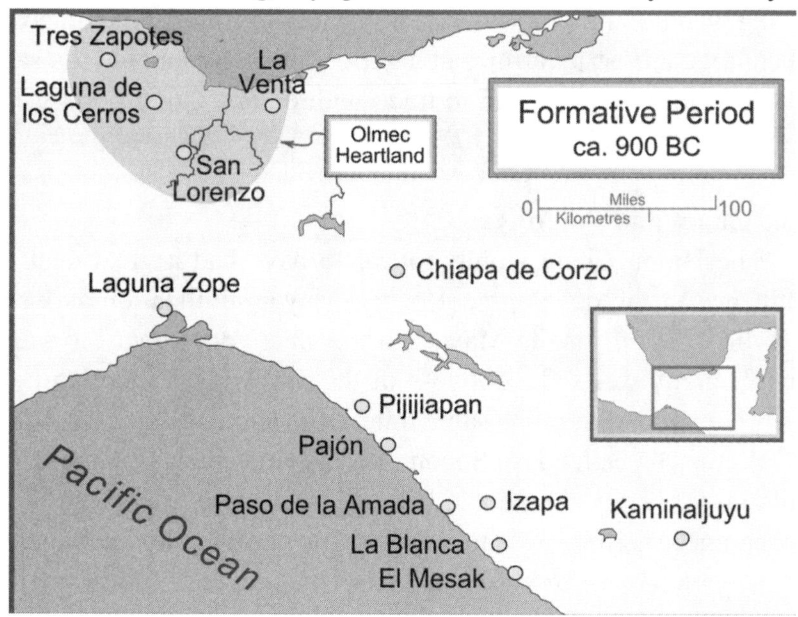

it was from the Shang the Cham learned to manage and build large seagoing vessels.

While the Olmecs civilization would seem to be older than the Cham, we can see that both started around 1000 BC. The Olmec may have been started by Shang Chinese at an early period and then the culture passed on to the Cham who were operating out of Sumatra, Java, Malaysia, Cambodia, Vietnam and the Cham Islands.

It would seem that the Shang and other Chinese naval forces would meet up at the Cham Islands in central Vietnam. From the Cham Islands the fleet of ships would voyage eastward into the Pacific, stopping first at Nan Madol in Micronesia and then continuing on to Samoa, the Marquesas and North America. When they landed they continued south to the tropical bays of Acapulco and further south to Tehuantepec. Here the early Olmec-Maya civilization was started by Chinese-Cham seafarers. In centuries to come they founded the Hohokam in Sonora and Arizona.

The Cham Islands are said to have been occupied by 1000 BC and only seafarers would have occupied this rocky granite island group. The beaches and bays of the Cham Islands were perfect for the gathering of large groups of ships and the trading of cargo. Being on an island that was far away enough from the mainland to keep large terrestrial armies at a good arm's length made it a safe place to harbor a ship and to trade with others. Other ports were nearby on the mainland.

The Cham and the Maya

The Hindu Cham would appear to have had a great deal of influence in the development of the Mayan civilization as well. The time frame for the Maya and the Cham are about the same and fit pretty well. The collapse of the Maya and the collapse of the Cham occurred at the same time, from about 700 to 900 AD.

As the Olmec lands of Soconusco and Guatemala became more culturally Mayan, the people became even more oriental in their appearance. As the British historian Graeme Kearsley documents in his book *Mayan Genesis*,[69] the art of the Mayan culture contains many Hindu elements, including hairstyles, decorative motifs, guardian demons, and the distinctive posture of arms, hands and fingers to communicate higher ideals. In Sanskrit such postures of the hands and fingers are known as mudras, and such postures have great meaning. We see these mudra postures in Mayan and Olmec statues and art. In a similar manner to the quizuo posture, the position of the arms, hands and fingers is universal and generally associated with Hinduism and Buddhism.

The areas that seem to be the earliest Pacific coast ports of the Cham or their predecessors are the sandy bays that start with the famous port of Acapulco and are found along the coast going south to the area known as Soconusco. These sandy bays were perfect for the Cham ships and the later Spanish galleons. The Cham were used to the sandy bays of the Cham Islands where they assembled their fleets from time to time. This was typical of the many islands of the Pacific.

The Spanish were essentially repeating the Cham and other transpacific voyages with their later Acapulco-Philippines trading. This trade enriched the Spanish traders in Acapulco and Mexico City, which was reached by mule train. Treasures were ultimately sent on to Spain.

Elephants were believed to have been carved on Mayan statues at the temple city of Copan on the border of Honduras and Guatemala. Many of the statues at Copan, as well as at nearby Quirigua, look very oriental in appearance. Both of these Mayan cities are located near

Maudslay's drawing a mahout at Copan.

the important jade mines in Motagua River Valley.

The British archaeologist Alfred P. Maudslay traveled to Copán in 1881 and began the excavation of the city. Excavation continues to this day with the Government of Honduras and the University of Pennsylvania directing the work.

When I first visited in 1992, I walked around the Great Plaza and marveled at the magnificent statues, steles and altars, some as high as four meters (12-13 feet). They are some of the most beautiful statues carved by the Maya, and have a controversial archaeological history. Stele B commemorates the accession of the ruler 18 Rabbit. Yin-Yang symbols literally cover the stele and are especially prominent on the belt. Above the ruler's head on either side of the top of the stele are what appear to be the heads of elephants.

When Maudslay first visited and drew the stele, a turbaned mahout or elephant driver, was depicted leaning on the head of the left elephant, and it would seem there would have been a similar depiction on the right side, but the stele was already damaged and that corner was missing. Curiously, the top left portion has now been destroyed, so that the mahout is no longer there. It is known that such a small figure was originally on the stele from Catherwood and Maudslay's early drawings, and others. Some European archaeologists have even accused American archaeologists of purposely defacing the stele.

Mainstream archeologists claim that instead of being an elephant with a mahout, they are stylized representations of the head of a macaw, with the beak curved backward in an exaggerated way to look like the trunk of an elephant. Why miniature turbaned men should be leaning on the stylized heads of these bizarre macaws has never been explained. It seems that this is a representation of an elephant and his mahout, both having been brought across the Pacific by the Cham!

Personally, I was amazed at the oriental look to all the statues. Having lived and travelled in China for several years, I was immediately struck at how Chinese-looking everything was. Many of the men had thin mustaches and thin wispy beards that are the exact caricature of the Fu Manchu-type of Chinese style. Had I not been completely aware that I was standing in the jungles of Central America, I would have thought that I was viewing a selection of statues from China or Vietnam!

Yin-Yang symbols were everywhere, and there was even a large stone ball, about three feet in diameter and weighing several tons, on which was carved a perfect yin-yang pattern. Around the edge was a braided rope effect and the whole stone was an oval-oyster shape, rather than being perfectly round.

Alfred Maudslay with one of the giant Mayan statues at Quiiqua.

Quiriguá and Copán share architectural and sculptural styles. Quiriguá is known for its wealth of sculpture, including the tallest stone monolith ever erected in the New World. These monolithic steles feature Mayan kings who are very oriental in appearance. They have whispy Chinese style mustaches and beards and could easily be kings from China or Vietnam.

Quiriguá was ideally positioned on the Motagua River flowing down from the Guatemalan highlands to control the trade of uncut jade, the majority of which was found in the middle reaches of the Motagua Valley. Quiriguá also controlled the flow of cacao, maize and other important commodities up and down the river. Both cacao and maize were grown in the area and Quiriguá could be reached from the Atlantic Ocean by travelling up the Motagua River. Mayan ports like Tulum could be found along the Atlantic coast and the Maya were known to have oceangoing boats that went to such islands as Cozumel. To the west the Mayans had ports along the Pacific coast as well and therefore had cities on both oceans. With this site the Maya, who began on the Pacific coast (as did the Olmecs), had access to the Atlantic Ocean and the Caribbean Sea.

The Shiva City of Monte Albán

I have been to Oaxaca near the west coast of Mexico a number of times. From Oaxaca City you can take a minibus to the mountaintop megalithic city of Monte Albán, less than an hour away from the city center. The ancient city is located on a low mountainous range rising above the plain in the central section of the Valley of Oaxaca. In fact the top of the mountain has been essentially cut off—artificially leveled—and great plazas, truncated pyramids and a court for playing the ball game known as tlachtli were constructed there. Monte Albán is also known for its underground passageways and at least 170 tombs, some of the most elaborate yet uncovered in the Americas. The great plaza atop the highest hill is flanked by four platforms; two temples stand on the platform to the south. Near the south end of this great plaza is a building thought to have been an astronomical observatory.

An overview painting of the mountaintop city of Monte Alban.

The plaza is large enough to land an airship on, and would make a great helicopter base.

One can see that its hilltop location is good for defense and for surveying the surrounding valleys of this area of the Isthmus of Tehuantepec, the narrowest area between the Atlantic and the Pacific Oceans. This was an area controlled by the early Olmecs. Later the Zapotec culture moved into the area, and after them the Mixtec culture arrived in the Oaxaca Valley. It is thought that the original building and mountain-slicing of Monte Albán began circa 800 BC, but that the Zapotecs didn't arrive until about 300 AD. Who were the mysterious early builders?

While archeologists seem confused as to who built Monte Albán, there seems to be no doubt that it was the Olmecs.

Many of the artifacts excavated at Monte Albán can be seen at the Museo Nacional de Antropologia in Mexico City and at the Museo Regional de Oaxaca in the ex-Convento de Santo Domingo de Guzmán in Oaxaca City. The Oaxaca museum houses, among others, many of the objects discovered in 1932 by Alfonso Caso in Monte Albán's Tomb 7, a Classic period Zapotec tomb that was opportunistically reused in Postclassic times for the burial of Mixtec elite individuals. These Zapotec-Mixtec individuals were accompanied by some of the most spectacular burial offerings discovered in North America including gold masks, figurines, jewelry and other objects.

On a recent trip with a group of World Explorers, we stopped at one platform where two round pillars were standing, once part of a building where they helped to hold up a stone ceiling that was now gone. The sign at the site said that the stone in these two pillars was a different kind of stone (it did not say which) than the stone that makes up most of Monte Albán, and was not from the area.

This meant that the large cylinders of stone, weighing several tons, had been brought from some other part of Oaxaca to the top of this mountain. In fact this platform with its stone pillars was one of the highest spots in all of Monte Albán. How had they brought these stones the great distance to the top of this mountain? Had they rolled them uphill on great roads, or was it possible that they were actually airlifted onto the top of the mountain? Why were these stones so important that they had to be brought from such a distance away? In actuality, we do not know exactly where

Olmec figures including some with beards at Monte Alban.

these great stone pillars came from.

One of the figures in the museum, I noticed, seemed to be of the Hindu elephant god Ganesh or Ganesha. Ganesh is the elephant-headed god in Hinduism. Ganesha is a very popular god in Hinduism, and was one of the most worshipped. Hindu tradition states that Ganesha is a god of wisdom, success and good luck. In Hindu tradition Ganesh is known as the Vighneshvara, which

A curious stele at Monte Alban that appears to show the Hindu god Ganesh.

means in Sanskrit "one who was the lord of obstacles or difficulties." Therefore, in Hindu tradition it is thought that by worshiping Ganesh, one can remove obstacles and difficulties. Hindus would often worship Ganesh before starting some new business or occupying a new household.

A scribe from Cuilapan, Oaxaca.

Ganesh is said to be the son of the Hindu god Shiva and his wife Parvati. He has the head of an elephant and typically has a garland of flowers around his neck and sometimes four arms. Unlike many Hindu gods, Ganesh is different almost every time he is depicted and has no formal look or way of holding his arms and hands, such as in the yogic mudra positions.

So, here was an elephant-headed god on a stele at the Monte Albán museum. Was it a depiction of a Hindu god in ancient Mexico? This would certainly fit in with what we know about the Olmecs and the Cham—that they were Hindu-Egyptians that arrived in fleets of boats from their Southeast Asia stronghold of Indonesia, Cambodia and Vietnam. The great Champa Museum in Da Nang, central Vietnam, holds hundreds of basalt and granite statues carved by the Cham of these same Hindu gods of Ganesh, Shiva and Parvati. Many of the statues at the museum look to be very similar to the Olmec art of Mexico.

Indeed, who were these ancient gods of Monte Albán who cut the top of a mountain off and created grand staircases and pyramids? Perhaps Monte Albán was originally to be one of the mountaintop fortresses occupied by the awesome Hindu god Shiva—King of the World.

The Shang-Cham-Olmec Connection

According to Chinese scholars the Chinese "invention" of writing goes back to the Shang Dynasty. The earliest Chinese characters are found on Shang Chinese oracle bones. These characters are similar to early Olmec characters.

As we have noted, in a *US News & World Report* story published November 4, 1996 reported that a Chinese language scholar named Han Ping Chen examined the Olmec figures and accompanying jade celts found at La Venta. He declared after examining some "writing" on the celts that, "Clearly, these are Chinese characters."

Says the article:

> For diffusionists, Olmec art offers a tempting arena for speculation. Carbon-dating places the Olmec era between 1000 and 1200 BC, coinciding with the Shang dynasty's fall in China. American archaeologists unearthed the group sculpture in 1955. Looking at the sculpture displayed in the National Gallery, as well as other Olmec pieces, some Mexican and American scholars have been struck by the resemblances to Chinese artifacts. In fact, archaeologists initially labeled the first Olmec figures found at the turn of the century as Chinese.
>
> … There are only about a dozen experts worldwide in the Shang script, which is largely unrecognizable to readers of modern Chinese. When Prof. Mike Xu, a professor of Chinese history at the University of Central Oklahoma, traveled to Beijing to ask Chen to examine his index of 146 markings from pre-Columbian objects, Chen refused, saying he had no interest in anything outside China. He relented only after a colleague familiar with Xu's work insisted that Chen, as China's leading authority, take a look. He did and found that all but three of Xu's markings could have come from China.
>
> Xu was at Chen's side in the National Gallery when the Shang scholar read the text on the Olmec celt in Chinese

> and translated: "The ruler and his chieftains establish the foundation for a kingdom." Chen located each of the characters on the celt in three well-worn Chinese dictionaries he had with him. Two adjacent characters are usually read as "master and subjects," but Chen decided that in this context they might mean "ruler and his chieftains." The character on the line below he recognized as the symbol for "kingdom" or "country"—two peaks for hills, a curving line underneath for river. The next character, Chen said, suggests a bird but means "waterfall" completing the description. The bottom character he read as "foundation" or "establish," implying the act of founding something important. If Chen is right, the celts not only offer the earliest writing in the New World, but mark the birth of a Chinese settlement more than 3,000 years ago.

The article ends by saying that more than 5,000 Shang characters have survived even though the soldiers who defeated the Shang forces murdered the scholars and burned or buried any object with writing on it. In a recent excavation in the Shang

The Olmec jade celts and figurines that feature early Shang glyphs.

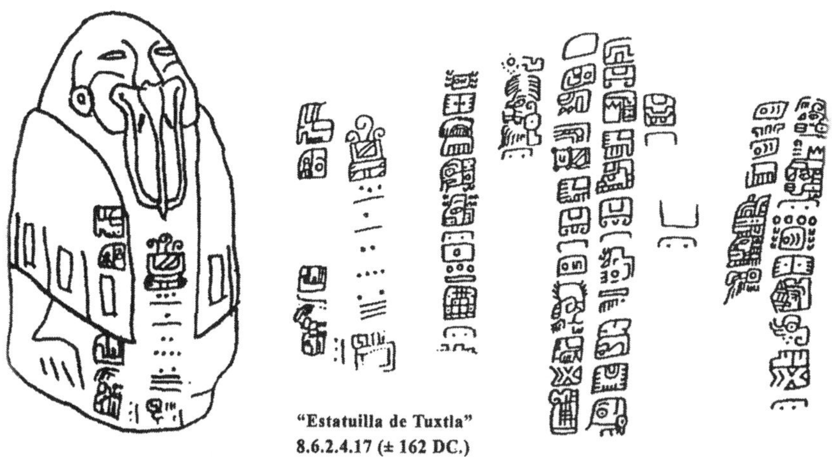

The Tuxtla Statue has early Olmec hieroglyphs on it.

capital of Anyang, archaeologists have found a buried library of turtle shells covered with characters. And at the entrance lay the skeleton of the librarian, stabbed in the back and clutching some writings to his breast.

Since the Olmec figurines and celts were buried in a special arrangement under white sand topped with alternate layers of brown and reddish-brown sand, Chen thinks that perhaps it was hidden to save it from the kind of rage that sought to wipe out the Shang and their memory.

In the same article, Betty Meggers of the Smithsonian Institution is quoted as saying, "Writing systems are too arbitrary and complex. They cannot be independently reinvented."

Is it possible that the Cham and their fleet at the Cham Islands were used to bring Shang Chinese priests and generals to Mexico? That would explain the strong Negoid presence in Olmec art and statuary. Indeed, the similarities between the Cham and the Olmecs are so strong that it is difficult to keep them from being connected in some way. Now we throw in Shang Chinese early writing and we have a scenario where the Hindu Cham of 1000 BC are using Vietnam and the Cham Islands to carry Chinese dignitaries eastward across the Pacific.

It is curious to think that the rise of the Olmec and later Mayan civilizations may have had something to do with the collapse of the capital back in China. The fortunes of many far-flung colonies would have been tied to events in the motherland. It would be an interesting course of study to review what we currently consider the "mysterious" rise and fall of certain civilizations to see if we can find correlations with the fortunes of cultures that have been heretofore considered unrelated. With the collapse of the Shang Dynasty in the year 1046 BC, the Chinese were no longer making special journeys across the Pacific. The Cham then made these voyages themselves until about 400 BC when something happened

The discovery of one of the colossal Olmec heads near Villahermosa.

that resulted in the destruction and elimination of the Olmecs.

The Maya now occupied the southern areas of the Olmecs while the central valleys of Mexico became Zapotec and Mixtec. Later the Aztec migrated from the north into this area. There is evidence to suggest that both Monte Alban and Teotihuacan were built by the Olmecs. The strange circular pyramid of Cuicuilco in the southern part of Mexico City, partially covered in a lava flow, was also probably built by the Olmecs.

So, with the collapse of the Shang civilization the Olmecs probably used the early Shang oracle script for a time, but this evolved into its own script and later evolved into Zapotec and Mayan script. Areas like Monte Alban and Comacalco were literal university campuses where ancient seafarers and locals alike

An Olmec cave painting from Oxtotitlan with a dragon and false penis.

learned different languages. See my book *The Mystery of the Olmecs*[22] for further information on the fascinating evolution of Olmec script.

Mayan became the dominant language on the Atlantic coast, while Zapotec became the dominant language inland and along the Pacific Coast. The exception to this would be Izapa and locations along the Pacific coast of Guatemala, which were in the Mayan sphere of influence.

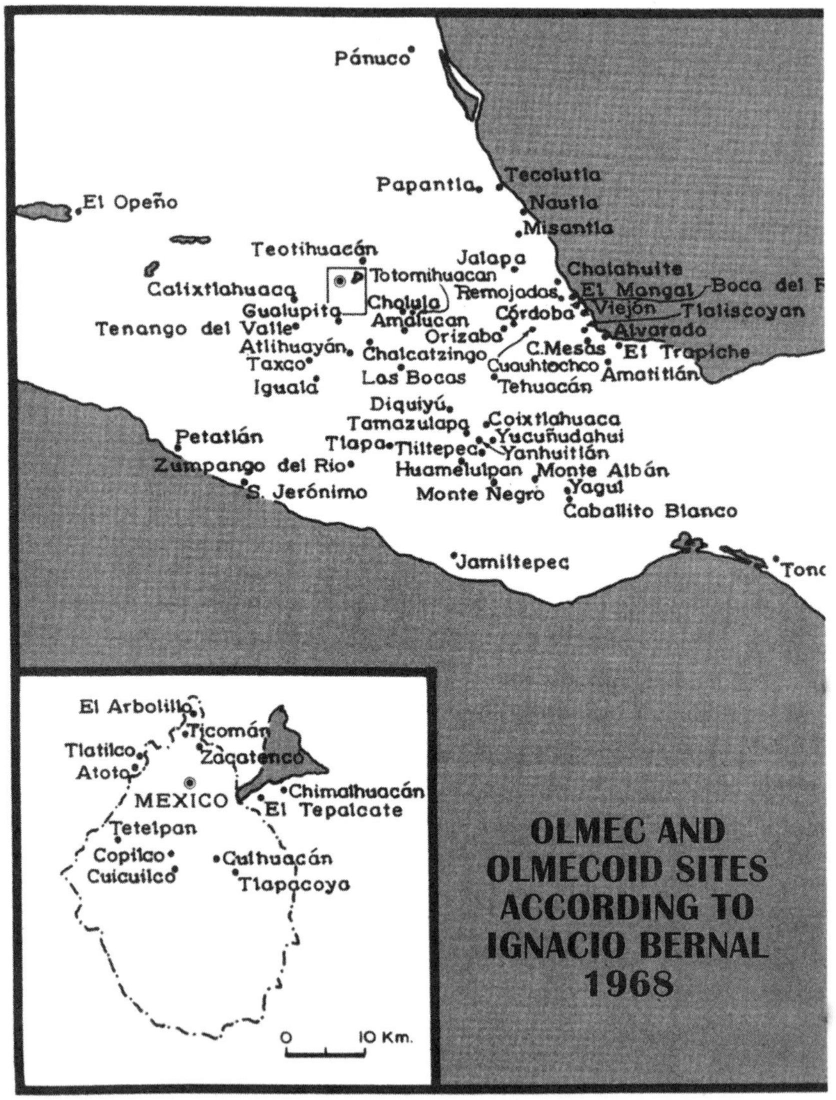

OLMEC AND OLMECOID SITES ACCORDING TO IGNACIO BERNAL 1968

The Hindu and Chinese influence on the Maya has been commented on by many historians and the use of the mudra hand and finger gestures suggests that the early Maya were Hindu-Buddhists, just like the Cham. In fact, it was in the Maya world where east literally met west. The Mayan lands on the Atlantic seaboard had ports, and Mayan trading ships went out to the Caribbean islands and around the Yucatan Peninsula to the Gulf of Mexico. The Mayan ships would certainly have crossed the Gulf of Mexico and gone up such rivers as the Mississippi and Alabama-Coosa. Mayan artifacts have reportedly been found at archeological digs in Georgia.

The Mayans had ports that were visited by transatlantic traders as well, including Phoenicians, Romans, Vikings and Africans. In many ways the Atlantic was a much easier ocean to cross than the Pacific and many cultures along the Atlantic Seaboard of Europe and Africa, such as the Basque, may have been travelling across the Atlantic for thousands of years. With the Cham, and their patrons the Chinese and Hindus, we have an organized and sustained movement of fleets of ships across the Pacific that seems to have begun about 1200 BC and continued until the collapse of the larger Cham Empire in Indonesia with the rise of Srivijaya in 650 AD.

Some approximate dates to take note of then:

2000 BC: Bada Valley, Sumatra, Sumba Island, etc. have tiki megaliths created.

1046 BC: The collapse of the Shang Dynasty in China. Olmecs in Mexico.

900 BC: King Solomon sends ships to Ophir and builds the First Temple.

480 BC: The great Hindu reformer Buddha dies.

400 BC: Olmecs come to an end and the Mayas dominate.

230 BC: End of the reign of Asoka in India, who became a Buddhist.

192 AD: First known Champa date at a temple in Vietnam.

650 AD: Rise of Srivijaya and beginning of end for the Cham.

900 AD: Mayan civilization collapses.

1471 AD: The Dai Viet conquer last of Champa.

1500 AD: Remaining Cham peoples move to Vietnamese highlands.

The Cham were probably sailing their fleets from Sumatra and other Indonesian islands to Vietnam starting around 1000 BC. It was only with some official inscriptions at My Son that historians got the date of 192 AD for the Cham. They had apparently occupied the Cham Islands since 1000 BC or before. The Cham, or whatever we want to call them, were making constant voyages across the Pacific—stopping at various islands—with huge fleets of ships ending in 650 AD. The Olmecs, Zapotecs and early Maya seemed to have been profoundly influenced by the Cham and their Chinese passengers.

But it would seem that the Cham and their tiki-face predecessors would not stop in Central America in their search for gold, gems and psychedelic drugs. There is strong evidence that these same people were in the mountains near the Pacific Coast of Colombia.

The Discovery of the Olmecs

When looking at Cham art, such as in the Museum of Cham Culture in Da Nang, the art of the Olmec naturally comes to mind. The statuary of both cultures is very similar. Both the Cham and the Olmecs are little understood. But first, who are the Olmecs?

Until the 1930s it was largely held that the oldest civilization in the Americas was that of the Maya. The great number of Mayan monuments, steles, pottery, statues and other artifacts discovered throughout the Yucatan, Guatemala and the Gulf Coast of Mexico had convinced archeologists that the Maya were the mother civilization of Central America.

But some "Mayan" artifacts were different from the main bulk of the artifacts in subtle ways. One difference was that some carvings of large heads had faces with more African-looking features than many of the other Mayan works. Mayan paintings and sculpture can be quite varied but the African-looking features seemed distinctly un-Mayan. These African-looking heads often had a curious frown and often wore masks or appeared to be half-jaguar-half-man beasts. This recurring motif did not fit in with other Mayan finds.

In 1929, Marshall H. Saville, the Director of the Museum of the American Indian in New York, classified these works as being from an entirely new culture not of Mayan heritage. Somewhat inappropriately, he called this culture Olmec (a name first assigned to it in 1927), which means "rubber people" in

A colossal Olmec head at San Lorenzo being excavated in the 1940s.

Nahuatl, the language of the Mexica (Aztec) people. Most of the early anomalous artifacts were found in the Tabasco and Veracruz regions of southern Mexico, a swampy region exploited for natural gas, but in ancient times a source point for rubber. Ancient Mesoamericans, spanning from the Olmecs to Aztecs, extracted latex from *Castilla elastica*, a type of rubber tree in the area. The juice of a local vine, *Ipomoea alba*, was then mixed with this latex to create rubber as early as 1600 BC (and possibly earlier). "Olmec" was the Aztec name for the people who lived in this area at the much later time of Aztec dominance.

The ancient Olmecs are now credited with creating the ball game that played such a significant role in all Mesoamerican civilizations, and the rubber balls that were used in the game. This game may be even older than the Olmecs, in fact. Ball courts and the Olmec-Mayan ball game were popular as far north as Arizona and Utah and as far south as Costa Rica and Panama.

According to the famous Mexican archeologist Ignacio Bernal,[59] Olmec-type art was first noticed as early as 1869, but as noted above, the term "Olmec," or "Rubber People," was first used in 1927. Naturally, a number of prominent Mayan archeologists, including Eric Thompson who helped decipher the Mayan calendar, refused to believe that this new culture called the Olmecs could be earlier than the Mayas. Not until a special meeting in Mexico City in 1942 was the matter largely settled that the Olmecs predated the Mayas. The date for the beginning of the Olmec culture was to remain a matter of great debate, however.

Bernal sums up this curious archeological episode in his book *A History of Mexican Archaeology*:

> …the whole Olmec culture is earlier than the Maya. This was anathema at the time because, as we have already seen, almost all the endeavors of the Carnegie and other institutions, North American in particular, had been directed towards Maya research, the consensus of opinion then being not only that the Maya culture was the oldest, but that all the other Mesoamerican cultures had stemmed

from it.

At the celebrated meeting held under the aegis of the Sociedad Mexicana de Antropología in 1942 to discuss the Olmec problem, archaeologists headed by Caso, Covarrubias and Noguera, along with Stirling, all maintained that the Olmecs belonged within the Archaic horizon. Caso claimed that the Olmec 'is beyond doubt the parent of such other cultures as the Maya, the Teotihuacan and that of El Tajín' (1942:46). Covarrubias held that 'whereas other cultural complexes share "Olmec" traits, this style contains no vestiges or elements taken over from other cultures, unless it be from those known as Archaic' (1943:48). Vaillant was one of the few North Americans to back up these theories and he did so because, in the course of his fine work on the Central Plateau with which we are already familiar, he had come across Archaic figurines displaying undoubted kinship with Olmec types. Eric Thompson, on the other hand, thought that the Olmec was a late culture within what we have now come to call the Post-Classic.

Olmec figures called the "Happy Chinamen" at the Xalapa Museum.

> And yet the name Olmec, first used by Beyer (1927) to designate this particular art style, has prevailed until today, incorrect though it may be. It is a source of confusion because it is lifted from historical sources which apply the term Olmec to very much later peoples. In 1942 Jiménez Moreno cleared the matter up by showing that the name Olmec properly refers to the inhabitants of the natural rubber-growing areas, but even so we have to distinguish clearly between the relatively recent bearers of the name and the archaeological Olmecs, which is why he proposed that these be called the 'La Venta people' to make confusion less confounded. But the name given at baptism was not to be shaken off, and is the one still used today.
>
> At the Mesa Redonda de Tuxtla in 1942 the Olmecs were given a provisional starting date around 300 BC. But somewhat later work at San Lorenzo, carried out with the aid of radiocarbon analysis—the use of which was spreading throughout the area—showed that 1200 BC was a more realistic date. This fitted in perfectly with what was being discovered all over Mesoamerica. It is a part of the general process that has already been discussed. Nineteenth-century scholars had often proposed fabulously early dates for the prehispanic peoples, and it produced in this century a vigorous counter-reaction which in its turn condensed them too drastically. But after 1950 this difficulty was to be overcome by the use of dating techniques that are not essentially archaeological.

The Olmecs had been discovered. However, this discovery created more questions than there were answers. The discovery of the Olmecs seemed to cast into doubt many of the old assumptions concerning the prehistory of the Americas. Suddenly, here was a diverse-looking people who built monumental sculptures with amazing skill, were the actual "inventors" of the number and writing system used by the Maya, played the ball game with its rubber balls, and even knew about the wheel (as evidenced by

Olmec clay statues of wheeled toys at the Xalapa Museum.

their wheeled toys).

A greater enigma beset the archeologists—who were the Olmecs?

When one begins to accept that the Olmecs were part of some sort of sophisticated transoceanic naval empire, at a time when the world was being explored by great navies—when the ancient sea kings ruled the earth.

One Olmec port on the Atlantic, called Comalcalco, later became a Mayan port. Comalcalco was a major Mayan port city that flourished between 700 and 900 AD. Like Cham cities, Comacalco was made of fired bricks. Many of these bricks have inscriptions on them. In 1977 and 1978, the National Institute of Anthropology and History (INAH) excavated the site and discovered that approximately three percent of the bricks which make up the site bore inscriptions.

In a study done by the archaeologist Neil Steede for the INAH it was discovered that 3671 bricks had inscriptions on them. Of these bricks, 2129 or 58 percent had Maya hieroglyphs on them. Old World inscriptions appeared on 499 of the bricks (or

13.6 percent) in languages such as Arabic, Phoenician, Libyan, Egyptian, Ogam, Tifinag, Chinese, Burmese and Paliburmese (which is related to the Cham script). Other bricks had drawings on them (735 bricks or 20 percent) and 308 bricks were mixed or unknown (8.4 percent). Some of the bricks even had inscriptions of elephants on them. Were these war elephants of the Cham, brought to Mexico? The presence of Chinese, Burmese and Paliburmese would indicate transpacific voyages such as those of the Hindu Shaivite Cham.

A colossal Olmec head showing long earlobes and insert (Xalapa Museum).

Chapter 8

Shiva and South America

Wooden ships on the water, very free (and easy)
Easy, you know the way it's supposed to be
Silver (people) on the shoreline, let us be
—*Wooden Ships*, Crosby, Stills & Nash

The search for Shiva in South America takes us to several countries, mainly those bordering on the Pacific Ocean. We have the gold mines at San Agustin in Colombia, the Inca and Pre-Inca ruins in Peru and Ecuador, plus the pre-Inca ruins of Tiwanaku and Puma Punku in Bolivia.

Let us begin with the advent of the Incas in 1438 AD, only a hundred years before the Spanish conquistadors would invade the land and end their empire which extended from Ecuador and western Peru to parts of Bolivia and northern Chile. Who were the Incas? Were they Polynesians who had arrived from Southeast Asia, Samoa and the Marquesas Islands? Did they inherit the megalithic buildings that exist around Lake Titicaca, including Cuzco? It would seem so.

From 1438 to 1533, the Inca Empire was centered on the Andean Mountains, using conquest and peaceful assimilation to rule over a large area from the capital of Cuzco. Later, Quito (in modern-day Ecuador) was to become a second, northern capital. The official language was Quechua, a language already in use by the Wari who lived around Lake Titicaca and Cuzco before the Incas arrived.

The Inca Empire supposedly existed without the use of the wheel or a system of writing. In the mountainous terrain of most of Peru and the Andes a wheel would not have been of much use. To get around they built elaborate rope bridges over chasms and rivers and used llamas and alpacas as draft animals, carrying a basket of food on either side of a saddle.

They had an extensive road network, good pottery and finely-woven textiles. They grew a wide variety of foods including over 150 types of potatoes. The empire had metals such as bronze and gold but there was no minted money, just the exchange of goods and payment of taxes that included spending some time working for the Inca rulers—who in theory owned everything. The Incas were a special group among the Wari and everyone in the Andes. They were tall with pale skin and had long earlobes.

They worshipped Inti—their sun god. The Incas considered their king, the Sapa Inca, to be the "son of the Sun." The Inca royalty as a whole were the "sons of the Sun." Gold was used to glorify Inti and the Qoricancha temple in Cuzco was wallpapered in sheets of gold leaf.

The story of the first Incas is a curious one. It apparently begins at a place of three caves (or alternatively, niches) near Lake Titicaca where the first family and their followers emerged. This place of three caves may have been on the Island of the Sun

A portrait of the first Inca, Manco Capac, at the Brooklyn Museum.

in Lake Titicaca. It was called the "house of production." This "house of production" was located on a hill called Tampu T'uqu, meaning in Quechua "window" or "niche."

Out of the central cave came the four brothers and sisters. They were: Ayar Manco, Ayar Cachi, Ayar Auca and Ayar Uchu; and Mama Ocllo, Mama Raua, Mama Huaco and Mama Coea. Out of the side caves came a group of people who were to be the forefathers of all the Inca royalty and clans, thus making the initial group of considerable size.

Says Wikipedia of the origin of Manco Capac/Ayar Manco:

> Ayar Manco carried a magic staff made of the finest gold. Where this staff landed, the people would live. They traveled for a long time. On the way, Ayar Cachi boasted about his strength and power. His siblings tricked him into returning to the cave to get a sacred llama. When he went into the cave, they trapped him inside to get rid of him.
>
> Ayar Uchu decided to stay on the top of the cave to look over the Inca people. The minute he proclaimed that, he turned to stone. They built a shrine around the stone and it became a sacred object. Ayar Auca grew tired of all this and decided to travel alone. Only Ayar Manco and his four sisters remained.
>
> Finally, they reached Cusco. The staff sank into the ground. Before they arrived, Mama Ocllo had already borne Ayar Manco a child, Sinchi Roca. The people who were already living in Cusco fought hard to keep their land, but Mama Huaca was a good fighter. When the enemy attacked, she threw her bolas (several stones tied together that spun through the air when thrown) at a soldier (gualla) and killed him instantly. The other people became afraid and ran away.
>
> After that, Ayar Manco became known as Manco Capac, the founder of the Inca Empire.

An old print of the three caves.

It is said that he and his sisters built the first Inca homes in the valley with their own hands. When the time came, Manco Capac turned to stone like his brothers before him. His son, Sinchi Roca, became the second emperor of the Inca.

So we learn from this story that the first Incas came from the Lake Titicaca area and found that Cusco was already inhabited.

 A drawing from 1615 of the Inca and his queen in a palanquin.

They fought with the inhabitants and ultimately gained control of a city that already existed. It would seem that Cuzco was originally a mining city, which would explain the many tunnels reported around the city.

Based on the archaeological evidence recovered from the Inca capital, Peruvian archeologists found that Cusco was conquered by the Wari in 600 AD. The Wari controlled areas west of Lake Titicaca and the Cusco Valley for around 300 years. When the Wari empire collapsed around 1000 to 1100 AD, the center of Wari power shifted to the Chuki Pukyu site in the Cusco Valley. The remnants of the Wari empire were then overthrown when the Inca empire rose to prominence circa 1438.

The Cusco Valley had long been in the periphery of the Lake Titicaca cultural sphere. Pottery and iconography from Tiwanaku are found in the Cusco area. Stone marks called keystone cuts can be seen at the Qoricancha in Cusco and at Tiwanaku in Bolivia. A major ancient road runs from the northern part of Lake Titicaca over a low pass and into the valley of Cusco. This is an obvious trade route used for thousands of years.

As I observe in my book *Ancient Technology in Peru and Bolivia*[38] it appears that the megaliths around Cuzco and the

An old drawing from India of a Maharaja in a palanquin.

Sacred Valley as well as Machu Picchu were built at the same time as the megaliths at Tiwanaku, Puma Punku, and around Lake Titicaca such as the towers at Sillustani and Cutimbo. Tiwanaku and Puma Punku were destroyed in an earthquake and tidal wave from Lake Titicaca circa 1000 AD. The megalithic structures in Cuzco, including towers that were later torn down by the Spanish, survived the earthquake and were not touched by the destructive wave from Lake Titicaca which went to the south destroying Tiwanaku and Puma Puma Punku, burying the sites in many feet of mud and muck. This deposit is still being excavated at Puma Punku to this day.

First European image of an Inca, 1533.

When the Incas got to Cusco, a city with megalithic walls and tunnels going into the mountain above the city, they decided to make this their capital. They rebuilt the roofs of the megalithic buildings and began to rebuild the many bridges and roads in the area. It was sort of like the legendary creation of Rome—expanding the trade routes and roads so that all roads led to Cusco in the new Inca order.

So what is the proof that the Inca culture came from Asia and the Pacific Islands?

In his 2003 book *Inca Origins,*[11] British archeologist Graeme Kearsley chronicles instance after instance of similarity between ancient India, Pacific Islands, and the cultures of Peru, Bolivia, Ecuador and Colombia. Kearsley's 866-page book is full of references and illustrations that seek to prove that Andean civilization and coastal Peru were strongly connected to Pacific Islands, ancient India and Hindu culture in general.

He correctly identifies the monuments at San Agustin in Colombia as statues of Shiva, Garuda, and other Hindu deities. He also compares the use of knotted ropes and notched sticks as communication devices in Peru, Pacific Islands and Southeast Asia. He also shows that the use of the litter or palanquin—a seat for the elite carried on two poles—was a custom that came from India.

Kearsely's exhaustive work is far too comprehensive to

comment on here but let us say that his many examples are intriguing. He has done the same thing for the Maya and Olmecs in his book *Mayan Genesis*[69] published in 2001.

The Home of the Gods

Some authors have claimed, often partially based on linguistics and comparative art, that the Sumerians, Phoenicians, Indus Valley Hindus, Egyptians and others came to South America in search of metals, hallucinogenic plants and other precious items.

One important book along these lines is *The God-Kings and the Titans* written by British historian James Bailey in 1973.[54] Bailey compares a great number of Old World and New World customs and artifacts such as pan pipes, gorgon heads, myths and construction techniques, and finds them to be identical. Bailey says that the Odyssey saga of Ulysses is a map-guide to the tin mines of Lake Titicaca. Bailey maintains that scholars still have no explanation as to where the huge amount of tin originated that enabled the Bronze Age to happen in the Middle East. He says that it came from Tiwanaku and the area around Lake Titicaca. Mythologists have tried to identify Ulysses' route by looking at sites around the Mediterranean, but on item after item, Bailey finds very interesting correspondences to what would have occurred on a boat trip from the Mediterranean to South America and concludes that the Odyssey was a transatlantic voyage to Brazil and then up

The Gate of the Sun at Tiwanaku. Viracocha stands in the center with two shafts.

the Rio La Plata to Bolivia, where the last part of the journey would have been conducted on foot.

Another archeologist who came to much the same conclusion as Bailey is the American history professor Hugh Fox of Michigan State University. In his book *Home of the Gods*,[55] Fox maintains that a Sumerian-Phoenician-Indus Valley collection of sea-kings crossed both the Pacific and the Atlantic in order to reach the rich tin mines of South America, particularly around Lake Titicaca. In addition, Fox says that the area around Tiwanaku and Lake Titicaca corresponds to the landscape of the classical Hindu myth of Mount Meru, the "Home of the Gods" and that this "mythical" Hindu mountain is Tiwanaku. He also claims that the language of the Incas is related to Sanskrit, and that ancient Sumerian words are used around Lake Titicaca, including "Anaku" which he says is the Sumerian name for "Tin Lands." Åéü

Fox says that he was influenced by James Bailey, and in his book quotes Bailey discussing *Book III* of the *Argonautica* (which is the famous story of Jason and the Golden Fleece):

> They passed from the ship beyond the reeds and the water to dry land [and] came from the plain to the palace of Aeétes [son of the sun god Helios] and they stood marveling at the entrance to the King's Court and the wide gates and columns which rose in ordered lines round the walls and, high up on the palace, a coping of stone rested on triglyphs. And here an inner court was built and round it were many well-fitted doors and chambers and all along each side was a richly wrought gallery. And on both sides loftier buildings stood obliquely…[54, 55]

Fox also discusses the Sumerian Gilgamesh story that he says describes a voyage across the ocean to Anaku, the Tin Lands, in search of a spiny thorn-apple that makes old men young again. This "apple" of eternal youth, Fox says, is representative of psychedelic drugs such as San Pedro cactus and ayahuasca.

Fox also highlights another episode in the *Argonautica* where Jason and the Argonauts arrive at the land of the Sun King and Jason is given a series of tasks to perform. One of them is to harness two fiery bulls and plow a field with them. These "bulls" are ovens or metal forges, with "feet of bronze and bronze mouths from which the breath came out in flame."[55]

Twins are part of the story of the land of Anaku, and Fox theorizes that the twins, including the two bulls breathing fire, are allegories for two different metals, tin and copper, which when mixed in the fire-breathing oven become the important final product, bronze. In Greek, he says, the twins are referred to as "anakes" which to him is a metaphor for this combining of the two metals. Gilgamesh was making his voyage to "Anaku" the land of tin—the "twins." Fox gives us this brief table:

Anakes—a Greek name for "The Twins."
Anaku—Sumerian name for the Tin Lands
Tiwanaku—The ancient House of the Sun in Bolivia right in the middle of tin country

Fox points out that the bronze twins (anakes) go to the ovens in the Tin Lands (Anaku) in order to be smelted. He says that metallurgy was "magic" and the metal worker himself was thought to be a magician who made chemical magic by marrying "the earth and the sky" or "twins," since an explanation of mineralogy and chemistry would have been impossible in the language of the time. The House of the Sun was an amazing complex for creating the bronze that would be the tears of sun. This same bronze was poured into the keystone cuts to create the clamps that held many of the giant blocks of granite together. Most of it, however, was exported, literally around the world!

Fox mentions that the land of Anaku is also spoken of as the home of the Annunaki, the elder gods. We see how part of Tiwanaku is found in the Anaku-Annunaki myths and that the Sumerian sky god, "An," is the King of the Annunaki. The area around Lake Titicaca was where the sky and earth met. Water was found here as well, a great inland sea. Also, Fox mentions the Sumerian words used in the local languages:

Titi-Tata: Father of Tin
Titi Wiyana: Altar of Tin to Adore the Sun Our King
Titi-Kaka/Thithi-Ccotta: Tin-Plated Cup that Contains All the Waters Reunited by the Four Winds of the Intis, Antillis, or Andes

Fox makes the point that the town of Oruru, south of Lake Titicaca, is another Bolivian mining center and derives its name from the Sumerian word "urruru" meaning "to smelt." Says Fox:

> So we have the tin at Tiwanaku/*anaku*, and the smelting at Oruru/*urruru*, although Arthur Posnansky, the great scholar who devoted much of his life to a study of Tiawanaku, was impressed by the size of the heaps of slag he saw at Tiawanaku when he first arrived there. The smelting wasn't all done at Oruru. The epithets connecting Lake Titicaca with charcoal and smelting intimately link the Sun King with intense metallurgical activity and again, the pre-Greek facts that are transformed into Greek myths link Helios [the Sun God] and Aeétes, his son, with Hephaistos, the smith of the gods, and the chief architect for the Sun King's palace: Tiawanaku.[55]

Indeed, with the discovery of the Fuente Magna Bowl and the Pokotia Monolith with their Sumerian inscriptions near Tiwanaku, it becomes clear that there is indeed some Sumerian connection with Lake Titicaca and the megalithic ruins found there. But if that is the case, then the building of these complexes and their use as smelting/mining/ceremonial centers must have been thousands of years earlier than the present-day researchers have concluded. A

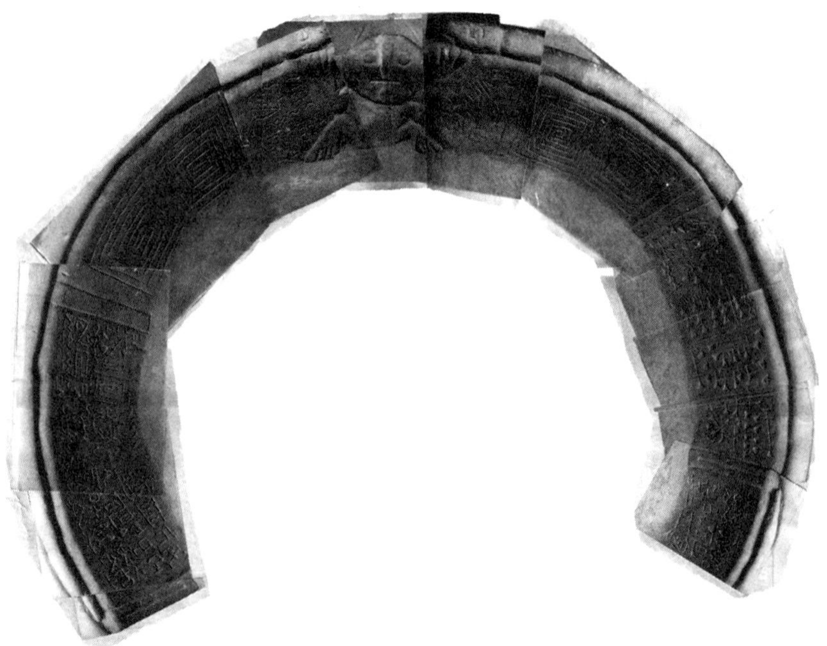

The Cuneiform inscriptions on the inside of the Fuente Magna Bowl.

storm is definitely brewing on the horizon of the Tiwanaku culture. The Great Lords, the En-Ka of the Sumerians, have yet to divulge all of their secrets to modern man.

Maximillian discovered the bowl.

The Fuente Magna Bowl was discovered on the property of the Manjon family, located somewhere near Tiwanaku. The area had not been subject to any archeological investigation up to that time, and probably very little since. Around 1959 a Bolivian archeologist, don Max Portugal-Zamora, learned of the existence of the bowl from a local priest named Pastor Manjon. They named the site *Fuente Magna* (Great Fountain).

Through the mediation and negotiation of General Armando Escobar Uria, the property was swapped for another parcel in the neighborhood of Sopocachi. Now safely under the protection of the honorable, municipal mayoralty, Mr. Portugal-Zamora began to restore the bowl by applying cement to the parts that showed chipping and deterioration. He apparently did not recognize the cuneiform script on the bowl, and thought it was some kind of unique indigenous writing, something akin to the rongorongo writing of Easter Island. For unknown reasons, the bowl remained an obscure artifact and, while it seems to have been in La Paz for many decades, it wasn't until 2002 that it resurfaced. This was the year that the Pokotia Monolith was being studied, and the writing on its side rekindled interest in the bowl. Both were put in the newly formed Museum of Precious Metals sometime around 2007.

Archeologists in Bolivia seemed to have no doubts as to the authenticity of both objects, and so the race was on to decipher the scripts. Dr. Alberto Marini analyzed the script on the Fuente Magna Bowl and reported that it was Sumerian. Then, ancient language expert Dr. Clyde A. Winters determined that the writing on the bowl was probably Proto-Sumerian, which is a script found on many artifacts from Mesopotamia. Winters said that an identical script was used by the Elamites, and called Proto-Elamite.

Dr. Winters said he compared the writing to the Libyco-Berber writing used in the Sahara 5,000 years ago. He claimed that this writing was used by the Proto-Dravidians (of the Indus Valley), Proto-Mande, Proto-Elamites and Proto-Sumerians.

As noted, he found that the Fuente Magna inscriptions are in the Proto-Sumerian script, and the symbols have several Proto-Sumerian signs joined together to represent words and sentences. Below is Winters' transliteration of the inscriptions on the right side of the Fuente Magna, reading from top to bottom and right to left:

1. *Pa ge gi*
2. *Mi lu du*
3. *I mi ki*
4. *me su du*
5. *Nia po*
6. *Pa*
7. *Mash*
8. *Nia mi*
9. *Du lu gi*
10. *Ka me lu*
11. *Zi*
12. *Nan na pa-I*

Winters then gave the following translation:

"(1) Girls take an oath to act justly (this) place. (2) (This is) a favorable oracle of the people. (3) Send forth a just divine decree. (4) The charm (the Fuente Magna) (is) full of Good. (5) The (Goddess) Nia is pure. (6) Take an oath (to her). (7) The Diviner. (8) The divine decree of Nia (is), (9) to surround the people with Goodness/Gladness. (10) Value the people's oracle. (11) The soul (to), (12) appear as a witness to the (Good that comes from faith in the Goddess Nia before) all mankind."

The transliteration of the inscriptions on the left side of the Fuente Magna is as follows:

1. *Tu ki a mash pa*

2a. *Lu me lu ki mi*

2b. *Pa be ge*

3. *Zi*
4. *lu na*

5. ge
6. du po
7. I tu po
8. lu mi du

This section was translated by Winters as:

> "(1) Make a libation (this) place for water (seminal fluid?) and seek virtue. (2a) (This is) a great amulet/charm, (2b) (this) place of the people is a phenomenal area of the deity (Nia's) power. (3) The soul (or breath of life). (4) Much incense, (5) to justly, (6) make the pure libation. (7) Capture the pure libation (or Appear (here) as a witness to the pure libation). (8) Divine good in this phenomenal proximity of the deity's power."

Winters says that the decipherment of the inscriptions on the Fuente Magna Bowl indicates that it was used to make libations to the Goddess Nia to request fertility. Plus, it was to offer thanks for the bountiful fauna and flora in the area that made it possible for these Sumerian explorers to support themselves in Bolivia.

Winters then turned his attention to the Pokotia Monolith. He says that the signs used to write the messages on the monolith were non-liguture Proto-Sumerian symbols. He deciphers the inscription under the hand on the Pokotia figure as saying:

> "The oracle Putaki conducts man to truth. (This) esteemed (and) precious oracle to sprout esteem, (now) witness (its) escape."

Winters' decipherment of the Proto-Sumerian inscription on the back of the statue is as follows:

> "Proclaim the establishment of character. The strong father (Putaki) to send forth the divination. Strong wisdom (in this) phenomenal area of the deity's power. Capture the speech (of the oracle). (The oracle is) very strong to benefit (and) nourish the sprouting (of) character. Tell human being(s) (the oracle's) benefit. The oracle to open (up) much (benefit for all). The ideal norm (is the) oracle (of Putaki). (This) oracle is (in) a phenomenal area of

> the deity's power. Distribute to all humanity (the divine decree). Snare a portion (of the) pure voice. (The oracle to) send forth gladness. Agitate the mouth (of the oracle), to send forth the divination. The diviner speaks good."

Winters comments:

> The writing on the Pokotia monument makes it clear that the Pokotia oracle was heard by many people in ancient Bolivia. This is interesting because the Pachacamac oracle was very popular in this area in historic times. ... satellite shrines of one or another of his offspring were worshipped by South Americans. During Inca (Sumerian: En-ka=*Enki*="Great Lord") times, the temple city of Pachacamac, contained the idol of Pachacamac which was a commanding oracle drawing devotees from Ecuador in the North through Bolivia in the South. People came from far and wide for a Pachacamac prophecy. (clyde.winters.tripod.com)

So here we see how the word Inca is related to ancient Sumerian and Indus Valley as "Great Lord" or "Enka" or "Enki."

What the evidence suggests is that Tiwanaku is over 5,000 years old, dating to circa 3500-3000 BC. It was built as an ore processing plant, extracting metals from the ore that was brought to Tiwanaku

An old print of scattered megalithic blocks at Tiwanaku.

An 1896 photo of Tiwanaku by Max Uhle showing megalithic blocks standing.

from the surrounding mountains. This metallurgical plant may have been operational until about 1000 AD. At Tiwanaku, metal workers created molten metals of various types, from pure gold to alloys like bronze. At the museum recently built at the site, a number of the bronze clamps from keystone cuts of the double-T shape can be seen, as well as gold and other metal artifacts. Even platinum, which requires a high melting point, has been found in South America, indicating some highly sophisticated metallurgical techniques.

It is interesting to speculate that mercury may have been produced by the complex at Tiwanaku as well. Perhaps the "tears of the Sun" actually represented the liquid metal that was highly valued by the ancients, though we do not know why. Mercury has been found in sealed Mayan bowls at Lake Atitlan in Guatemala, and was famously used to form flowing rivers in the tomb of the ancient Chinese emperor Chi Huang-Ti.

Mercury is derived from the mineral cinnabar, which is a Greek word that is thought to be derived ultimately from Persian and Sanskrit. Cinnabar is a red crystal associated with volcanic activity; it can be crushed and smelted to extract mercury, also known as quicksilver. Pure mercury separates from sulfur in a rotary kiln and easily evaporates. This creates a mercury vapor, and a "condensing column" is used to collect the liquid metal, which in Greek and Roman times was most often transported in iron flasks. Ceramic vessels can also be used to hold the liquid metal and this was common in China and the Americas.

The major cinnabar-mercury deposits of South America are near the town known as Huancavelica in Peru, northwest of Lake

Titicaca. Huancavelica was known in pre-Inca times as the area of "Wankas." The Spanish took note of the area early in the conquest and founded the city of Huancavelica in 1572. The mines had been shown to the conquistador Jeronimo Luis de Cabrera in 1564 by the Indian Nahuincopa, who was his servant. Huancavelica became the main source for mercury in all of Spanish America, including all of Central America and Mexico. Mercury is often used to extract silver or gold from ores and the mercury from Huancavelica was used in the extraction of silver from the very important mines at Potosi, just south of Lake Titicaca.

This area was known as "Alto Peru" in colonial times. The Potosi mines and their silver were the single most important source

A trench dug by Arthur Posnansky in 1945 showing destruction at Tiwanaku.

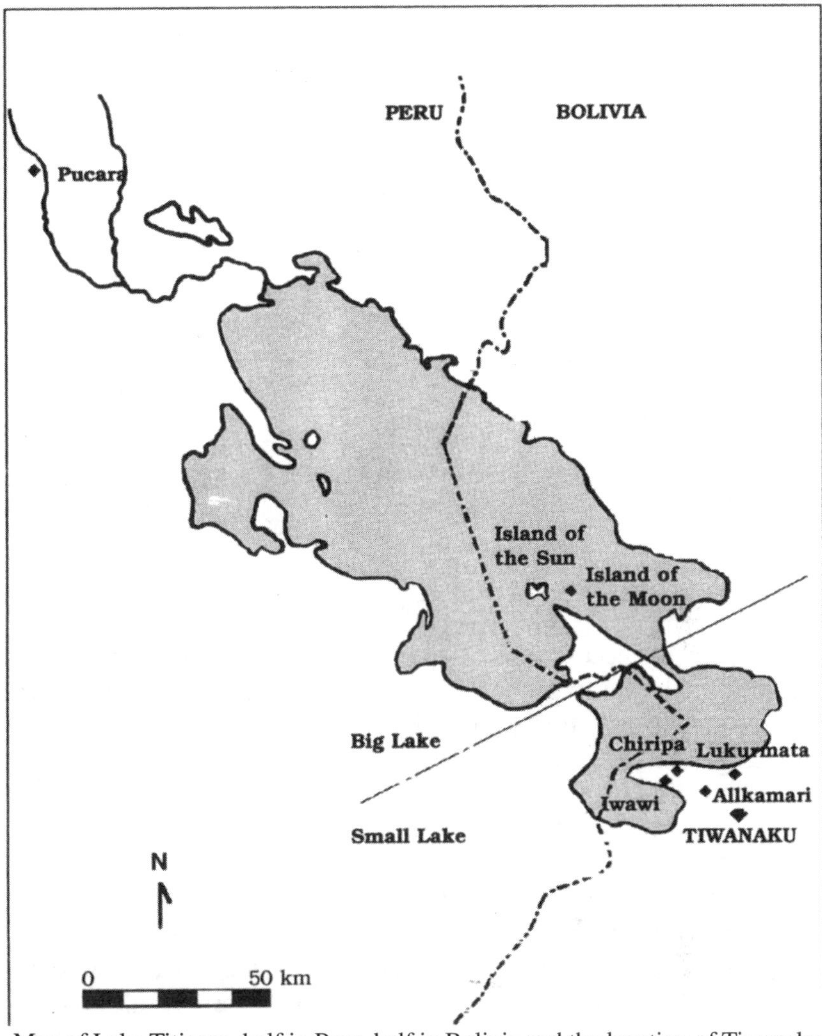

Map of Lake Titicaca, half in Peru, half in Bolivia and the location of Tiwanaku.

of wealth for the Spanish in colonial America and it was the mercury from Huancavelica that made it possible. After the conquest, the entire world was flooded with Spanish "pieces of eight," the Spanish doubloon made of Potosi silver.

So, the question is: was the cinnabar and mercury from Huancavelica exploited in ancient times by the early megalith builders at Tiwanaku and possibly Chavin? Activity is known to go back to at least 1400 BC. If not these mines of cinnabar, then perhaps some other mines now exhausted or undiscovered were the source?

Mercury is mentioned in the ancient vimana texts in Sanskrit,

texts that talk about ancient flying vehicles and other high tech devices, including weapons. Mercury was apparently a part of the vortex technology that powered the vimana aircraft. Mercury is also said to have been behind the Nazi "foo fighter" technology that produced glowing, pulsing globes that appeared to be some sort of flying gyro. Foo fighters were used in the final days of WWII by the Germans as a last ditch defense against the squadrons of Allied bombers that were flying over Germany at the time. The Germans had hoped that swarms of pulsing foo fighters emitting an electromagnetic field would interfere with the electrical systems of the bombers. Though it didn't work on a large scale, the foo fighters caused some RAF pilots to return home before dropping their ordnance. It is thought that modified versions of foo fighters were used as the plasma-gyro engines in the experimental designs of flying disks that the Germans were starting to develop.

The people building the amazing South American complexes—Sumerian Annunaki, or whomever—must have had power tools to do some of the things they did, and we still don't know how the largest blocks of stone at Puma Punku, Tiwanaku, Chavin, Sacsayhuaman or Ollantaytambo were moved. If these people had electricity, giant saws and equipment to move very large blocks, did they have flight as well? Ancient legends say that they did. They were the Birdmen who are depicted around the world, including on

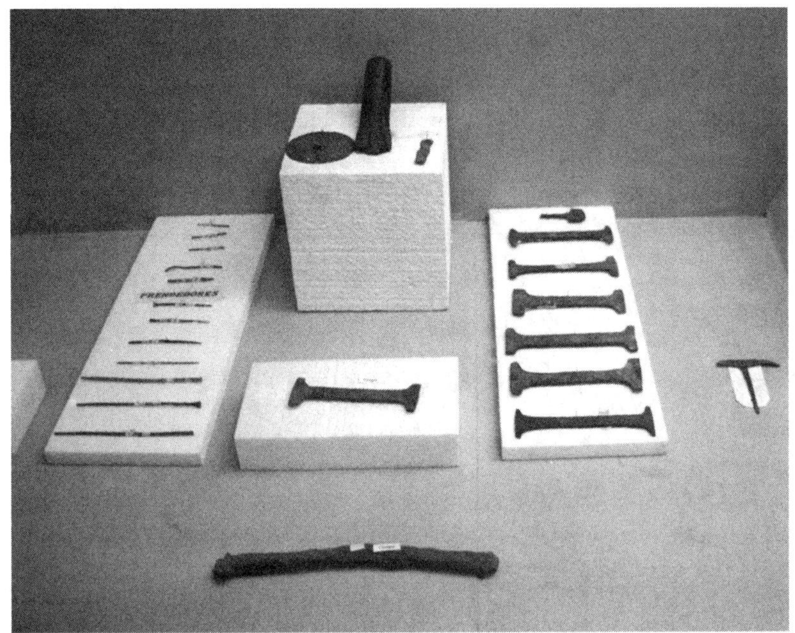

Metal clamps of bronze on display at the Tiwanaku Museum.

the Gate of the Sun at Tiwanaku.

The City of the Sun and the Voyage Across the Pacific

Were Tiwanaku and Puma Punku the Mount Meru of the ancient Hindus and the City of the Sun of the ancient Sumerians and Greeks? Mainstream archeologists are baffled as to why such a sophisticated city was built here on the southern shores of Lake Titicaca. Was it just a cult center? Who were these geniuses and what were they after?

We know now that they included Sumerians. Indus Valley Hindus probably began voyaging into the Indian Ocean, Persian Gulf and Western Pacific at a very early date. A descendant of these people, the "Phoenicians of the Pacific," were the Cham people of Southeast Asia. These Hindu-Buddhist megalithic people, who also used the curious T-shaped keystone cuts and clamps, were found in Malaysia, Indonesia, Thailand, Laos, Cambodia (Cham-Bodia) and Vietnam. Their capital was Cham Island off the coast of Danang, Vietnam. Megalithic complexes like Borobadur in central Java are associated with the Cham, who built several megalithic stone temples throughout the region.

This amazing group of Hindu-Buddhists made excellent granite and basalt statues of Shiva and Buddha. I think the Cham

An old print of the Qoricancha Temple in Cuzco from 1869.

traveled from Southeast Asia past the Philippines and New Guinea into the vast Pacific Ocean where they made their way to Tonga, Tahiti, the Marquesas and finally the Americas. The way back was to go south to Peru and return via Easter Island and Rarotonga, to Samoa, Fiji and Tonga. It was a long voyage, but Polynesians had made such long trips many times before. Vikings, Phoenicians, Chinese, Micronesians, Portuguese, Basques, Egyptians and others were to make many such long journeys to the Americas before Columbus.

Oceans are highways, not barriers, as I have often pointed out. The easy way to go someplace far away is to go by water, not to walk there. The idea that all native Americans had to have walked to the two continents of North and South America is absurd. People have been using boats for over 30,000 years as archeologists freely admit. And they could easily have made their way along the coasts of all the continents, including Antarctica, in the remote past.

Seafaring is a natural activity of human beings, who are uniquely aquatic and land mammals at the same time. Even in the most fierce weather of the remote sea passages at the poles, mankind is able to adapt himself to the ocean. He can catch rainwater, fish for food and manage a mini-village on board his large ship. Most ocean going ships in ancient times held up to 300 people, such as the Tongaraki double-canoes of Tonga. Some Chinese ships held 800 people or more.

I hold that Tiwanaku, Puma Punku, and possibly some sunken

A photo of keystone cuts on a block of stone at the Qoricancha.

cities in Lake Titicaca were part of an early transoceanic quest for metals that culminated in the creation of a huge metallurgical plant and ceremonial city that processed metals from around the lake. According to my theory, many mines were located in the large region in all directions from Lake Titicaca. There were stone quarry sites as well. Megalithic towers like those at Sillustani were built around this time. The Cuzco area was also a mining town and it is likely that metals were processed there as well.

Ore came by boat to the foundries and agricultural towns connected to the lake by a series of canals. At Puma Punku and Tiwanaku there were stone-lined canals, and even pyramids with lakes at the top, to provide hydraulic pressure on the ores to wash them and prepare them for the furnaces. Here high temperatures had to be generated to melt the ores and create the molten metals, the "tears of the sun." These metals were copper, tin, silver and bronze. Iron must have been smelted as well, and it seems that only steel tools—combined with power in the form of electricity—could have made some of these articulated megaliths.

A giant, high tech, megalithic and nearly indestructible complex was made that included the diverting of the Tiwanaku River to feed the washing process of the ore to the now vanished metallurgical forges that once existed at Tiwanaku and Puma Punku. Other sites were part of the network and were spread out around Lake Titicaca, including Sillustani, Cutimbo, Cuzco, Pisac,

Ollantaytambo and Machu Picchu.

I believe that on a basic level, this network was an outpost of the metallurgical masterminds of Armenia, Kurdistan and Sumeria circa 3000 BC. They crossed the Pacific and Atlantic with their ships based in both the Mediterranean and the Persian Gulf. They brought with them iron tools and simple electric devices to power mechanical saws and drills.

On a more sophisticated level, they came with much more. They came with knowledge of mechanical machines and computers. They were interested in creating a huge stone factory that had to be situated near a source of large stones. In the case of Machu Picchu there are granite outcroppings in the immediate vicinity, which is naturally advantageous.

I think they had airships and portable power plants. They knew about rotating magnetic fields being the source of AC power (same as we currently use)—and set up hydroelectric or wave stations to generate a large amount of power. In the most advanced level of this theory, they had ways to send power via microwaves to satellites and then redirect them to the remote parts of the earth as a form of usable power.

They had airships that could fly great distances that are described in the ancient Hindu and Buddhist epics. They are known as vimanas. They had aerial vehicles to take passengers from one town to another. They were capable of aerial warfare as well, with weapons and defensive tactics. These airships could presumably take cargo.

Most of the cargo would go by ship, just as most cargo is moved in today's modern age. This cargo would be ingots and other forms of precious metals. Other cargo would include psychedelic mushrooms (dried or suspended in honey) and other precious substances.

The Gold Mines of Colombia

Colombia is a mountainous and ethnically diverse country. It was one of the earliest areas of Spanish exploration, with the Admiral Alonso de Ojeda (who had been one of the early explorers with Columbus) landing on the Atlantic coast in 1499.

By the year 1533 the important port of Cartagena was founded, and before that the ports of Santa Maria la Antiqua del Darien (1510) and Santa Marta (1525) were in use.

By April of 1536 the Spanish conquistador Gonzalo Jiménez

de Quesada led an expedition to the interior and christened the districts through which he passed the "New Kingdom of Granada." Marching inland in August 1538, he founded the city of Santa Fé de Bogota as the capital. During this same period the conquistador Sebastián de Belalcázar, conqueror of Quito, an Inca capital, traveled into what is now Colombia and founded Cali (1536), and then Popayan (1537). The German conquistador Nikolaus Federmann crossed the mountains of the Llanos Orientales and went over the Cordillera Oriental during the years 1536 to 1539, spurred on by the persistent legend of El Dorado, the "city of gold."

This legend of a city of gold, and the many gold artifacts found in Colombia, continued to play a pivotal role in luring explorers from all over Europe to New Granada during the 16th and 17th centuries. Their goal was to find the fabled lost city of unimaginable wealth.

The German conquistadors Georg von Speyer and Nikolaus Federmann separately searched the Venezuelan lowlands, then into the Colombian plateaus, and then the Orinoco Basin for the lost city of gold. Tradition had the gold city on an island, presumably in the jungles of the Amazon basin, which was yet to be explored—and remains today a vast area of little-known land. Federmann and von Speyer completely missed the megalithic sites of San Agustin and Tierradentro, which were high in the mountains and long lost to history. They would not be discovered until hundreds of years later.

Von Speyer was accompanied by the German conquistador Philipp von Hutten on an expedition (1536-38) in which they journeyed through Colombia and reached the headwaters of the Rio Japura in southwest Colombia, near the current border with Ecuador. Hutten led an exploring party of about 150 men in 1541, mostly horsemen, from Santa Ana de Coro on the coast of Venezuela into Colombia in search of El Dorado. This group wandered for several years, but were continually harassed by the natives and finally returned to Santa Ana de Coro in Venezuela in 1546.

The stories of a golden city drew the Spanish conquistador Gonzalo Jimenez de Quesada and his army of 800 men away from their mission to find an overland route to Peru. From 1537 to 1538 Quesada's army moved into the Andean homeland of the Muisca people and essentially conquered them. His men noticed that the

Muisca had a large number of small gold artifacts. In September of 1540 his brother, conquistador Hernan Perez de Quesada, set out with 270 Spaniards and thousands of Indian porters to explore the Orinoco Basin, but they found no golden city—mostly hostile jungle—and returned to Bogota.

News of the gold artifacts from the Muisca area of Colombia and stories told by the natives of the special rites that took place at Lake Guatavita convinced the Spanish that a kingdom of tremendous wealth existed somewhere in the area. The rites at Lake Guatavita included the gold dusting of a king who jumped into the crater lake, as well as throwing items made of gold into the waters.

Colombia: The Land of El Dorado

With Guiana being the focus of the quest for El Dorado for centuries, the original location of the City of Gold—Colombia—became lost to history. But the discoveries at San Agustin—starting in the late 1800s and continuing up to the 1970s—showed that a megalithic culture that mined gold and made astonishing monuments existed in the mountains of western Colombia. This area, high in the Colombian Massif, was virtually unknown to the early Spanish colonizers of Colombia. Even today the extent of this amazing civilization is just beginning to be understood.

El Dorado was said to be a source of emeralds and gold. Colombia is today the largest producer of emeralds in the world. It also produces many other gems but it has a virtual corner on the emerald market, holding an estimated 95% of the world's emerald-bearing rock. It is interesting to consider that some of the world's emeralds in ancient treasuries may have come from old trading ports on the Atlantic and Pacific coasts of Colombia. Other sources of emeralds are India, Afghanistan, Canada, Australia, Madagascar, and Russia. Indonesia, Thailand, Cambodia and Vietnam are not significant emerald producers so the Cham were likely to get their emeralds from India or Colombia.

Gold production in Colombia began by at least 400 BC, according to Wikipedia and other sources. Curiously, the gold trade was said to be centered on the Pacific Coast of Colombia, rather than the Atlantic. At any rate, one would think that gold work in Colombia, and South America in general, would be much earlier than 400 BC. A date like 4000 BC would seem more correct, but since gold artifacts, such as those from Lake Guanavita or San

Agustin, cannot be dated by carbon dating or other methods, we simply do not know how old many of these gold artifacts are.

Many of the artifacts are of a gold-copper alloy called tumbaga. Because of the plentiful amount of gold in Colombia and Peru, tumbaga was a common metal used to make artifacts; it was harder than copper by itself, plus other metals could be added to it. It had a fairly low melting point, lower than copper or gold on their own, and furthermore, an acid mixture such as lime juice could eat away at the outer copper surface—leaving only the gold molecules which could then be polished into a shiny gold burnish, a process known as depletion gilding.

Says Wikipedia:

> The earliest examples of gold mining and goldwork have been attributed to the Tumaco people of the Pacific coast and date to around 325 BCE.
>
> Gold would play a pivotal role in luring the Spanish conquistadores to the area during the 16th century.
>
> Gold was considered sacred by most of the precolumbian civilizations of the area. In Muisca mythology, Gold (Chiminigagua) was considered itself a deity, and the force of creation. Copper mining was very important for the classic Quimbaya civilization, which developed the tumbaga alloy.

Much of the gold in Bogota's famous gold museum probably came from San Agustin and Tierradentro, as it would seem that the entire purpose for building these sites was the mining of gold and other metals. Bogota's Gold Museum is one of the greatest collections in the world and probably Colombia's most important museum and tourist attraction. Gold was plentiful throughout the Andean countries, and museums in Ecuador, Peru and Bolivia also have substantial gold and tumbaga collections.

The Strange Megaliths of San Agustin

On the first day in Bogota of a World Explorers trip to Colombia, our group visited the Gold Museum which has room after room of over 55,000 pieces of gold and other materials from all the major pre-Hispanic cultures in Colombia. Some of the gold objects were of some pretty interesting-looking people, wearing all sorts of strange headgear and clothes. Some literally looked like spacemen of some sort.

One of the rooms in the museum holds the famous display of gold "airplanes" that appear to be miniature models of winged craft, complete with a cockpit, wings and airplane-style tail. Mainstream archeologists insist that the objects must depict flying fish or birds. However, birds and fish do not have tails like these golden models—only airplanes have such tails. Could they actually depict flying craft from thousands of years ago? Are these what some vimanas from ancient India or Sumeria looked like? Ancient astronaut theorists would say yes, but mainstream archeologists cannot believe that such advanced technology existed in the past—only our own civilization has been capable of this technology, they insist. But in 1994, German enthusiasts Peter Belting and Conrad Lubbers fashioned radio-controlled scale models of some of the planes and proved that they could fly.

We left Bogota in a private minibus from our hotel for the long day's journey into the mountains of western Colombia. As dusk was falling on the small mountain hamlet of San Agustin our minibus pulled up to our hotel a few blocks from the main square of the small, but bustling, tourist town. The next morning we visited the main museum and megalithic site and after lunch we visited some of the other sites around San Agustin. San Agustin is a UNESCO World Heritage Site so let us get some official information from that organization.

The UNESCO website (http://whc.unesco.org/en/list/744) says that the San Agustin Archaeological Park is the:

> …largest group of religious monuments and megalithic sculptures in South America [and] stands in a wild, spectacular landscape. Gods and mythical animals are skillfully represented in styles ranging from abstract to realist. These works of art display the creativity and imagination of a northern Andean culture that flourished from the 1st to the 8th century.
>
> The San Agustin Archaeological Park includes four separate sites, with boundaries defined so as to include the main concentrations of burial mounds with megalithic statues of the Regional Classic (1-900 AD) period. A third of the 600 known San Agustin statues and half of 40 known monumental burial mounds that are dispersed throughout the Alto Magdalena region are located inside the boundaries of the archaeological park. These 20 burial mounds include the largest and also the most elaborate examples. The "Mesitas" site, 80 ha of the park, includes 8 mounds, more than a hundred statues, and the entire core of the largest demographic and ceremonial centers—containing not only the oldest and largest tombs—Mesita A and Mesita C—sites, but also the residential remains of the elite families that ruled over their society, constructed the monuments and used them as burials for their main leaders. Thus, the park includes not only a series of separate monuments but

also the vestiges of the central communities that constructed and lived beside them. In spite of the impacts of natural phenomena on the material remains, conservation actions have preserved their material integrity. Challenges remain in maintaining the integrity of such a vast area in light of pressures for extended agricultural use and growth of local communities.

The UNESCO site goes on to say:

> In the pre-agricultural period, from c 3300 to c 600 BC, San Agustin was occupied by a society with a rudimentary stone technology using unretouched basalt chips; their principal food was wild fruits, but hunting cannot be ruled out.

UNESCO defines the period from 3300 BC to 600 BC as "pre-agricultural," but it seems doubtful that this society did not have maize, beans or other cultivated crops until 600 BC. It would seem likely that they had corn (maize), squash, beans and other agricultural crops common to Peru and Mexico at the time. Probably they had all of this, plus bananas, sweet potatoes, cassava-yucca, and even quinoa and other grains common to Peru,

A dolmen at San Agustin of a fanged Shiva with clubbed protectors.

Ecuador and Bolivia.

In fact, it is reported that in ancient times corn (maize) was grown from Argentina to the American Southwest, Kansas, and Nebraska. It was probably also grown at the mound sites at Cahokia in Illinois and other sites in Indiana, Kentucky, Tennessee and Ohio. That maize was not being grown at sites in Colombia seems almost impossible. Archeologists argue about the origin of corn, much like bananas, sweet potatoes, cotton and other crops. While archeologists in Peru claim that maize was first cultivated there, archeologists in Mexico claim that maize was first grown in the highlands of central Mexico by the mysterious Olmecs.

Corn grown in Peru can be very large, much larger than that in North America, and it seems likely that people in the highlands of

A statue at San Agustin of a fanged Shiva, similar to tikis at Bada Valley.

Colombia and Ecuador were growing large crops of maize for many thousands of years. It may be that the Olmecs first domesticated maize in Mexico and spread it to South America, or perhaps it came to Mexico from South America—also with the Olmecs. The Fuente Magna Bowl at the Museum of Precious Metals in La Paz, Bolivia, indicates that the Sumerians were in Peru and Bolivia by 3000 BC. Possibly they brought maize from Mexico to Peru, or vice versa. Either way, it is likely that Colombia had maize cultivation by at least 4000 BC. Bio-archeologists currently put the cultivation of a domesticated maize—either in Peru or Mexico—at 9000 BC. The banana was genetically engineered into a seedless fruit about the same time.

UNESCO and mainstream archeologists maintain that the earlier megalithic mining culture of Colombia came to a sudden halt around 700 AD and that sophisticated terrace building and drainage projects, as seen at San Agustin, came to an end. Essentially, the culture underwent a slow decline until nothing was really left, some 800 years before the European explorations of rediscovery. The demise of the San Agustin culture came at the same time as the decline of the Cham, circa 700 AD, which was driven by the rise of Srivijaya and the Khmer.

The mystery of these imaginative and industrious people and

A dolmen at San Agustin of a fanged Shiva with clubbed protectors.

where they came from persists today. San Agustin is similar to and of the same level of stonework and megalithic artistry as the work of the Olmecs in Mexico and Guatemala, the stone balls of Costa Rica and the statues at Tiwanaku.

Giant granite boulders from the mountain streams, some weighing many tons, were moved to artificial mound sites and then carved into grand monuments, some as tall 21 feet (7 meters). It is estimated that more than 600 statues are scattered over a wide area in the green hills surrounding San Agustin. Many of the statues are of fang-toothed men holding clubs or babies, while others resemble masked monsters. Many have unusual hats or helmets on. Some hold their arms over their heart and stomach in the classic "tiki" pose. There are also sculptures depicting animals such as an eagle, frog and jaguar. There is a similarity between the San Agustin tiki statues and those at Bada Valley and Sumatra.

Nowhere in the park are we told how these astonishing statues were carved, or why. We are told that these statues had magical and protective qualities and some of them were "guardians" of the monumental tombs, complete with gigantic sarcophagi, that are scattered among the hills. The effort that all this must have taken, including the huge earthworks, is considerable. Archeologists portray these people as an isolated culture that suddenly decided to put their efforts into carving gigantic statues with an unmistakable artistic flair. Yet, the similarity with the Olmecs and the early tiki statuary in Indonesia is very much evident, and it would seem that there are links to the early Cham here.

The UNESCO site goes on to say that:

> The Alto de los Idolos is on the right bank of the Magdalena River and the smaller Alto de las Piedras lies further north: both are in the municipality of San José de Isnos. Like the main San Agustin area, they are rich in monuments of all kinds. Much of the area is a rich archaeological landscape, with evidence of ancient tracks, field boundaries, drainage ditches and artificial platforms, as well as funerary monuments. This was a sacred land, a place of pilgrimage and ancestors worship. These hieratic guards, some more than 4 m high weighing several tonnes, are carved in blocks of tuff and volcanic rock. They protected the funeral rooms, the monolithic sarcophagus and the burial sites.

> The main archaeological monuments are Las Mesitas, containing artificial mounds, terraces, funerary structures and stone statuary; the Fuente de Lavapatas, a religious monument carved in the stone bed of a stream; and the Bosque de Las Estatuas, where there are examples of stone statues from the whole region.
>
> A new society appeared in the region in the 7th century BC: the people cultivated maize on the flat land or gentle slopes and lived in dispersed houses near the main rivers, possibly in simple groups headed by chiefs. The extended burials were in vertical shaft tombs, with simple grave-goods. The period probably lasted until the 3rd or even the 2nd century BC.
>
> Around the 1st century AD there were profound cultural changes in the area: this was a time of a great flowering of monumental lithic art and the so-called Agustinian Culture. Links with other regions of the south-west grew, population density increased markedly, and earlier settlements were reoccupied. New house sites on the hilltops were also settled and occupied over long periods. There was considerable social consolidation and the concentration of substantial power in the hands of the chiefs made possible the production of gigantic works: hundreds of elaborate stone statues were carved, some in complex relief and large in size. The huge monumental platforms, terraces and mounds and the temple-like architecture reflect a complex system of religious and magical belief. Some 300 enormous sculptures (divinities with threatening faces, warriors armed with clubs, round eyes and jaguars' teeth of mythical heroes) stand in the region of Agustin in the heart of the Andes, El Huila Province.

Marveling at the many dolmens, statues and sarcophagi, I couldn't help noticing the similarity to Olmec statues and monumental works that can be found on the Gulf Coast of Mexico as well as on the Pacific Coast and in southern Mexico. The sharp features in the carving also made me think that these statues were not bashed out with a rock hammer. It would seem that metal chisels were being used, and possibly even power tools.

The similarity of San Agustin to places like the Bada Valley in Indonesia, the Plain of Jars in Laos and even the Cham statues of central Vietnam was evident to me. These stoneworkers cut and moved huge blocks of granite and basalt, like the Olmecs, and were known to have metals such as gold, bronze and iron. If the search for gold by the Cham and their predecessors had brought them to Colombia, they would have found it.

When the Spanish (and Portuguese) came to the Americas, explorers would carry various samples of metals, gems and minerals with them to show to the natives that they encountered. It was hoped that helpful natives would direct them to gold and copper deposits plus the sites of other valuable minerals. Did the Cham and their Tiki-Sumerian predecessors come to Colombia with nuggets of gold and copper seeking the source of these metals for their technological devices, statuary and the glorification of Shiva and Buddha?

Officially, the origin of the carvers remains a mystery, and the site is largely unexcavated. Who were these amazing stoneworkers, here to mine gold and leave curious megalithic monuments behind? I learned on a visit to San Agustin in May of 2019 that many of the

A Nepalese copper mask of the Bhairava aspect of Shiva with fangs.

statues were of Shiva!

During that visit, for an episode of the History Channel's *Ancient Aliens* show in 2019, I met Praveen Mohan, a writer and researcher from the south of India. We walked through the archeological park and Praveen explained to me that the main fanged statues were statues of Shiva in his aspect as the frightful deity Bhairava. He also explained to me that the statues in some of the dolmens, where there were three figures, two men with clubs on either side of a larger fanged figure in the middle, were also of Shiva and his two protectors. He added further that the statue of a bird with a snake in its mouth was a statue of the Hindu deity Garuda, the bird that Vishnu rode, who was commonly depicted as having a snake in its mouth.

I was fascinated by his explanation and it made perfect sense to me that these were statues of Shiva, as a fanged Shiva is often seen in Nepal where I have spent quite a bit of time. Nepal is essentially a Shaivite country and hilly terrain is where large numbers of sadhus roam, worshippers of Shiva. Wikipedia gives us a good definition of Bhairava and points out that, while a fearsome monster, he is also the serene god Shiva who lives on Mount Kailash in Tibet with his long hair in a topknot:

> Bhairava (Maha Kala Bhairava) (Sanskrit: भैरव, lit. frightful) is a Shaivite deity worshiped by Hindus. In Shaivism, he is a fierce manifestation of Shiva associated with annihilation. In the Trika system Bhairava represents Supreme Reality, synonymous to Para Brahman. Generally in Hinduism, Bhairava is also called Dandapani (as he holds a rod or Danda to punish sinners) and Swaswa meaning "whose vehicle is a dog." In Vajrayana Buddhism, he is considered a fierce emanation of boddhisatva Mañjuśrī and also called Heruka, Vajrabhairava and Yamantaka. He is worshiped throughout India, Nepal and Sri Lanka as well as in Tibetan Buddhism. Tamilnadu has the largest number of Kala Bhairava temples in India.

So we now see how the empire of Shiva spanned the entire Pacific Ocean to South America. When the Conquistadors entered the city of Cuzco in Peru there were a number of statues in the Qoricancha Temple but they were mostly destroyed. Today a few bits of granite statues can be seen at the Qoricancha Museum, but it is hard to make out what they might have been. They might have been statues of Shiva.

Was San Agustin part of a transoceanic trade network that included Asians, Olmecs, Africans and Phoenicians? Because of their practice of child sacrifice, the Phoenicians were known to have statuary of men holding babies—babies that were about to be consecrated to the gods.

A statue at San Agustin of the Bhairava aspect of Shiva with fangs.

The Road to Tierradentro

Our group left San Agustin early one morning and drove over the mountains to Popayan, the capital of Cauca Department. It was an all-day drive, passing through some beautiful and remote mountain country. As noted above, Popayan was founded by Spanish conquistador Sebastián de Belalcázar in 1537. It is also an area of gold mining that produced Escudo gold coins and silver Reales for the Spanish crown from 1760 through 1819.

We spent the night in Popayan's charming old town, and then our chartered bus took us back into the mountains to the curious archeological site of Tierradentro located about 40 miles (100 km) from the city.

Tierradentro ("Inner Earth") is the second-most important archaeological site in Colombia, after San Agustin, but gets far fewer visitors. The rough mountain road, much of it very muddy from the frequent rains, was along steep mountain valleys and it was clear that parts of the road would wash out from time to time. A lot of road construction was taking place at the time of our journey!

There are some statues, like those at San Agustin, but Tierradentro is mainly known for its elaborate underground tombs. So far, archaeologists have discovered about 100 of these unusual funeral temples that are cut into solid rock and painted with geometric patterns. These underground funerary temples are known as hypogea (or a hypogeum in the singular).

These hypogea are scattered on various hills around the town with names such as Alto del Aguacate (Avocado Hill), Alto de Segovia, Alto de San Andrés, Alto del Duende and El Tablón. There are also two museums and an open-air granite statuary park.

The typical hypogeum has an entry, like a trap door, with a spiral hewn-stone staircase leading steeply down to the main chamber, usually 15 to 30 feet below the surface. Some of the tombs have several lesser chambers around the central chamber. Each would probably have contained a large ceramic pot in which the cremated remains of the deceased were kept. Some of these urns can be seen at the museums.

The walls of the tombs are painted with geometric, anthropomorphic and zoomorphic patterns in red, black and white. The domed ceilings of the largest hypogea are supported by pillars that are part of the solid rock. Most of the tombs have been looted, but the museums in town still have plenty of ceramic objects and fabrics on display. There are some monumental statues as well, which archeologists admit are very similar to those at San Agustin. Indeed, were they the same culture?

A statue of Garuda at San Agustin?

The time frame for Tierradentro is about the same as San Agustin, approximately 300 AD to 600 AD, though it seems that no really good dating has been done at Tierradentro. The rock-cut tombs would probably have been used over and over again through the centuries, and one would think that the statues in Tierradentro were made at about the same time as those in San Agustin. Indeed, Tierradentro was apparently a gold mining area in ancient times, like San Agustin. Gold artifacts have been discovered at Tierradento and some are now at the Gold Museum in Bogota.

We spent several days in Tierradentro, visiting the museums and hiking around the hills to the tombs that were generally kept under lock and key by guards. The steps of the cut-stone spiral staircases were often quite big, making me wonder if the people were literal giants who could walk down such staircases with ease.

Mainstream archeologists think that megalithic cultures like those at San Agustin and Tierradentro were isolated peoples who, for unknown reasons, independently began carving granite boulders into elaborate, beautiful and bizarre statues. They created artificial mounds and cut tombs into solid rock and must have had some pretty large houses, as well as kilns for firing the ceramic objects and even forges for working the metals.

Statues at Tierradentro were finely made of granite, a very hard rock, and in some cases the people depicted were as bizarre as the ones in San Agustin, with large eyes and strange hats. Mainstream archeologists would likely say that stone hammers and chisels were used in the making of the statues and the rock-cut tombs, but they are so well made that I would have to say that iron chisels and even power tools were used in their manufacture.

Indeed, what appears to have happened at Tierradentro and San Agustin is that a sophisticated group of foreigners arrived in Colombia and started two mining operations in the western mountains. With sophisticated mining tools, including possibly power tools, they began extracting tons of gold from the mountain streams and nearby gold mines. When not extracting gold or copper they built large homes with farms, and industries like ceramics. And, in their spare time, they used their mining tools to carve granite boulders into statuary. This statuary probably had some sort of magical or religious purpose though in some cases it may just represent some of the lords or ladies of this extended mining camp. One large boulder by the school in the center of town had a number of drill marks on it, seemingly made by a large power tool.

The way that the statues were dressed and the unusual ways that they held their hands and arms, often with a baby or club in their hands, made me think of the tiki statues in the Marquesas Islands and Tahiti, as well as the Kon Tiki statue at Tiwanaku in Bolivia. The Olmecs and Phoenicians also produced similar statues making unusual hand and arm gestures. As has been discussed, in Hindu sculptures such arm, hand and figure positions are known as "mudras" and every different position has a different meaning. The mysterious statues in Colombia seem be also communicating in some way.

As we left Tierradentro, I looked back at the steep mountain valleys that the road clung to. We stopped briefly at a spot where the road had collapsed and a bulldozer was pushing dirt and mud around to clear the road. Even today travel in this area is relatively difficult, and it must have been even more difficult in ancient times. Coming by helicopter or airship would be the easiest way to arrive in Tierradentro. Maybe the gold airplanes back in Bogota were souvenirs from the ancient airports that once existed at San Agustin and Tierradentro. The strange world of ancient Colombia was one in which it seemed anything could have happened.

The bizarre statuary and jewelry of Tierradentro, San Agustin and the Gold Museum speak for themselves. The mysterious ancient megaliths of Colombia and impressive gold artifacts were done by a sophisticated culture that was capable of exporting this gold to distant lands. In fact, the gold of ancient Colombia may have been taken as far away as Champa, helping to enrich the temples of stone, brick, gold and silver there.

Still, in order to do the mining and the stonework, large machines and power tools would have to have been brought to the site. This would need to be done by air, with some sort of vimana airship to transport such expensive and necessary machinery. Other trips to the gold-bearing areas of Colombia and other parts of South America would be done by ship, utilizing the massive fleet of the Cham. Just as we have aircraft (and spacecraft) today, we still use ships—some of them gigantically huge—for the transfer of minerals, goods and machinery from continent to continent.

Contact between civilizations on both sides of the Pacific and Atlantic Oceans must have been going for at least 3,000 years, and probably earlier. Oceans are not barriers to travel but rather highways on which small or large groups of people are able to trade or migrate to distant lands. In fact, walking to some of these distant lands would either be very difficult or impossible—because they are islands! Ultimately traveling most places by boat is quicker and safer. You just have to know where you are going, and this was accomplished by watching the stars.

Historians around the world admit that Egypt, Sumeria, India and China had a significant number of ships—literal navies—by at least 3000 BC, and probably much before. But certain areas of the world are left off of this list of ancient navies—places such as South America, West Africa, and Southeast Asia—and seem to not have this history of shipbuilding and maritime navigation over large distances. But in the case of Southeast Asia, this is ridiculous. In no other area of the world, except Polynesia and the Caribbean, is there such a plethora of islands. In addition, Indonesia and Southeast Asia in general are extremely productive in terms of agricultural output and the exploitation of mineral wealth. Because of the volcanic nature of many Indonesian and Melanesian islands, those who search for gold and other valuable minerals are likely to be richly rewarded.

It is an interesting thought to think of the larger area of Southeast Asia as Cham or Champa and as Suvarnabhumi—the land of gold. Yet the Cham themselves not only exploited the gold of Indonesia but made the longer journeys to Mexico and South America. Colombia, like Peru and Bolivia, may have been key in this transoceanic quest for gold and larger and larger sources. The creation of newer and stronger (or, alternatively, longer lasting) alloys was probably also part of their quest. Mexico, although it has a number of gold mines, has never been a significant producer of gold. South America, on the other hand, has been.

The gold of Colombia seems to have been exploited by a

number of ancient civilizations, including the Cham. Perhaps the ships of the Polynesians and the Cham proceeded south to ports in Peru such as Chan Chan or Paracas and continued to take on cargo. From these ports, below the equator, they departed to the west, into the South Pacific. Perhaps their next stop, if they could find it, was Easter Island. Otherwise they would continue northwestward until they reached the Tubuai Islands and Tahiti.

The rise of the mysterious San Agustin culture circa 100 AD is a period in which the Cham ships were gathering at My Son and the Cham Islands. The demise of the San Agustin culture is also the time of the decline of the Cham. Once the wars with Srivijaya and the Khmer started in 650 AD the great fleets of ships stopped their transpacific voyages to Mexico, Colombia and Peru. Did the wars in Sumatra, Java, Cambodia and Vietnam resulting in the collapse of the Cham cause the downfall of the San Agustin culture in Colombia?

So we see how Peru and Tiwanaku are part of the great Empire of Shiva that spanned from the Middle East to ancient India and Southeast Asia to Pacific Islands and on to North and South America. Both North and South America (at least the Pacific Coast areas) were colonized by Hindu-Cham-Polynesians who not only started such civilizations as the Hohokam and the Maya, but took over or inherited other early cultures such as the Olmecs and Tiwanaku. The Incas were a later group of Polynesians who ventured to Lake Titicaca and then founded their short-lived empire on the still-standing megalithic ruins of Cuzco.

The Spanish put an end to the Incas by about 1540 and this was the end of the influence of Shiva on that continent. Except for the snake worship in Peru the rituals are largely gone except for the burning of incense at offering places. This is still popular among the Quiche Mayans in Guatemala and Mexico today.

Chapter 9

Mount Kailash, Tibet and Vimanas

So, maybe I will see you on the Sacred Way
—which we all travel.
—Dan Vadis

Well, I am an idiot walking a tightrope of fortune and fame
I am an acrobat swinging trapezes through circles of flame
If you've never stared off into the distance, then your life is a shame
...Oh, you can see a million miles tonight, but you can't get very far
—*Mrs. Potter's Lullaby*, Counting Crows

According to Hindu myth and doctrine the god Shiva lives on, or inside of, a mountain in Tibet called Mount Kailash. Tibet holds such mysteries as the Potala Palace in Lhasa, the secret city of Shambhala, Shiva's home in Mount Kailash, and numerous other enigmas in remote or hidden spots. The landscape of Tibet is typically high desert with snowcapped mountains and icy cold streams and rivers. There are many sheltered valleys in Tibet where farming and animal husbandry occur. Parts of eastern Tibet are very mountainous and green, especially along the borders of Sikkim, Bhutan and Assam.

Mount Kailash is also known as Gang Rinpoche in Chinese, which means "snow jewel mountain." The mountain is known as "Kailāsa" in Sanskrit. The name may be derived from the word "kelāsa" which means "crystal." Indeed, the mountain looks like a giant pyramid or "crystal." The official elevation of the mountain is 21,778 feet (6,638 meters). Mount Kailash is located close to the important lakes Manasarovar and Rakshastal. The sources of four rivers (Indus, Sutlej, Brahmaputra, and Ghaghara) lie in the vicinity. Mount Kailash is sacred in Buddhism, Bon, Hinduism, and Jainism. Pilgrims from China, Nepal, India, and other

A photo of the north side of Mount Kailash.

countries undertake a sacred pilgrimage that involves trekking towards Lake Manasarovar and a circumambulation of Mount Kailash at it lowest levels.

Wikipedia reports that in 1926, Hugh Ruttledge, the deputy commissioner of Almora, visited the area to meet the Garpön (local Tibetan leader) of Ngari. As the Garpön was away, he circumambulated Mount Kailash while studying it. Ruttledge believed the mountain was about 20,000 feet (6,000 meters) high and utterly unclimbable. He thought about an ascent along the northeast ridge and had been exploring the area with Colonel R. C. Wilson, who then went to the other side of the mountain with a Sherpa named Tseten. Wilson said that Tseten told him that the southeast ridge represented a feasible route to the summit. Wilson explained that although they attempted to climb the mountain, they ran into heavy snowfall, making the ascent impossible.

The Austrian geologist and climber Herbert Tichy visited the area in 1936, attempting to climb the mountain. When he asked the local people whether Kailash was climbable, a Garpön replied to him: "Only a man entirely free of sin could climb Kailash. And he wouldn't have to actually scale the sheer walls of ice to do it—he'd just turn himself into a bird and fly to the summit." To date, there have been no known successful ascents of the mountain and the Chinese government has forbidden anyone to attempt the climb. Tichy went on to be part of the first ascent of the nearby peak Cho Oyu in 1954.

Mount Kailash and Lake Manasarovar are mentioned in the Hindu epics *Ramayana* and *Mahabharata.* In Hindu art and literature, the mountain is described as the abode of Shiva, who is depicted as residing there along with his consort Parvati and their children, Ganesha and Kartikeya.

In Hindu mythology, Mount Meru is considered as a stairway to heaven, where the devas reside. The *Vishnu Purana* states that it lies in the center of the world surrounded by six mountain ranges similar to a lotus, with one of these mountain ranges being the Himalayas. Mount Kailash came to be identified with Meru over time, though Mount Meru is a mythical mountain and Kailash is a physical peak. The mysterious megalithic site of Borobadur in central Java is supposed to represent Mount Meru and is in the form of a stone mandala.

The early Hindu texts mention a mythical Mount Meru and Lake Manasa. The mythical Manasa lake is described as one created through the mind of Brahma as the preferred abode of his vahana hamsa (the bird that serves as his vehicle). In the *Ramayana*, the rishi Vishvamitra tells Rama that Brahma created a lake out of his consciousness (Manas), hence the name Manas Sarovar (lake of consciousness) and a river was born out of that lake called Sarayu, which flowed through the kingdom of Ayodhya. This is the holy river Ganges that was tamed by Shiva and sent to nourish the

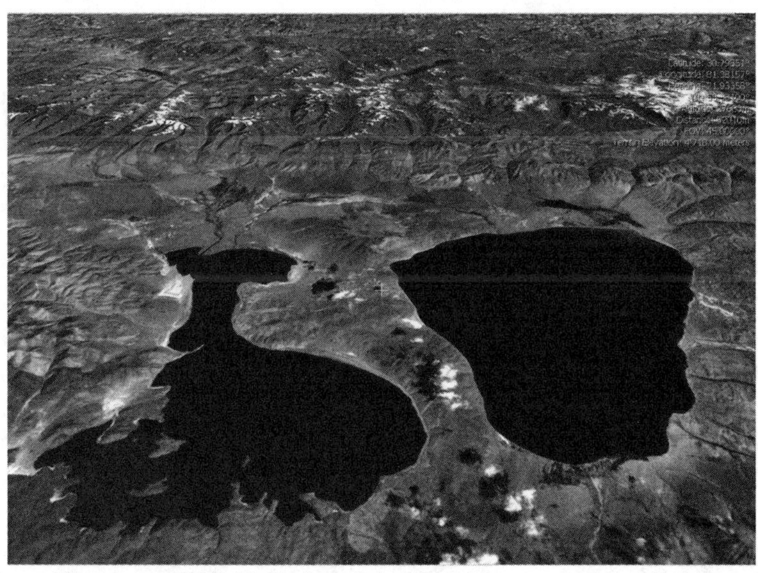

A satellite photo of Mt. Kailash and the lakes Manasarovar and Rakshastal.

A painting of Shiva on Mount Kailash. Note the long hair and topknot.

fertile valleys below the Himalayas (one of four rivers emanating from Mount Kailash).

Shiva is described as sitting in a lotus position, engaged in meditation within the confines of Mount Kailash. According to the Hindu scriptures the demon-king Ravana shook the mountain after he was refused entry to Kailash. This enraged Shiva, who pressed his toe upon the mountain, trapping Ravana. Ravana sang hymns in praise of Shiva for a thousand years before he was released. This representation of Shiva is also referred to as Ravananugraha (meaning "form showing favor to Ravana").

At the end of the *Mahabharata* seven rishis (sages or holy men) are trekking through the dangerous paths of the Himalayas on a pilgrimage to Mount Kailash. As they trek along the mountain trails they are followed by a stray dog. At the end of the book the stray dog turns out to be Shiva in disguise.

In these legends we get the idea that Mount Kailash has an interior that can be entered. Shiva and his family are living within the mountain. Ravana is attempting to enter the mountain. Could it be that Mount Kailash has an interior? Could it be a secret mountain fortress with a secret entrance, perhaps near the top of the mountain? We will discuss this later in this chapter.

The mountain is also central to the Jain religion, a form of Hinduism. According to Jain scriptures, Rishabhadeva, the first Tirthankar of Jainism attained moksha (liberation) on Mount Kailash. His death is believed in Jainism to have occurred on Ashtapada (the Jain name for Mount Kailash). It is believed by Jains that the Jain emperor Bharata Chakravartin constructed three stupas and 24 shrines of the 24 tirthankaras (supreme preachers) somewhere near Mount Kailash. The idols at the shrines were said to be studded with precious stones. This group of stupas and jeweled shrines was called Sinhnishdha. Bharata Chakravartin also performed two weeks of worship at the mountain and attained moksha. No trace of these gem-studded idols remains, if they ever existed. Jain tradition says that large pits were dug around the mountain and the River Ganges was made to flow through it. This may refer to passages in the Himalayas that the Ganges flows down—sometimes in wondrous ways.

Wikipedia tells us that tradition says that the 24th and the last Jain Tirthankara, Mahavira (599 BC–527 BC), was taken to the summit of Meru (Kailash) by Indra shortly after his birth, after Indra put his mother into deep slumber. There he was anointed with precious unctions.

In Buddhist texts, Mount Kailash is also known as the mythological Mount Meru. Wikipedia says that in Buddhism, Kailash represents the father of the world and Lake Manasarovar symbolizes the mother.

Wikipedia also says that Vajrayana Buddhists believe that the Tibetan saint Milarepa (c. 1052—c. 1135) had a challenge with Naro Böncham, a follower of the Bön religion of Tibet. The two engaged in a battle of wits with neither able to gain a decisive advantage. Finally, it was agreed that whoever could reach the summit of Mount Kailash first would be the victor. While Naro sat on a magic drum to climb up the slope, Milarepa reached the summit riding on the rays of the sun, thus winning the contest. Milarepa then bequeathed a nearby mountain to Naro, since that time known as Mount Bönri.

According to the website travellersquest.com:

> Geologists have been studying the landscape of Mount

Kailash for decades. They state that the mountain is hollow from the inside and its geometry is pyramidal in structure, which faces four directions of the compass. So, one of the mysteries of Mount Kailash is that researchers believe the structure emits positive energy in all directions.

...Mount Kailash features four faces, each of them facing a different direction of a compass. According to Vedas, mount Kailash is a gateway or a bridge to connect earth and heaven. The idea is an exciting mystery of Mount Kailash as the summit of the mountain is regarded as the entrance to heaven in religions such as Jainism, Buddhism, and Hinduism. It is a popular theory that Draupadi and Pandavas reached Moksha after summiting Mount Kailash's peak. However, currently, it is considered blasphemy to most religions if a person attempts to climb a sacred mountain.

...One of the eerie mysteries surrounding Mount Kailash is that numerous visitors have experienced unusual events. One of them is the quick passing of time—travelers have expressed that the growth of their hair and nails have accelerated near the mountains. They have experienced significant growth in a matter of days, which usually takes around two to three weeks in normal conditions. This phenomenon is linked to the alleged arcane energies surrounding Mount Kailash. Besides, the accelerated growth theory has yet to be proved whether it is merely perspective or real.

...Several researchers and investigators from America and Russia conclude that the holy mountain is the center of the globe or axis mundi. So, mount Kailash is regarded as the center of the world and is commonly referred to as the world pillar, world tree, world axis and cosmic axis. The sacred peak is also referred to as the center of the world in Ramayana and ancient Hindu Vedas. Further, another mystery of Mount Kailash is that it connects several global monuments worldwide, such as Stonehenge, the North Pole and the South Pole.

The Tibetan tour website called greattibettour.com makes the following astonishing claims:

Scientists have discovered that the top of Mt. Kailash is actually a man-made vacuum pyramid. It is surrounded by more than 100 other small pyramids. According to preliminary estimates, the direct height of the pyramid complex is between 100 and 1,800 meters, while the Egyptian pyramid is only 146 meters. If true, it would be larger than any known pyramid today.

...The Kailash Pyramids miracle was probably built by an advanced civilization that understood the subtle laws of energy (the twist field) and how to control energy and time.

...Kailash Mountain is considered the axis of the universe, the center of the world, the pillar of the world. It is the place where the earth connects with heaven. As you can see from Google Maps, the distance from Stonehenge in the UK to Mt Kailash is 6,666 kilometers, which is also the distance from Kailash Range to the North Pole. The distance from Mt Kailash to the South Pole is 13,332 kilometers, which is exactly twice the distance to the North Pole or Stonehenge.

... Mt Kailash is the center of a worldwide system that connects mystical sites and energy sites from around the world, including the Pyramids of Egypt, the Pyramids of Mexico, Easter Island, Stonehenge, and the North Pole... which constitute the global energy grid system.

...Some scientists believe that the Kailash range is a vortex of energy that lifts the body and mind. It is said that people who spend 12 hours in the vicinity of Kailash experience accelerated hair and fingernails growth, which is equivalent to two weeks of normal time.

A Google search turned up this odd bit on supposed NASA scans of Mount Kailash. The AI overview of the search said this:

Electromagnetic Activity: NASA satellite scans have reportedly detected strong and erratic electromagnetic radiation emanating from Mount Kailash, causing compasses to malfunction and electronic devices to behave erratically. Some scientists speculate this could be due to rare earth minerals or a magnetic field beneath the mountain.

Time Distortion: There are reports of visitors experiencing rapid hair and nail growth while near the mountain, suggesting a possible time distortion effect. NASA has confirmed magnetic distortions in the area, though their impact on biological functions is not fully understood.

Underground Structures: Radar mapping has revealed potential hollow areas and tunnels beneath the mountain's surface, leading to speculation about undiscovered structures. Some theorists suggest the possibility of ancient, unknown structures hidden within.

Pyramid Shape: Some researchers propose that Mount Kailash itself is a massive, hollow pyramid, possibly part of a larger pyramid complex.

Other Observations: There are also reports of unusual lights appearing near the mountain, potentially linked to the magnetic field, and the mountain's snow cap is said to never melt.

So we learn that time seems to shift around Mount Kailash. Unusual lights are apparently seen around the mountain. Apparently some studies indicate that there might be hollow spaces within the mountain.

The Bon Religion Began 18,000 Years Ago

Tibet is famous for being a Buddhist country, but what was it like before Buddhism took hold? The Bon or Bonpo are a Tibetan people who inhabited Tibet before the current Buddhist lamas were in control. It is generally agreed that modern Tibetan culture originated in an ancient kingdom located in what is now western and northwestern Tibet called Zhangzhung or Shangshung.

Zhangzhung is associated with the Bon religion, the pre-Buddhist religion of the area. The Bon religion remained a distinct religion in Tibet and Nepal and influenced some of the practices and philosophies of Tibetan Buddhism. Bon monasteries, similar to Buddhist monasteries, still exist in parts of western Tibet and the Mustang region of Nepal. The Bon use as their symbol a swastika that goes to the left, instead of to the right as in a Buddhist swastika. Mount Kailash has a giant swastika seen on the south face of the pyramidical peak. The Bon religion of Tibet claims the mountain is sacred to them.

A photo of the south side of Mount Kailash showing the swastika.

For the Bon people, Mount Kailash is the abode of sky goddess Sipaimen and the mountain was the center of the ancient Bon empire of Zhangzhung. The mountain was the center of the universe Mandala and the source of the mythical Lion, Horse, Peacock, and Elephant Rivers which flowed in the four cardinal directions.

The Bon religion is said to have been founded by Tonpa Shenrab, also known as Shenrab Miwo. According to Bon doctrine, Tonpa Shenrab lived 18,000 years ago. This is 15,500 years before Gautama Buddha, who lived circa 500 BC. Practitioners of Bon believe that Tonpa Shenrab first studied the Bon doctrine in the land of Tagzig Olmo Lung Ring, at the end of which he pledged to Shenlha Okar, the god of compassion, that he would guide the peoples of this world to liberation.

Like Guatama Buddha, Tonpa Shenrab was of royal birth. Tonpa Shenrab renounced his royal inheritance at the age of thirty-one to travel the path of enlightenment. Tonpa Shenrab embraced the life of a renunciate and commenced austerities, spreading the doctrine of Bon. Eventually he arrived in the land of Zhangzhung, which is the area around Mount Kailash.

Accounts of Tonpa Shenrab's life are to be found in three principal sources: the Dodü, a manuscript from the 19th century, and two sources of oral lineage called Zermik and Ziji. The story of Tonpa Shenrab is also told in a fourteenth century terma

A Tibetan painting of Tag-Zig Olmo Lung Ring.

("treasure" in Buddhism, a secret doctrine, written or oral) of Loden Nyingpo.

The Bon religion, called Yungdrung Bön, is essentially the root religion, and therefore culture, of Tibet. According to Latri Khenpo Nyima Dakpa Rinpoche in the book *Opening the Door To Bön* (Snow Lion Publications, 2005), Tonpa Shenrab:

> ...was born in a completely pure and spiritual land named Tag-Zig Olmo Lung Ring (hereafter Olmo Lung Ring), which is beyond the impure nature of this existing world. This is the birthplace of all enlightened ones, it is a perfected realm where peace and true joy last forever and it is free from any danger of destruction by any of the elements of nature.

The land of Olmo Lung Ring lies to the west of Mount

Kailash and is the shape of an eight-petaled lotus divided into four parts: the inner, middle, and outer parts, and the boundary. Its sky is like an eight-spoked wheel. Olmo Lung Ring is filled with beautiful gardens, stupas, parks, and snow-covered mountains. Yungdrung Gutsek, a pyramid-shaped mountain with nine Yungdrungs [swastikas] ascending like a staircase to the top, is in the center of Olmo Lung Ring. While a single Yungdrung symbolizes the everlasting and indestructible essence of mind, the nine Yungdrungs symbolize the nine ways or stages of Bön. On each step of the mountain are temples of both male and female deities, and beautiful stupas that symbolize the mind of enlightenment.

Four rivers flow from Yungdrung Gutsek. The mountain has four sides that face in the four directions, and these rivers flow from the corners at the mountain's base, from formations that resemble the heads of four different animals. From the east, the snow lion is the source of the river Narazara; from the north, the horse is the source of the river Pakshi; from west, the peacock is the source of the river Gyim Shang; and from the south, the elephant is the source of the river Sindhu.

Some scholars identify Mount Kailash in northwestern Tibet as Olmo Lung Ring, due to the lakes and snow covered mountains that surround the area and four rivers that flow from it. The followers of Bön do not accept this explanation. This is because Olmo Lung Ring is not a physical place that can be visited by ordinary human beings. In order to reach Olmo Lung Ring one must practice, become purified of all negativities, and achieve enlightenment. Bönpos pray to be born in Olmo Lung Ring because this can occur only after achieving enlightenment. Visiting Mount Kailash is possible before enlightenment is reached, as long as one is determined to accept the physical challenges. This is proof to Bönpos that Mount Kailash is not Olmo Lung Ring.

Historical Bön texts state very clearly that the holy mountain Mount Kailash was in the center of the Kingdom of Zhang Zhung, which was the closest neighboring kingdom to Tibet and existed until the end of the eighth century. Zhang Zhung was integrated into Tibet after the death of the Emperor Ligmincha, its last ruler. In early times the Kingdom of Zhang Zhung extended from what is today the upper part of western Tibet, through parts of Nepal, northern India (Ladhak, Zangskar, Kinnaur, Spiti, etc.), to Pakistan (Kashmir) and to China (the Karakoram area). Most of the Bön teachings have been translated from the Zhang Zhung language into Tibetan.

Mount Kailash is a holy place for Bönpos and is blessed by the Zhang Zhung deity Me Ri. The Me Ri teachings were among the main practices of the Zhang Zhungpa (people of Zhang Zhung) and were later introduced into Tibet. The lineage of this practice has been preserved, and it continues to the present time.

The Land of Zhangzhung

So, the land of Zhangzhung appears to be centered around Mount Kailash and includes considerable territory to the west, north and east of the sacred mountain. This territory also stretched to the south into parts of northern India and present-day Nepal. It should be noted the southeastern side of Mount Kailash, the side facing the two sacred lakes, has what appears to be a swastika on its impressive sheer face. This gigantic swastika is the result of a huge slash down the center of the mountain face and a large parallel slash across the face. It is most apparent when there is recent snowfall on the mountain.

The Land of Zhangzhung and its people are frequently mentioned in Tibetan texts. Tradition has it that Zhangzhung consisted "of three different regions: sGob-ba, the outer; Phug-pa, the inner; and Bar-ba, the middle. The outer section is thought to extend as far as Gilgit in Pakistan and even to the Kirgiz Mountains of Kirgizstan, which is directly north of Gilgit. Ladakh, including Lahaul and Spiti, was part of sGob-ba. The other areas are yet to be identified but may be areas of central Tibet and even the Altai Himalaya in western Mongolia. Archeological work on the Chang Tang plateau of central Tibet in 2010 found possible evidence of an Iron Age culture in the area which some have tentatively identified as that of the Zhangzhung. Don't forget, the first Bon avatar was supposedly born in 16000 BC.

The capital city of Zhangzhung was called Khyunglung the "Silver Palace of Garuda." It supposedly lay southwest of Mount Kailash (Mount Ti-se in the Zhangzhung language). The remains of palaces in the upper Sutlej Valley are thought to be the ruins of this city.

According to Rolf Alfred Stein, author of *Tibetan Civilization*, the area of Zhangzhung (which he calls Shangshung) was not historically a part of Tibet and was a distinctly foreign territory to the Tibetans. Says Stein:

> ...then further west, the Tibetans encountered a distinctly foreign nation—Shangshung, with its capital at Khyunglung. Mt. Kailash (Tise) and Lake Manasarovar formed part of this country, whose language has come down to us through early documents. Though still unidentified, it seems to be Indo European.... Geographically the country was certainly open to India, both through Nepal and by way of Kashmir and Ladakh. Kailash is a holy place for the Indians, who make pilgrimages to it. No one knows how long they have done so, but the cult may well go back to the times when Shangshung was still independent of Tibet. How far Shangshung stretched to the north, east and west is a mystery.... We have already had an occasion to remark that Shangshung, embracing Kailash sacred Mount of the Hindus, may once have had a religion largely borrowed

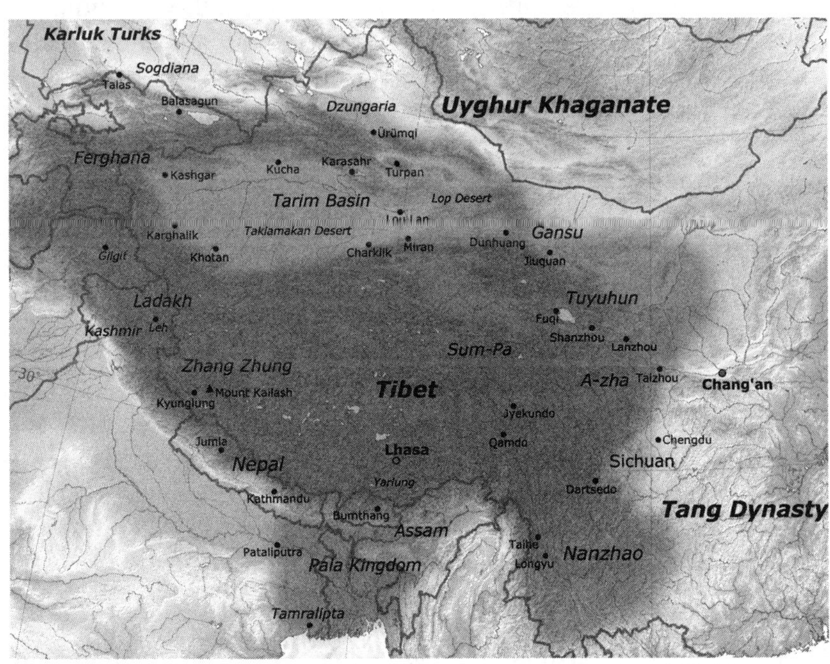

A map of the Tibetan empire at its greatest extent, circa 800 AD.

> from Hinduism. The situation may even have lasted for quite a long time. In fact, about 950, the Hindu King of Kabul had a statue of Vishnu, of the Kashmiri type (with three heads), which he claimed had been given him by the king of the Bhota (Tibetans) who, in turn had obtained it from Kailash.

Not much is really known about Zhangzhung during the literally thousands of years of pilgrims, mainly from India, making the pilgrimage to Mount Kailash to see the sacred mountain. This would have been a major part of the economy, as would farming and yak herding in the valleys of what is now western Tibet. Trade with India, a source of exotic goods and metal utensils, would have been very important. Salt was a major export from western Tibet to India, including the popular Himalayan pink salt. Quartz crystals and gold were also products of western Tibet.

At some time around 634 AD Zhangzhung was conquered from an area of central Tibet by the king Songtsen Gampo. Songtsen Gampo then united with the country of Yangtong and conquered more tribes before threatening the Songzhou Chinese emperor with an army of more than 200,000 men. He then sent an envoy with gifts of gold and silk to the Chinese emperor to ask for a Chinese princess in marriage and, when refused, attacked Songzhou. He apparently finally retreated and apologized, and later the emperor granted his request for the marriage of his daughter.

Stein says Tibetan accounts relate that the central Tibetan king (this area is today Chinghai, formerly known as Amdo Tibet) and the king of Zhangzhung had married each other's sisters in a political alliance. However, the Tibetan wife of the king of the Zhangzhung complained of poor treatment by the king's principal wife. War ensued, and through the treachery of the Tibetan princess, according to Stein: "King Ligmikya of Zhangzhung, while on his way to Sum-ba (Amdo province) was ambushed and killed by King Srongtsen Gampo's soldiers. As a consequence, Zhangzhung was annexed to Bod (Central Tibet). Thereafter the new kingdom born of the unification of Zhangzhung and Bod was known as Bod rGyal-khab." R. A. Stein places the conquest of Zhangzhung in 645. There was a brief revolt in 677 AD but it was brought under control by the son of Songtsen Gampo, by the "firm governance of the great leaders of the Mgar clan."

A handful of Zhangzhung texts and 11th century bilingual

Tibetan documents attest to a Zhangzhung language that was related to Kinnauri, a language spoken by certain tribes in Himachal Pradesh. The Bonpo claim that the Tibetan writing system is derived from the Zhangzhung alphabet, while modern scholars recognize the clear derivation of Tibetan script from a north Indian script. Possibly both are correct and it is clear that modern Tibetan script is derived from north Indian Sanskrit scripts.

The Secret City of Shambhala

The Bonpos claim that Tonpa Shenrab lived some 18,000 years ago, and visited Tibet from the land of Tagzig Olmo Lung Ring, which they say is another name for Shambhala. Bonpos also suggest that during this time Lord Shenrab's teaching permeated the entire subcontinent of India and was partly responsible for the development of the Vedic religion. They give as an example Mount Kailash, which is the center of Zhangzhung culture, and is also the most sacred mountain to Hindus. As a result, the Bonpos claim that the supposedly much later Hindu teaching owes its origin, partially, to Tonpa Shenrab and the Bon religion. Hindus would probably say that Vedic Hinduism is older than 18,000 years. Certainly, we know that Hindus believe that the god Shiva (also known as Shankar) lives upon (or inside) the mountain called Kailash.

In Tibetan Buddhist tradition, Shambhala is a spiritual kingdom and is mentioned in the Buddhist text known as the Kalachakra tantra. As we have seen, the Bon scriptures speak of a closely related land called Tagzig Olmo Lung Ring, which they say is the same place as Shambhala.

According to Wikipedia, the Sanskrit name Shambhala is taken from the name of a city mentioned in the Hindu Puranas, probably in reference to Sambhal in Uttar Pradesh. The mythological relevance of the place originates with a prophecy in Vishnu Purana (4.24) according to which Shambhala will be the birthplace of Kalki, the next incarnation of Vishnu, who will usher in a new age (Satya Yuga); it is also the prophesied ruling Kingdom of Maitreya, the future Buddha.

So, Shambhala is said to be ruled by the future Buddha Maitreya. In the narrative of the Kalachakra tantra, coming from Dolpopa Sherab Gyaltsen (d. 1361 AD), King Manjuśrīkīrṭi is said to have been born in 159 BC and ruled over a kingdom of 300,510 followers of the Mlechha religion, some of whom worshiped the

Sun. He is said to have expelled 20,000 people from his domain who clung to Surya Samadhi (solar worship) rather than convert to Kalachakra (Wheel of Time) Buddhism. After realizing these were the wisest and best of his people and how much he was in need of them, he later asked them to return and some did. Those who did not return are said to have set up the city of Shambhala. Manjuśrīkīrti initiated the preaching of the Kalachakra teachings in order to try to convert those who returned and were still under his rule. In 59 BC he abdicated his throne to his son, Puṇḍārika, and died soon afterward, entering the Sambhogakaya of Buddhahood.

The Kalachakra tantra prophesies that when the world declines into war and greed, and all is lost, the 25th Kalki king Maitreya will emerge from Shambhala with a huge army to vanquish Dark Forces and usher in a worldwide Golden Age. This final battle is prophesied for the year 2424 or 2425 (in the 3304th year after the death of Buddha). Thereafter, Buddhism would survive another 1,800 years.

Westerners first learned about Shambhala when one of the explorers in Tibet, the Portuguese missionary Estêvão Cacella, heard about it (transcribed as Xembala) and thought it was another name for Cathay or China. Cacella in 1627 headed to Tashilhunpo, the seat of the Panchen Lama and, discovering his mistake, returned to his base in India.

Then the Hungarian scholar Sándor Kőrösi Csoma, writing in 1833, provided the first geographic account of "a fabulous country in the north... situated between 45' and 50' north latitude."

Theosophical Society co-founder Helena Blavatsky (1831-1891) alluded to the Shambhala myth in her books starting in 1877 with the publication of *Isis Unveiled.* Blavatsky, who claimed to be in contact with a Great White Lodge of Himalayan Adepts, mentions Shambhala in several places, but without giving it especially great emphasis.

Another Theosophist, Alice A. Bailey, claimed Shambhala was

Helena Blavatsky.

an extra-dimensional place on the astral plane, a spiritual center where the governing deity of Earth, Sanat Kumara, dwells as the highest Avatar of the Planetary Logos of Earth.

In 1924 Nicholas and Helena Roerich led an expedition aimed at Shambhala. They believed that Belukha Mountain in the Altai Mountains was an entrance to Shambhala, a common belief in that region.

Wikipedia tells us that, inspired by Theosophical lore and several visiting Mongol lamas, Gleb Bokii, the chief Bolshevik cryptographer and one of the bosses of the Soviet secret police, along with his writer friend Alexander Barchenko, embarked on a quest for Shambhala in an attempt to merge the Kalachakra tantra and ideas of Communism in the early 1920s.

Among other things, in a clandestine laboratory affiliated with the secret police, Bokii and Barchenko experimented with Buddhist spiritual techniques to try to find a key for engineering perfect communist human beings. They contemplated a special expedition to Mongolia and Tibet to retrieve the wisdom of Shambhala. However, the project fell through as a result of intrigues within the Soviet intelligence service, as well as rival efforts of the Soviet Foreign Commissariat that sent its own expedition to Tibet in 1924.

The French Buddhist explorer Alexandra David-Neel associated Shambhala with Balkh in present-day Afghanistan, also offering the Persian Sham-i-Bala, "elevated candle" as an etymology of its name. Similarly, the Gurdjieffian J. G. Bennett published speculation that Shambhala was Shams-i-Balkh, a Bactrian sun temple.

The Nazis sent several expeditions to Tibet in the 1930s "to contact the Agartha and Shambhala" as part of Nazi esotericism. It has been speculated the SS created a secret base in Tibet during this time and promised to arm the Tibetans against Britain and China.

Shambhala was probably the inspiration for Shangri-La, a paradise on Earth hidden in a Tibetan valley, which features in the 1933 novel *Lost Horizon* by British author James Hilton and was made into a Hollywood movie.

Tag-Zig and Tajikistan

Some scholars think that the origin of the Bon and Tonpa Shenrab is Tajikistan and that Tag-Zig of Tagzig Olmo Lung

Ring is Tajikistan. Some ancient Bonpo scriptures refer to today's Tajikistan, as the Zhangzhung word "Tag-Zig" refers to today's "Ta-jik", and "-istan" is the Persian word applied after Islamic rule. At the time of the 7th century AD Tibetan king Songsten Gampo, the Tajik area was under Tibetan rule. It is thought by some Bon scholars that Tonpa Shenrab was born in the Tajik area.

Recently the first proto-historical agricultural society in Central Asia was discovered near the ancient town of Sarazm in Kyrgyzstan, just north of Tajikistan. Sarazm was the first city in Central Asia to maintain economic relations with a network of settlements covering a vast territory from the Turkmenistan steppes and the Aral Sea (in the north and northwest) to the Iranian Plateau and the Indus (in the south and southeast).

The archaeological site of the ancient city of Sarazm is located near Sohibnazar, a village situated on the left bank of the river Zeravshan, near the border with Uzbekistan. Located 15 kilometers west of the city of Panjakent, the site occupies an area of about 1.5 km in length and 400 to 900m in width. At the peak of the occupation, the site would have covered an area of up to 90 hectares.

Following surface discoveries unearthed due to agricultural activity, the first excavation of the site started in 1977 and was conducted by Abdullah Isakov of the Academy of Science of Tajikistan. During that first excavation, eight soundings in different locations were conducted and three areas were excavated. In 1987, seven areas were excavated and twenty soundings were conducted.

The territory that now constitutes Tajikistan and Kyrgyzstan was previously home to several ancient cultures, including the city of Sarazm of the Neolithic and the Bronze Age and was later home to kingdoms ruled by people of different faiths and cultures, including the Oxus civilization, and Andronovo culture. Dominant faiths have been Buddhism, Nestorian Christianity, Hinduism, Zoroastrianism, Manichaeism, and Islam. The area has been ruled by numerous empires and dynasties, including the Achaemenid Empire, Sasanian Empire, Hephthalite Empire, Samanid Empire, and Mongol Empire.

Wikipedia tells us that the earliest recorded history of the region dates back to about 500 BC when much, if not all, of modern Tajikistan was part of the Achaemenid Empire. Some authors have also suggested that in the seventh and sixth centuries BC, parts of modern Tajikistan, including territories in the Zeravshan valley,

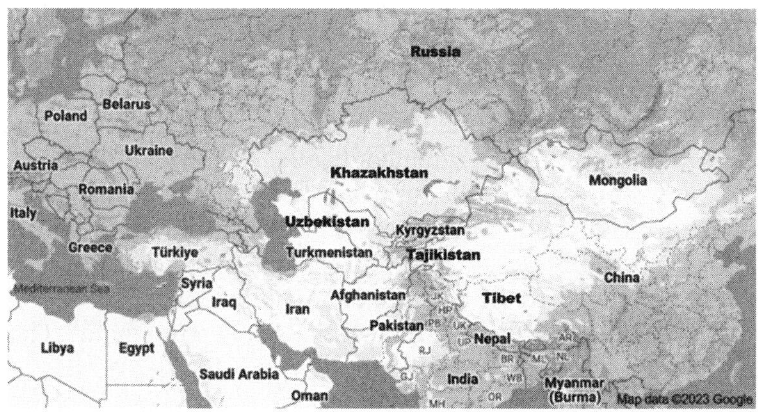

A map of Tibetan and Central Asia.

formed part of the ancient Hindu Kambojas tribe before it became part of the Achaemenid Empire.

After the region's conquest by Alexander the Great it became part of the Greco-Bactrian Kingdom, a successor state of Alexander's empire. The Silk Road passed through the region and, following the expedition of Chinese explorer Zhang Qian during the reign of Wudi (141 BC–87 BC), commercial relations between the Han Empire and Sogdiana flourished. Sogdians played a major role in facilitating trade and also worked in other capacities as farmers, carpetweavers, glassmakers, and woodcarvers.

The Kushan Empire, a collection of Yuezhi tribes, took control of the region in the first century AD and ruled until the fourth century AD during which time Buddhism, Nestorian Christianity, Zoroastrianism, and Manichaeism were all practiced in the region. Later the Hephthalite Empire, a collection of nomadic tribes, moved into the region and Arabs brought Islam in the early eighth century. Central Asia continued in its role as a commercial crossroads, linking China, the steppes to the north, and the Islamic heartland via the Silk Road.

Tajikistan and Kyrgyzstan were briefly under the control of the Tibetan Empire and the Tang dynasty from 650 to 680 AD and then under the control of the Umayyads in 710 AD.

The Samanid Empire, 819 to 999, restored Persian control of the region and enlarged the cities of Samarkand and Bukhara (both cities are today part of Uzbekistan) that became the cultural centers of Iran, and the region was known as Khorasan. The empire was centered in Khorasan and Transoxiana; at its greatest extent it encompassed modern-day Afghanistan, large parts of

Iran, Tajikistan, Turkmenistan, Uzbekistan, Kyrgyzstan, parts of Kazakhstan, and Pakistan.

What is important here is that Kyrgyzstan and Tajikistan were originally Tibetan countries that practiced the Bon religion and later Buddhism and were often controlled by Tibet. It would seem that Zhangzhung originally stretched from Mount Kailash all the way to Tajikistan and Kirgizstan. Did the Bon religion really start in Tajikistan 18,000 years ago? Did it then spread eastward across the Tibetan plateau to the area around Mount Kailash? Prior to 500 BC was Tajikistan ruled by Zhangzhung as a Bon state? That is what Bon scholars apparently believe.

Vimanas and Mount Kailash

Hindu and Buddhist literature abounds with tales of flying machines called vimanas in Sanskrit. The ancient Indians themselves apparently wrote entire flight manuals on the operation of various types of vimanas, of which there were as many as five different kinds including: the Pushpaka vimana; the Shakuna Vimana; the Sundara Vimana; the Rukma Vimana; and the Tripura Vimana.

Says the *Ramayana* about the Pushpaka vimana:

> The Pushpaka vimana that resembles the Sun and belongs to my brother was brought by the powerful Ravana; that aerial and excellent chariot going everywhere at will… that chariot resembling a bright cloud in the sky… and the King [Rama] got in, and the excellent chariot at the command of the Raghira, rose up into the higher atmosphere.

The great British/American biologist, author and researcher Ivan T. Sanderson wrote in his 1970 book *Invisible Residents*[9] (reprinted by AUP) that a curious text called the *Samarangana Sutrahara* seemed to describe a spinning flying saucer of some type. Sanderson, who also makes reference to Desmond Leslie, the British co-author of George Adamski's classic 1953 book *Flying Saucers Have Landed,* says that the *Samarangana Sutradhara* is a technological text of a type called *Manusa:*

> It is, moreover, from these authenticated texts, mostly in poetic form, that some truly astonishing concepts

have been derived. Poetic they may be, and nothing more than myth, legend, or folklore may they purport to record, but they make statements that are more than just surprising. Several are, what is more, couched in perfectly straightforward terms and are, time and time again, stated to be not legendary but technological, and thus called *Manusa*. These are said by the writers to explain how certain devices were constructed for aerial flight, but not how to so construct them because the inventors and the establishment did not want such things to be mass-produced and get into the hands of any other than the rulers, commonly called "kings" and "princes." What is more, among the non-technical works devoted to the more poetic stories, and known as *Daiva*, there would appear to be more than ample suggestion, if not evidence, that such airships could be and were put to the most gruesome and devastating use in wartime.

...In the *Manusa*, the most elaborate details for building (such aerial machines) are set down. The *Samarangana Sutradhara* says that they were made of light material, with a strong, well-shaped body. Iron, copper, and lead were used in their construction. They could fly to great distances and were propelled by air. This text, according to Leslie, devotes 230 stanzas to the building of these machines, and their uses in peace and war.

Sanderson then goes on to give this quote from the *Samarangana Sutrahara* that comes from Leslie's 1953 book:

Strong and durable must the body be made, like a great flying bird, of light material. Inside it one must place the mercury-engine with its iron heating apparatus beneath. By means of the power latent in the mercury which sets the driving whirlwind in motion, a man sitting inside may travel a great distance in the sky in a most marvelous manner.

Similarly by using the prescribed processes one can build a vimana as large as the temple of the God-in-motion. Four strong mercury containers must be built into the interior structure. When these have been heated by controlled fire from iron containers, the vimana develops

> thunder-power through the mercury. And at once it becomes a pearl in the sky.
>
> Moreover, if this iron engine with properly welded joints be filled with mercury, and the fire be conducted to the upper part it develops power with the roar of a lion.

Sanderson then continues to comment on the important mention of the liquid metal mercury:

> Leslie and several others who at least tried to take a serious view of these odd statements subsequently indulged in some perfectly valid speculations as to just what the significance of mercury might be. These are both sensible and permissible but lead off into matters that do not concern us here. Needless to say, they did not encompass the basic observation that a circular dish of mercury revolves in a contrary manner to a naked flame circulated below it, and that it gathers speed until it exceeds the speed of revolution of said flame. I fancy that Mr. Leslie will be enchanted with this new observation.
>
> Here is the projection of energy by an exceedingly simple process. Should the ancients have stumbled across this process—though how in the dickens they might have done so is almost beyond comprehension—they might well have followed up the lead and ended up by finding out how to tap and channel such energy. Take this lead far enough and one can suggest the development of an "engine" employing it and being put to use to do (as the engineers say) work.
>
> Desmond Leslie's theme is that this was one type of engine developed for aerial flight, and he extrapolates therefrom to the suggestion that it may have been developed far enough for space travel, and that something on this principle powers some UFOs.

Sanderson was keenly interested in all sorts of mysteries, including UFOs and the ability of some craft to fly through the air and go underwater as well. He felt that the subject of vimanas was a credible ancient mystery and one that deserved greater attention. Sanderson's book came out in the early 1970s, basically during the popular Chariots of the Gods-Ancient Astronauts period. By the

1980s scholars in India were getting more interested in what their ancient texts said about space travel, ancient flight and vimanas.

At the World Space Conference on October 11, 1988 in Bangalore, India, as reported in the local newspaper *The Hindu*, an Italian by the name of Dr. Roberto Pinotti addressed the delegates and spoke on ancient Indian vimanas. After briefly telling them what vimanas were, he went on to say that the Tripura Vimana was powered by motive power generated by solar rays and had an elongated form similar to a modern blimp.

He went on to say that the "ancient Aryans knew the use of the element 'fire' as could be seen from their 'Astra' weapons that included soposamhara (a flame-belching missile), Prasvapna (which caused sleep) and four kinds of Agni Astras that traveled in sheets of flame and produced thunder."

While Dr. Pinotti concluded his talk by telling the delegates that they should take the subject of vimanas seriously, he was really speaking to the foreign delegates, as most Indians, especially Hindus or those of religions derived from Hinduism such as Buddhism or Jainism, already believed that their ancestors had such technology.

Pinotti also mentioned the *Samarangana Sutradhara,* saying that it is a scientific treatise dealing with every possible angle of air travel in a vimana. Pinotti said that there are 230 stanzas dealing with construction, takeoff, cruising for thousands of miles, normal and forced landings, and even possible collisions with birds.

In Control of Three Planetary Systems?

There are many other ancient texts from India that provide fascinating and incredible information on the highly technological ancient world, of which ancient India was only a part. *The Bhagavad Gita* (known as Srimad-Bhagavatam to Hindus) is part of the *Mahabharata*. In text 19 of the Third Canto we read (as translated by Bhaktivedanta Swami Prabhupada, founder of the Hare Krishna movement):

> The elder child, Hiranyakasipu, was unafraid of death from anyone within the three worlds because he received a benediction from Lord Brahma. He was proud and puffed up due to this benediction and was able to bring all three planetary systems under his control.

That Hiranyakasipu was in control of three planetary systems is an incredible statement, and one that seems a bit out of line for a supposedly primitive people whose main interest was growing food, hunting and gathering, and fending off wild animals. Yet, these "cavemen" were, by their own written records, quite sophisticated and in possession of not only aircraft, but spacecraft as well.

It is interesting to conjecture as to which three planetary systems they are talking about. It may be assumed that earth is one of these systems. Considering the fascinating photos of pyramids and other structures found on Mars by NASA, we may believe Mars to have been a planet worthy of "bringing under control." Perhaps Venus (sometimes referred to as Hesperus) is the third planet. Even more interestingly, perhaps this third planet is a planet that supposedly once existed between Mars and Jupiter, where the asteroid belt exists today. The populace of this planet allegedly blew it up many thousands of years ago, while playing around with some very dangerous and destructive technology—a lesson that the people of our planet at this point in time and space might well learn before we repeat such a cosmic disaster.

Bringing three planetary systems under control would seem to require physical travel in a spaceship. The fascinating book *Easy Journey to Other Planets* was written by Bhaktivedanta Swami Prabhupada, the aforementioned founder of the ISKCON movement. This book is about astral travel, however, and not about visiting other planets in mechanical devices.

One Sanskrit authority who has held to the idea of the vimanas of ancient Indian texts being genuine flying machines of the past is Dr. V. Raghavan, who wrote the classic book *Yantras or Mechanical Contrivances in Ancient India.* This book was first published in 1952 by The Indian Institute of Culture in Bangalore and was republished in 1956 with a second introduction by the author.

The short book, meant to be used as a school text by students of ancient Indian literature and science, is a reference to all kinds of mechanical contrivances (including robots, war machines and aircraft) mentioned in classical Indian literature. Dr. Raghavan, a professor at the University of Madras, answers his critics in the preface to the second edition (1956) by saying:

> Regarding these critics I only want to emphasize what

> I have clearly stated in the opening of my lecture as to my exact intention in presenting this material. In the whole thesis, I have not myself made any claim or argued that aeroplanes were roaring across the skies in ancient India. I have not pressed into service any unpublished manuscript said to exist in secret or private possession and claiming to contain precious information on the construction of Vimanas or aerial vehicles. I have, on the contrary, used only the most reputed works, the references to different yantras in which have to be explained, if one does not want to close his eyes to them.

Indeed, Dr. Raghavan is possibly referring to such secret libraries as James Churchward, author of several books about the mysterious lost continent of Mu, claimed to have consulted (of dubious value to the scholar, certainly). All of Raghavan's references are from freely available sources. One need not turn to obscure sources on vimanas when a great deal of public material is available. Dr. Raghavan's question to those critics who object to his discussions of ancient Indian aircraft is, "What meaning do the critics propose to attach to the manifold yantra references in the epics...?"

Dr. Raghavan quotes many sources and his book is filled with classical stories of people and their flying machines, artisans whose specialty is to construct aircraft, and amusing tales of robots and other strange, exotic "contrivances." He quotes at length from the *Samarangana Sutradhara* attributed to the 11th century philosopher king Bhoja. As we have seen, this ancient text, "in many ways, a rare treatise in Sanskrit literature" according to Raghavan, is particularly revealing because it goes into great detail on the construction, propulsion and uses of aircraft. Bhoja, with Raghavan's commentary, gives certain details on the mercury engine that propelled the craft.

Dr. Raghavan also gives details on how vimanas were used to frighten war elephants, which were commonly used in skirmishes between clashing forces in ancient India. He also discusses mechanical birds that flew, mainly toys and amusement devices.

The Controversial Book: *War in Ancient India*

Another book that mentions the *Samaragana Sutradhara* is the scholarly book by a historian from southern India named

Ramachandra Dikshitar. His 1944 book (later republished by the Oxford University Press with an additional foreword) *War in Ancient India*[66] contained a fascinating chapter entitled "Aerial Warfare in Ancient India" that had the scholars of his day looking at him through their spectacles with amusement. How could there have been aerial warfare in ancient India when quite obviously—as every scientist knows—the ancient Indians could not possibly have had airships.

Yet, the scholarly professor defended himself and said that he only wrote about these things because the ancient texts described such events as people flying in machines, well known as vimanas, and that these aircraft were also used in military actions. Aerial warfare, then and now, is an attractive option in that it is likely to inflict the most damage on the enemy with the least loss of life on the attacker's side. Aerial warfare, including the use of rockets and missiles, is a superior way to wage war, as long as one has that technology, advanced as it is.

Vishnampet R. Ramachandra Dikshitar was born in 1896 in the southern Indian state of Tamil Nadu, and was a historian, Indologist and Dravidologist. He was a professor of history and archaeology at the University of Madras and authored a number of standard textbooks on Indian history. In 1928, he was appointed as a lecturer at the University of Madras. He was promoted to reader in 1946 and made Professor in 1947. Dikshitar specialized in Indian history in general, and Tamil history in particular. He was a renowned Sanskrit scholar of his time. In his book *Origin and Spread of the Tamils* (1947), he maintained that Polynesia and Australia were to the South Indian traders, which would support my assertion that they brought Shiva worship to these regions.

Dr. Dikshitar was someone who did not follow the official dogma of his time and instead pursued the ancient texts—wherever they led him. Let us now look at what he concluded from the ancient texts in his book *War in Ancient India.*

The Contribution of Ancient India to the Science of Aeronautics

Dr. Dikshitar begins his chapter called "Aerial Warfare in Ancient India" with several paragraphs on how interesting it is that India was an early contributor to the then newly emerging science of aeronautics, including airplanes, zeppelins, blimps and other aircraft:

No question can be more interesting in the present circumstance of the world than India's contribution to the science of aeronautics. There are numerous illustrations in our vast Puranic and epic literature to show how well and wonderfully the ancient Indians conquered the air. To glibly characterize everything found in this literature as imaginary and summarily dismiss it as unreal has been the practice of both Western and Eastern scholars until very recently. The very idea indeed was ridiculed and people went so far as to assert that it was physically impossible for man to use flying machines. But today what with balloons, aeroplanes and other flying machines a great change has come over our ideas on the subject.

...Turning to Vedic literature, in one of the *Brahmanas* occurs the concept of a ship that sails heavenwards. The ship is the Agnihotra of which the Ahavaniya and Garhapatya fires represent the two sides bound heavenward, and the steersman is the Agnihotrin who offers milk to the three Agnis. Again in the still earlier *Rg Veda Samhita* we read that the Asvins conveyed the rescued Bhujya safely by means of winged ships. The latter may refer to the aerial navigation in the earliest times.

In the recently published *Samarangana Sutradhara* of Bhoja, a whole chapter of about 230 stanzas is devoted to the principles of construction underlying the various flying machines and other engines used for military and other purposes. The various advantages of using machines, especially flying ones, are given elaborately. Special mention is made of their attacking visible as well a invisible objects, of their use at one's will and pleasure, of their uninterrupted movements, of their strength and durability, in short of their capability to do in the air all that is done on earth. After enumerating and explaining a number of other advantages, the author concludes that even impossible things could be affected through them. Three movements are usually ascribed to these machines—ascending, cruising thousands of miles in different directions in the atmosphere and lastly descending. It is said that in an aerial car one can mount up to the Suryamandala 'solar region' and the Naksatra mandala (stellar region) and also travel throughout the regions of air above the sea and the earth.

> These cars are said to move so fast as to make a noise that could be heard faintly from the ground. Still some writers have expressed a doubt and asked 'Was that true?' But the evidence in its favor is overwhelming.[66]

Bringing the vimana debate up to modern times, in a report published online by The Tibet Post International (thetibetpost.com) on March 16, 2011 the news source said under the headline of "UFO Photographed in Eastern Tibet":

> Dharamshala: The photograph above (see a zoomed in image of the UFO below) comes from the Karze, eastern region of Tibet. A group of friends were on their way to a nearby airport when the car they were travelling started having engine problems. According to "All News Web," the group got out to move the car off the road when one of the group spotted a UFO hovering overhead and managed to take a photo of it.
>
> This UFO event occurred on February 20 of this year. The UFO seen in the photo is a classic metallic flying saucer. The witnesses have submitted the photo to researchers for analysis.
>
> Tibet has had an association with UFOs that might

A photo of a disk-shaped flying object in eastern Tibet on February 20, 2011.

well go back thousands of years, "All News Web," reported. It has long been rumored that a secret UFO base exists in the area. It is also believed that a giant UFO is buried somewhere under mountains in the region. In the 10th century AD, Tibetan monks adorned pages of sacred Buddhist manuscripts with depictions of metallic flying saucers they had seen in the skies above the area.

In an article written on November 6, 2012 on the Indian news site "The Register" (theregister.com) it was reported that UFOs and a "mystery robot" were seen by Indian troops along the Indo-Tibetan border region which includes the western Tibetan state of Ladahk, currently administered by India and disputed with China.

The article, under the title of "Mystery robot-bringing UFOs sighted by Indian troops on Tibet border" said:

> Mysterious UFOs have returned to a remote region on the Tibetan border, according to sightings by Indian troops stationed in the area. The UFOs, which have been reported for years, are said to have included a strange "robot like" figure seen by Indian scientists in 2004 walking along a mountain valley—which then "rapidly became airborne" and flew away.
>
> We learn of the latest military sightings through the trenchant journalism of *India Today*, which says that Indian army troops and gendarmerie units of the Indo-Tibetan Border Police Force (ITBP) have been submitting reports of strange luminous airborne objects since the summer above the Ladakh region. Ladakh is a remote, mostly uninhabited but heavily militarized zone along the border with Tibet and China.
>
> It seems that the Indian army has checked carefully and the UFOs in question are not manned or unmanned aircraft: these are routinely sighted in the area but can picked up on radar—unlike the UFOs. Indian army radars have been unable to track the strange shining objects. An unmanned aircraft dispatched towards one UFO did sight it, but then "lost sight of the object."
>
> According to *India Today*, the Indian government—stimulated to curiosity by the frequent reports from the military—dispatched a scientific expedition to the region

A photo of the "Robot-like figure" at Samudra Tapu in 2004.

in September [2012]. The Indian boffins saw the UFOs but were unable to establish what they were.

The paper reports, magnificently: Scientists say the mysterious objects are not necessarily from outer space.

We also learn that UFOs have been reported in the Ladakh region for many years, with the best of these reports coming from a group of Indian government scientists who were in the area in 2004 studying glaciers:

> A five-member group of geologists and glaciologists led by Dr. Anil Kulkarni of the isro's Space Applications Centre in Ahmedabad were on a research trip through the barren Samudra Tapu Valley. They filmed a four-foot tall 'robot-like' figure, that 'walked' along the valley, 50 m away from them. The humanoid object then rapidly became airborne and disappeared. The encounter lasted 40 minutes. It was seen by 14 persons including the six scientists.

Though Dr. Kulkarni's report was comprehensive, it appears to have been mysteriously ignored by the Indian government. A clue as to just why can be found in the IT report; we note that Kulkarni's description—in addition to its submission via scientific channels—was also supplied to unnamed "intelligence agencies… the matter was buried soon after."

This interesting report includes a photo of the "robot" heavily illuminated apparently taking to the air in a remote valley of western Tibet's Ladahk. Check the color section for a good photograph of the incident in 2004.

We have to wonder if this report has something to do with Mount Kailash, which is east of this curious incident in Ladahk. It does not seem to be of Indian military origin but might be of Chinese military origin, as this is an area of conflict between these two countries. This area discussed in the article is in a neutral zone of Lakahk that the two countries are fighting over. Is this some activity that has to do with Shambhala and the vimanas of ancient India and Tibet?

The Airships of King Solomon

A number of historical characters have been said to have had airships or flying chariots. One such famous person was the Hebrew King Solomon the Wise, the son of David. Solomon was the last ruler of a United Israel and ruled circa 970-931 BC. After his death Israel split into Judah in the south and Israel in the north. His descendants ruled Judah.

He was known for being very worldly, having many wives (many from far-off countries), and for sending Phoenician ships on a mysterious three-year journey a land of plentiful gold: Ophir. They could have gone quite a distance in one year—and would certainly have traveled beyond the near countries in the Indian Ocean during that time. They were probably going to Australia, Indonesia and even Peru in their search for shiploads of gold. The Bible says such treasure was collected, along with valuable spices, feathers and even exotic animals such as apes.

Solomon was known as someone who was very wise and it seems that he had been to remote lands and possessed a vimana of some sort. According to the *Kebra Negast* (a sort of Ethiopian Old Testament), King Solomon would visit the Queen of Sheba, who bore his son Menelik, by flying in a "heavenly car." Like today's aircraft passengers, he flew in one day a great distance:

> The king... and all who obeyed his word, flew on the wagon without pain and suffering, and without sweat or exhaustion, and traveled in one day a distance which took three months to traverse [on foot].

We have here a portrait of a king who literally had everything, including his own Air Force One to take on special trips throughout Asia and Africa. Had Solomon ever flown across the Pacific to Tonga, Easter Island and Peru? There are legends in Asia that Solomon did make visits to Central Asia and Tibet. Throughout the Middle East, as far as Kashmir, are mountains known as the "Thrones of Solomon," including one in northwestern Iran, a flat-topped mountain called Takht-i-Suleiman (Throne of Solomon). It has been conjectured that these may have been landing bases for Solomon's airship.

The Russian-American explorer, mystic and painter Nicholas Roerich testifies that throughout Central Asia it is widely believed that Solomon flew about in an airship:

> Up to now, in the people's conception, King Solomon soars on his miraculous flying device over the vast spaces of Asia. Many mountains in Asia are either with ruins or stones bearing the imprint of his foot or of his knees, as evidence of his long-enduring prayers. These are the so-called thrones of Solomon. The Great King flew to these mountains, he reached all heights, he left behind him the cares of rulership and here refreshed his spirit.

Roerich described in his book *Altai-Himalaya* a UFO sighting in 1926 of a silvery oval-shaped object in northern China as he headed to Tibet:

> On August fifth—something remarkable! We were in our camp in the Kukunor district not far from the Humbolt Chain. In the morning about half-past nine some of our caravaneers noticed a remarkably big black eagle flying above us. Seven of us began to watch the unusual bird. At this same moment another of our caravaneers remarked "There is something above the bird."
>
> And he shouted in his astonishement. We all saw, in a direction north to south, something big and shiny reflecting sun, like a huge oval moving at great speed. Crossing our camp this thing changed in its direction from south to southwest. And we saw how it disappeared in the intense blue sky. We even had time to take our field glasses and saw quite distinctly an oval form with shiny surface, one

side of which was brilliant from the sun.

Roerich and his wife Helena collected very large quartz crystals on their journeys, plus they were the authors of a number of mystical books that included discussions of vimanas and the great Buddhist-Hindu past of Masters who still possessed vimanas, magical machines and hidden fortresses deep in the remotest parts of the Altai Himalaya, Gobi Desert and Tibet. Roerich was familiar with Madame Blavatsky and the Theosophical Society and he recognized that much of her work was derived from Central Asian legends of vimanas and the Land of the Immortals in the Kunlun Range of northern Tibet—the land of Hsi Wang Mu. This Shangri-La place held a "cave of the ancients" with a secret city inside a mountain, various Arhats, Immortals and Masters did what they could to guide mankind in a spiritual direction from this fortress of solitude.

Did King Solomon have some flying vehicle with which he flew to Persia, India and Tibet? With whom did he meet there? Did he visit Mount Kailash in his vimana? Given the many stories of flying vehicles from the ancient Indian epics, this is not so unusual. Mountains with ruins on their summits that include large grassy areas, do indeed exist all over the world. The megalithic structures of Sacsayhuaman and Machu Picchu are two such "airports" in Peru.

Modern Vimana Sightings in Tibet

Frank Smythe (1900-1949), was an English mountaineer, author, photographer and botanist. He is best remembered for his mountaineering in the Alps as well as in the Himalayas, where he identified a region that he named the "Valley of Flowers," now a protected park in Uttarakhand state near the Tibetan border.

Smythe was a member of Hugh Ruttledge's 1933 Everest expedition. During the expedition, Smythe witnessed two spots hovering and pulsating in the sky. This was reported in Champak Chatterji's 1993 article "The Climbing Partner—The Other Experience in the Himalaya" published in *Himalayan Journal.*

Wikipedia reports that on March 25, 1968 at around 8.15 pm the residents of Batulechaur in Pokhara district, Nepal, witnessed "a blazing object, flashing intermittently, accompanied by big thunder sound" disintegrating over the Kaski region. A huge metallic disk shaped object with a six-foot base and 4 feet in height was found in a crater in Baltichaur five miles northeast of the town of Pokhara. Years later the CIA drew up a report on this curious, unexplained incident. What happened to this "metallic disk" is not known.

Closer to our own time period, a report from *India Today* (indiatoday.in) appearing on November 7, 2012 under the headline "Mystery Sighting Spooks Soldiers Army, astronomers and DRDO have been unable to establish the origins of the unidentified luminous flying objects over India's Himalayan border with China" said:

> Units of the Indian Army and the Indo-Tibetan Border Police Force (ITBP) have reported Unidentified Flying Objects (UFOS) in the Ladakh region of Jammu and Kashmir. An ITBP unit based in Thakung, close to the Pangong Tso Lake, reported over 100 sightings of luminous objects between August 1 and October 15 this year. In reports sent to their Delhi headquarters in September, and to the Prime Minister's Office (PMO), they described sighting "Unidentified Luminous Objects" at day and by night. The yellowish spheres appear to lift off from the horizon on the Chinese side and slowly traverse the sky for three to five hours before disappearing. These were not unmanned aerial vehicles (UAVS), drones or even low earth-orbiting satellites, say Army officials who have studied the hazy photographs taken by ITBP.
>
> Drone sightings are verified and logged separately. The Army has reported 99 sightings of Chinese drones between January and August this year: 62 sightings were reported in the western sector, the Ladakh region, and 37 in the eastern sector in Arunachal Pradesh. Three of these drones intruded into territory claimed by India along the 365-km-long border with China in Ladakh, manned by ITBP. Such mysterious lights have been sighted before in Ladakh, a barren, 86,000 sq km heavily militarized zone wedged between Pakistan-occupied-Kashmir and Chinese-occupied Aksai Chin. The persistent sightings by the ITBP this year, however, worried the Army's Leh-based 14 Corps. The ITBP, did not respond to a detailed *India Today* questionnaire.
>
> In September, the Army moved a mobile ground-

based radar unit and a spectrum analyzer—that picks up frequencies emitted from any object—to a mountaintop near the 160-km-long, ribbon-shaped Pangong Lake that lies between India and China. The radar could not detect the object that was being tracked visually, indicating it was non-metallic. The spectrum analyzer could not detect any signals being emitted from them. The Army also flew a reconnaissance drone in the direction of the floating object, but it proved a futile exercise. The drone reached its maximum altitude but lost sight of the floating object.

In late September this year, a team of astronomers from the Indian Astronomical Observatory at Hanle, 150 km south of the lake, studied the airborne phenomena for three days. The team spotted the flying objects, Army officials say, but could not conclusively establish what they were. They did, however, say that the objects were "non celestial" and ruled out meteors and planets.

Scientists however say, the harsh geography and sparse demography of the great Himalayan range that separates Kashmir Valley from Ladakh, lends itself to unusual sightings. "The region is snowbound in winter, has few roads and is one of the most isolated places in India," says Sunil Dhar, a geologist at the government Post Graduate College in Dharamshala, who has studied glaciers in the region for 15 years.

Yet, none of the experts from the National Technical

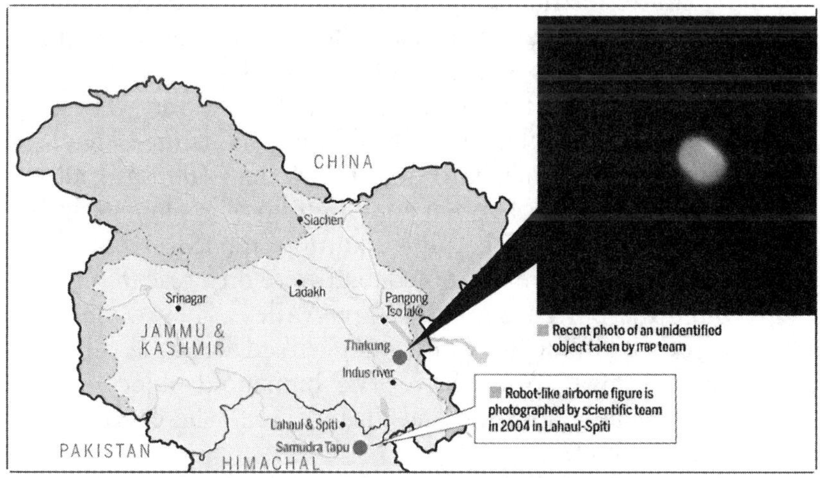

A map and photo of the UFO activity in Ladakh and at Samudra Tapu in 2004.

Research Organisation (NTRO)—in charge of technical intelligence—and Defence Research Development Organisation (DRDO), has been able to identify the objects. This has caused embarrassment rather than fear in the establishment. "Something is clearly wrong, if our combined scientific resources can't explain the phenomena," says a senior Army official in Delhi. Intelligence officials say these objects could be a crude psychological operation by China, or sophisticated probes attempting to ascertain India's defences in Ladakh.

"We can't ignore these sightings. We need to probe what new technology might have been deployed there," says former Indian Air Force (IAF) chief Air Chief Marshal (retired) P.V. Naik. In 2010, the IAF probed and dismissed Army sightings of such luminous objects as Chinese lanterns. UFO sightings have been endemic to Ladakh over the past decade. In late 2003, 14 Corps sent a detailed report on sightings of luminous objects to Army headquarters. Army troops on posts along Siachen had seen floating lights on the Chinese side. But reporting such phenomena risks inviting ridicule. When told about them at a northern command presentation in Leh, the then army chief, General N.C. Vij, had angrily dismissed the reports as hallucinations.

Scientists say the mysterious objects are not necessarily from outer space. There is no evidence of UFOS being of extra-terrestrial origin, says reputed Pune-based astrophysicist Jayant Narlikar. The implication of them being alien objects is fancy, not fact, he says.

There is still no explanation, however, for what is believed to be the clearest UFO sighting yet, in the Lahaul-Spiti region of Himachal Pradesh less than 100 km south of Ladakh in 2004. A five-member group of geologists and glaciologists led by Dr Anil Kulkarni of the ISRO's Space Applications Centre in Ahmedabad were on a research trip through the barren Samudra Tapu Valley. They filmed a four-foot tall robot-like figure, that walked along the valley, 50 meters away from them. The humanoid object then rapidly became airborne and disappeared. The encounter lasted 40 minutes.

It was seen by 14 persons including the six scientists.

Kulkarni then interviewed each expedition member separately to verify what the team had seen. Copies of his detailed report were circulated to the PMO, ISRO, the Army and several intelligence agencies. Kulkarni established his team hadn't seen a natural phenomenon. The matter, however, was buried soon after.

Sunil Dhar, who was part of the 2004 expedition, terms the sighting of the unidentified object an unforgettable experience. Locals, he says, have reported sighting mysterious objects for many years. These are unsolved mysteries that need more intensive study, he says. Left unexplained, the Ladakh sightings risk slipping into the crack between fact and science fiction.

Men and Gods in Mongolia

The British publisher Kegan Paul of London published two curious books on Mongolia in the 1930s, *In Secret Mongolia*[13] (originally titled *Tents in Mongolia*) (1934) and *Men and Gods in Mongolia* (1935).[14] The books were written by Henning Haslund, a Danish explorer who accompanied Sven Hedin and other explorers into Mongolia and Central Asia in the 1920s and 30s. In these exciting books, Haslund takes us into the barely known world of Mongolia of 1921, a land of god-kings, bandits, vast mountain wilderness and a Russian army running amok.

Starting in Peking, Haslund journeyed to Mongolia as part of the Krebs Expedition—a mission to establish a Danish butter farm in a remote corner of northern Mongolia. Along the way, he smuggled guns and nitroglycerin, got thrown into a prison by the new Communist regime, battled various Robber Princes and more. Haslund met the "Mad Baron" Ungern-Sternberg and his renegade Russian army, the many characters of Urga's fledgling foreign community, and the last god-king of Mongolia, Seng Chen Gegen, the fifth reincarnation of the Tiger god and the ,ruler of all Torguts."

Aside from the esoteric and mystical material, there is plenty of just plain adventure. Haslund encounters a Mongolian werewolf, is ambushed along the trail, escapes from prison and fights terrifying blizzards—but all in good humor, which makes us wonder at the amazing character of this intrepid adventurer.

In the 1935 sequel, *Men and Gods in Mongolia,* Haslund continues his adventures, taking us to the lost city of Karakota in the Gobi Desert where we meet Dambin Jansang, the dreaded warlord of the forbidden expanse of desert known as the Black Gobi. There is even material in this incredible book on the Himori, an "airhorse" that flies through the sky and carries with it the sacred stone of Chintamani.

A Mountaintop Mystery

Haslund includes a very curious story in *Men and Gods in Mongolia* that may be helpful in the search for the secret fortresses of the ancients—military bases, kept for thousands of years and staffed by men and women, that include vimanas and underground or inside-mountain hangars. Hiding military installations is exactly what is done today by governments that prefer to keep their fighter squadrons in underground hangars that are virtually invisible. A modern jet can take off from one of these hangars in a matter of minutes while the source of the craft, including the runways, remains hidden from view. Just like today, did ancient cultures hollow out mountains and create self-sufficient survival centers?

Haslund, toward the end of his second book, discusses his meetings with the Toin Lama, who was the senior Buddhist Lama for the region of far western Mongolia and Sinkiang. Haslund tells us that this elderly lama was fascinated by aeroplanes and air travel and asked him many questions about the subject.

Says Haslund:

> It was illustrated papers that were to open the way to the first intimacy between *Toin Lama* and me. He was the most eager of all my auditors, and every evening we went in detail through the pictures in a year-old weekly paper with all the matter for discussion to which each picture gave rise.
>
> The number containing Charles Lindbergh's Atlantic flight lasted three evenings, and I wonder whether the exploit of that blond scion of Scandinavia with the monstrous *nisdeg telleg*, "ether-carriage," anywhere produced more astonishment and delight than among the Torguts of "the Mountains of Heaven."
>
> The marvelous news of man's ability to follow the flight of the bird gave birth to a plan for the future in the primitive but progress-loving mind of *Toin Lama.* Of course it would be only a question of time before the Torguts would have

their own "ether carriages" and with their aid one of the country's greatest riddles would be solved.

Deep within the mountains rises a sky-piercing peak with steep sides and topped by an irregular plateau like a gigantic watchtower. The bare gray precipices of the mountain are clothed at the top with pallid glaciers, and it needs courage to attempt to climb it. Yet the mountain has been climbed by two hunters of a former generation. They reached the top of the alpine tower and came back with an account of what they had seen. Those two hunters are dead long since, but the account of their wonderful experience survives and has tempted many a hunter of later times to the same climb, but none has been able to accomplish it. For terrifying sounds were heard from the sides of the mountain, and long before they reached the top they were seized with confusion of thought. Many have been entirely lost, but others have been found later at the foot of the mountain with no memory of what had happened after their minds were clouded and no knowledge of how they came down from the heights.

But the sight that the two hunters saw was worth the hardships of the climb, for up there was a paradise for Mongols. High up, the mountainsides ended in a mighty circular crater the slopes of which were covered with luxuriant vegetation. Through the green alpine meadows flowed foaming rivers, and on the slopes fat sheep and goats were grazing and multitudes of game. Deep down in the crater valley lay a blue lake on whose fertile banks and surrounding steppes cattle grazed in countless multitudes. White tents were scattered over the steppe and from their smoke-vents the heat of fires trembled in the pure air. But no human beings were to be seen. The tents stood uninhabited, the horses played in unsaddled freedom and nature smiled in secure blessedness.

This strange story of a secret city on top of a mountain may be pure legend, but what legend is not based on something real? Was this possibly a secret vimana base? A mirage on the summit of a mountain? Could there be some lost paradise on top of a mountain in the Altai Himalaya? Haslund did not give this mountain a name, but it is apparently in western China, the Pamirs, or the Altai

Himalaya.

Once again we are reminded of the stories of Mount Kailash, the abode of Shiva. Tibet is certainly the land of Shiva and it would seem that Mongolia is also the land of Shiva. Do certain mountains exist in Tibet and Mongolia that are ancient bases for vimanas and other technology?

Do the lights seen in western Tibet by Indian army officers come from one of these secret mountain bases? Are the flying saucers that have been seen since the 1920s in Tibet, Mongolia and the Himalayas coming from a hidden hangar inside of a mountain? Many modern Hindus and Tibetans seem to believe this and for them Shiva is very real as well. His empire spans many thousands of years and vast amounts of the planet Earth. Hindus would probably believe that Shiva once ruled the entire planet tens of thousands of years ago—an age that is lost in time and legend.

In his book *Proof of Vedic Culture's Global Existence*[21] the author Stephen Knapp says:

> Does this mean that these are ancient vimanas that still exist today? Are they stored in some underground caverns somewhere? Or are they simply modern-built using the ancient designes as described in the Vedic texts? The UFOs that have been seen around the world may not be from some distant galaxy, but may be from a secret human society, or even military installation. However, many of the Vedic texts do describe interplanetary travel. So even if these space machines are from some other planet, they may be using the same principles of propulsion that have already been described in the universal Vedic literature. The answer awaits us.[21]

Bibliography

1. *Champa: Ancient Towers, Reality & Legend*, Ngo Van Doanh, 2002, Gioi Publishers, Hanoi.
2. *My Son Sanctuary*, Thanh Dia, 2005, Hanoi.
3. *Cu Lao Cham: An Introduction to the Islands*, Di Tich and Danh Thang, 2005, Da Nang.
4. *Cham Sculpture and Indian Mythology*, Huynh Thi Duoc, 2007, Hanoi.
5. *Minorities of Central Vietnam*, Jacques Dournes, 1980, Minorities Rights Group, London.
6. *Ancient Angkor,* M, Freeman and C. Jacques, 2003, River Books, Bangkok.
7. *Eden in the East,* Stephen Oppenheimer, 1998, Weidenfield & Nicolson, London.
8. *The Lost World of Cham*, David Hatcher Childress, 2017, Adventures Unlimited Press, Kempton, IL.
9. *Invisible Residents*, Ivan T. Sanderson, 1970, Adventures Unlimited Press, Kempton.
10. *When China Ruled the Seas*, Louise Levathes, 1994, Simon & Schuster, New York.
11. *Inca Origins*, Graeme Kearsley, 2003, Yelsraek Publishers, London.
12. *The Lost Continent of Mu*, James Churchward, 1926. Reprinted by Adventures Unlimited Press, Kempton, IL.
13. *In Secret Mongolia*, Henning Haslund, 1934, Kegan Paul, London. Reprinted by Adventures Unlimited Press, Kempton, IL.
14. *Men and Gods in Mongolia*, Henning Haslund, 1935, Kegan Paul, London. Reprinted by Adventures Unlimited Press, Kempton, IL.
15. *The African Presence in Early Asia*, edited by Runoko Rashidi and Ivan Van Sertima, 1988, Transaction Publishers, New Brunswick, NJ.

16. *The African Presence in Early America*, edited by Ivan Van Sertima, 1987, Transaction Publishers, New Brunswick, NJ.
17. *Borobudur and Temples of Java*, 2008, Ariswara Publishers, Magelong, Indonesia.
18. *Ark of God*, David Hatcher Childress, 2015, Adventures Unlimited Press, Kempton, IL.
19. *The Gods of Eden*, Andrew Collins, 1998, Headline, London.
20. *Harscha Charita of Bana*, translated by E.B. Cowell and F.H. Thomas, 1897, Oriental Translation Fund, London.
21. *Proof of Vedic Culture's Global Existence*, Stephen Knapp, 2000, The World Relief Network, Detroit, MI.
22. *The Mystery of the Olmecs*, David Hatcher Childress, 2003, Adventures Unlimited Press, Kempton, IL.
23. *They Came Before Columbus: The African Presence in Ancient America,* Ivan Van Sertima, 1977, Random House, New York.
24. *The Children of the Sun*, W. J. Perry, 1923, Hutchinson, London. Reprinted by Adventures Unlimited Press, Kempton, IL.
25. *Esoteric Egypt: the Sacred Science of the Land of Khem*, J.S. Gordon, 2015, Inner Traditions, Rochester, VT.
26. *Ancient Technology in Peru & Bolivia,* David Hatcher Childress, 2012, Adventures Unlimited Press, Kempton, IL.
27. *Saga America*, Barry Fell, 1980, New York Times Books, New York.
28. *Maps of the Ancient Sea Kings*, Charles Hapgood, 1966, Chilton Books. Reprinted by Adventures Unlimited Press, Kempton, IL.
29. *The Megalithic Culture in Indonesia,* W.J. Perry, 1918, University of Manchester Press, Manchester, UK.
30. *The Indo-Sumerian Seals Deciphered*, L.A. Waddell, 1925, London.
31. *Hindu America?,* Chaman Lal, 1960, Bharatiya Vidya Bhavan, Bombay (Mumbai).
32. *The Mystery of Easter Island*, Katherine Routledge, 1919, London. Reprinted by AUP, Kempton.
33. *The Riddle of the Pacific*, John MacMillan Brown, 1924 Reprinted by AUP, Kempton, IL.
34. *Mysteries of Easter Island*, Francis Maziere, 1968, W.W. Norton, New York.
35. *The Caroline Islands,* F.W. Christian, 1899, London.

36. *Aku-Aku,* Thor Heyerdahl, 1958, Rand McNally Co., Chicago.
37. *Kon Tiki*, Thor Heyerdahl, 1950, Rand McNally Co., Chicago.
38. *Ancient Technology in Peru and Bolivia*, David Hatcher Childress, 2012, Adventures Unlimited Press, Kempton, IL.
39. *The Civilization of Angkor*, C. Higham, 2001, Weidenfeld & Nicolson, London.
40. *War in Ancient India*, Ramachandra Dikshitar, 1944, Oxford Press, UK.
41. *Axis of the World,* Igor Witkowski, 2008, Adventures Unlimited Press, Kempton, IL.
42. *In Search of Quetzalcoatl*, Pierre Honoré, 1963, Hutchinson & Co. London. Reprinted by AUP, Kempton, IL. (Original title: *In Quest of the White God*)
43. *Ancient Man: A Handbook of Puzzling Artifacts*, William Corliss, 1974, The Sourcebook Project, Glen Arm, MD.
44. *Chavin and the Origins of Andean Civilization*, Richard L. Burger, 1992, Thames and Hudson, London.
45. *Notes on Inka Architecture*, Luis Oscar Chara Zereceda, 2006, Cuzco.
46. *Early Metal Mining and Production*, P. Craddock, 1995, Edinburgh University Press Ltd, Edinburgh.
47. *We Are Not the First*, Andrew Tomas, 1971, Souvenir Press, London.
48. *Megalithic Finds in Central Celebes*, Walter Kaudern, 1938, Goteborg Ethnographical Museum, Goteborg, Sweden.
49. *Jade: A Study in Chinese Archaeology and Religion*, Berthold Laufer, 1912, Dover Books, New York (reprinted 1974).
50. *Inca Architecture and Construction at Ollantaytambo,* Jean-Pierre Protzen, 1993, Oxford University Press, Oxford.
51. *Arquitectura Y Construccion Incas en Ollantaytambo,* Jean-Pierre Protzen, 2005, Fondo Editorial de la Pontificia Universidad Catolica del Peru, Lima (Spanish language edition of the Oxford Press book).
52. *Upon a Stone Altar*, David Hanlon, 1988, University of Hawaii Press, Honolulu.
53. *Lost City of Stone*, Bill Ballinger, 1978, Simon & Schuster, New York.
54. *The God-Kings and the Titans*, James Bailey, 1973, St. Martin's Press, New York.

55. *Home of the Gods*, Hugh Fox, 2005, Galde Press, Minneapolis.
56. *Lost Cities of Ancient Lemuria & the Pacific*, David Hatcher Childress, 1988, Adventures Unlimited Press, Kempton, IL.
57. *South Seas Myths and Legends*, Donald Mackenzie, 1930, Senate Books, London.
58. *The Olmecs: America's First Civilization,* Richard A. Diehl, 2004, Thames & Hudson, New York.
59. *The Olmec World*, Ignacio Bernal, 1999, University of California Press, Berkeley.
60. *Xalapa Museum of Anthropology: A Guided Tour*, 2004, Governors of the Museum, Xalapa, Mexico.
61. *The Enigma of Cranial Deformation*, David Hatcher Childress and Brien Foerster, 2012, Adventures Unlimited Press, Kempton, IL.
62. *The Ra Expeditions,* Thor Heyerdahl, 1965, Hutchinson, London.
63. *The Zuni Enigma*, Nancy Yaw Davis, 2001, Norton & Co., New York.
64. *Man's Conquest of the Pacific,* Peter Bellwood, 1978, William Collins, London.
65. *The Nan Madol Area of Ponape: Researches Into Bounding and Stabilizing an Ancient Administrative Center*, Dr. Arthur Saxe, 1980, Office of the High Commissioner, Trust Territory of the Pacific, Saipan, Marianas Islands.
66. *War in Ancient India*, Ramachandra Dikshitar, 1944, Oxford University Press, Oxford.
67. *Vimana*, David Hatcher Childress, 2015, AUP, Kempton, IL.
68. *A Guide to Ponape*, Gene Ashby, 1983, Rainy Day Press, Eugene, Oregon.
69. *Mayan Genesis: South Asian Myths, Migrations and Iconography in Mesoamerica*, Graeme Kearsley, 2001, Yelsraek Publishers, London.
70. *Incidents of Travel in Central America, Chiapas and Yucatan,* Stevens and Catherwood, 1843, Harper and Sons, New York.

Get these fascinating books from your nearest bookstore or directly from: Adventures Unlimited Press

www.adventuresunlimitedpress.com

ANCIENT TECHNOLOGY IN PERU & BOLIVIA
By David Hatcher Childress

Childress speculates on the existence of a sunken city in Lake Titicaca and reveals new evidence that the Sumerians may have arrived in South America 4,000 years ago. He demonstrates that the use of "keystone cuts" with metal clamps poured into them to secure megalithic construction was an advanced technology used all over the world, from the Andes to Egypt, Greece and Southeast Asia. He maintains that only power tools could have made the intricate articulation and drill holes found in extremely hard granite and basalt blocks in Bolivia and Peru, and that the megalith builders had to have had advanced methods for moving and stacking gigantic blocks of stone, some weighing over 100 tons.

340 Pages. 6x9 Paperback. Illustrated.. $19.95 Code: ATP

THE ENIGMA OF CRANIAL DEFORMATION
Elongated Skulls of the Ancients
By David Hatcher Childress and Brien Foerster

In a book filled with over a hundred astonishing photos and a color photo section, Childress and Foerster take us to Peru, Bolivia, Egypt, Malta, China, Mexico and other places in search of strange elongated skulls and other cranial deformation. The puzzle of why diverse ancient people—even on remote Pacific Islands—would use head-binding to create elongated heads is mystifying. Where did they even get this idea? Did some people naturally look this way—with long narrow heads? Were they some alien race? Were they an elite race that roamed the entire planet? Why do anthropologists rarely talk about cranial deformation and know so little about it? Color Section.

250 Pages. 6x9 Paperback. Illustrated. $19.95. Code: ECD

ARK OF GOD
The Incredible Power of the Ark of the Covenant
By David Hatcher Childress

Childress takes us on an incredible journey in search of the truth about (and science behind) the fantastic biblical artifact known as the Ark of the Covenant. This object made by Moses at Mount Sinai—part wooden-metal box and part golden statue—had the power to create "lightning" to kill people, and also to fly and lead people through the wilderness. The Ark of the Covenant suddenly disappears from the Bible record and what happened to it is not mentioned. Was it hidden in the underground passages of King Solomon's temple and later discovered by the Knights Templar? Was it taken through Egypt to Ethiopia as many Coptic Christians believe? Childress looks into hidden history, astonishing ancient technology, and a 3,000-year-old mystery that continues to fascinate millions of people today. Color section.

420 Pages. 6x9 Paperback. Illustrated. $22.00 Code: AOG

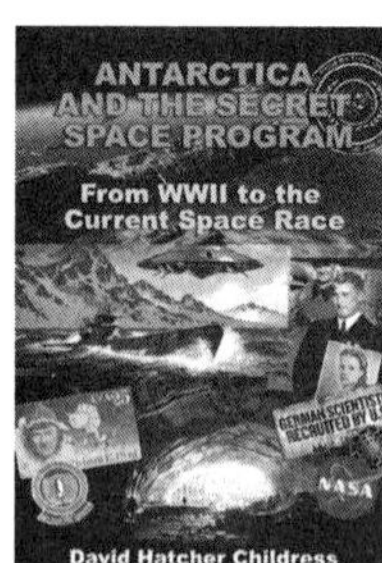

ANTARCTICA AND THE SECRET SPACE PROGRAM

David Hatcher Childress

David Childress, popular author and star of the History Channel's show *Ancient Aliens*, brings us the incredible tale of Nazi submarines and secret weapons in Antarctica and elsewhere. He then examines Operation High-Jump with Admiral Richard Byrd in 1947 and the battle that he apparently had in Antarctica with flying saucers. Through "Operation Paperclip," the Nazis infiltrated aerospace companies, banking, media, and the US government, including NASA and the CIA after WWII. Does the US Navy have a secret space program that includes huge ships and hundreds of astronauts?

392 Pages. 6x9 Paperback. Illustrated. $22.00 Code: ASSP

HAUNEBU: THE SECRET FILES

The Greatest UFO Secret of All Time

By David Hatcher Childress

Childress brings us the incredible tale of the German flying disk known as the Haunebu. Although rumors of German flying disks have been around since the late years of WWII it was not until 1989 when a German researcher named Ralf Ettl living in London received an anonymous packet of photographs and documents concerning the planning and development of at least three types of unusual craft. Chapters include: A Saucer Full of Secrets; WWII as an Oil War; A Saucer Called Vril; Secret Cities of the Black Sun; The Strange World of Miguel Serrano; Set the Controls for the Heart of the Sun; Dark Side of the Moon: more. Includes a 16-page color section. Over 120 photographs and diagrams.

352 Pages. 6x9 Paperback. Illustrated. $22.00 Code: HBU

ANDROMEDA: THE SECRET FILES

The Flying Submarines of the SS

By David Hatcher Childress

Childress brings us the amazing story of the German Andromeda craft, designed and built during WWII. Along with flying discs, the Germans were making long, cylindrical airships that are commonly called motherships—large craft that house several smaller disc craft. It was not until 1989 that a German researcher named Ralf Ettl, living in London, received an anonymous packet of photographs and documents concerning the planning and development of at least three types of unusual craft—including the Andromeda. Chapters include: Gravity's Rainbow; The Motherships; The MJ-12, UFOs and the Korean War; The Strange Case of Reinhold Schmidt; Secret Cities of the Winged Serpent; The Green Fireballs; Submarines That Can Fly; The Breakaway Civilization; more. Includes a 16-page color section.

382 Pages. 6x9 Paperback. Illustrated. $22.00 Code: ASF

VRIL: SECRETS OF THE BLACK SUN

By David Childress

A remnant of the Nazi military—particularly the SS—continued to operate aircraft and submarines around the world in the decades after the end of the war. This volume closes with how the SS operates today in the Ukraine and how the Wagner second in command, Dimitry Utkin, killed in the fiery crash of Yevgeny Prigozhin's private jet between Moscow and St. Petersburg in August of 2023, had SS tattoos on his shoulders and often signed his name with the SS runes. Chapters include: Secrets of the Black Sun; The Extra-Territorial Reich; The Rise of the SS; The SS Never Surrendered; Secret Submarines, Antarctica & Argentina; The Marconi Connection; Yellow Submarine; Ukraine and the Battalion of the Black Sun; more. Includes an 8-page color section.

382 Pages. 6x9 Paperback. Illustrated. $22.00 Code: VSBS